"*Easy Target* is a riveting story. Tom Smith had one of the most dangerous assignments in Vietnam, especially near Black Virgin Mountain in 1960 and 1970. . . . This is one of the best books about going to Vietnam I've ever read."
—Kevin Buckley, former Saigon bureau chief for *Newsweek*

"Excellent . . . Smith recounts his typically grueling experiences in basic training, the tough and proudly elitist atmosphere in flight school, and his arrival in Vietnam. . . . Skillfully evokes the frequently terrifying combat action and the close camaraderie among pilots."
—*Library Journal*

"Fast-paced . . . illuminating . . . [a] tell-it-like-it-was account. Indifferent to rules and regulations, Smith and his fellow pilots nevertheless flew their ships like teenage hot-rodders, going into super-hot LZs for wounded grunts and tracking the enemy at tree-top level. Smith describes these reluctant but courageous pilots well."
—Keith Nolan

"A winner! Very funny and sometimes powerfully moving. . . . Smith possesses the great American qualities in abundance: heart, sense of humor, resourcefulness, resilience. . . . It has movie written all over it."
—Alex Shoumatoff

"Flying scout helicopters in Vietnam was the aerial counterpart of walking point. . . . [A] visceral memoir . . . gritty enough to appeal to adventure fans."
—*Publishers Weekly*

"The Vietnam war produced a number of excellent first-hand accounts of helicopter warfare. At the top of the list are *Chickenhawk, Low Level Hell,* and *CW2*—all classics and among the finest accounts of aerial warfare ever written. Now *Easy Target* joins these elite ranks."
—*Richmond Times-Dispatch*

EASY TARGET

The Riveting True Story of a Scout Pilot in Vietnam

Tom Smith

AN ONYX BOOK

ONYX
Published by the Penguin Group
Penguin Putnam Inc., 375 Hudson Street,
New York, New York 10014, U.S.A.
Penguin Books Ltd, 27 Wrights Lane,
London W8 5TZ, England
Penguin Books Australia Ltd, Ringwood,
Victoria, Australia
Penguin Books Canada Ltd, 10 Alcorn Avenue,
Toronto, Ontario, Canada M4V 3B2
Penguin Books (N.Z.) Ltd, 182–190 Wairau Road,
Auckland 10, New Zealand

Penguin Books Ltd, Registered Offices:
Harmondsworth, Middlesex, England

First published by Onyx, an imprint of Dutton Signet,
a member of Penguin Putnam Inc.
This is an authorized reprint of a hardcover edition published by Presidio
Press.
For information address Presidio Press, 505B San Marin Drive, Suite 300,
Novato, California, 94949.

First Onyx Printing, November, 1997
10 9 8 7 6 5 4 3 2 1

REGISTERED TRADEMARK—MARCA REGISTRADA

Printed in the United States of America

The events in *Easy Target* and their chronology are all precisely as they
occurred. The documents and letters presented in the text are quoted exactly,
and all of the dialogue provided has been reconstructed to the best ability
of the author. All of the individuals described are real people; however, the
names have in many instances been changed (except for nicknames and call
signs, which have been faithfully preserved).

BOOKS ARE AVAILABLE AT QUANTITY DISCOUNTS WHEN USED TO PROMOTE PROD-
UCTS OR SERVICES. FOR INFORMATION PLEASE WRITE TO PREMIUM MARKETING DIVI-
SION, PENGUIN PUTNAM INC., 375 HUDSON STREET, NEW YORK, NEW YORK 10014.

*To Kathy and Tiger
And to Cisco*

Contents

Acknowledgments

Carl Borowski, Craig Fielding, Mike Foster, Ken Gardiner, Jon Harris, Rich Houghton, Ron McNevin, David Miles, Alan Smith, Marvin Stokes, Jim Wilhite, Keith Zulke, and many other young men of our company whose names I have forgotten, I am glad I was there with you.

Thanks to Roberta Arnold, Pat and Kitty Merle-Smith, Toby and Lee Schoyer, and Blakie and Bob Worth for their help and encouragement. Special thanks to George McClelland and Arthur Westing, first and final editors. Kat, without your direction and support *Easy Target* would not have been started or finished. I love you.

1

Trials and Errors

A Prologue

The pilot sitting to my left, the farm boy flying the helicopter, probably thought I was recoiling in my seat in a mindless reflex to dodge the tracer rounds that were flashing all about us.

"If you can see the tracers, the little piss-ants have missed us!" Hunched over the controls, his eyes fixed straight ahead, he was grinning as he pointed the nose of the Huey at the rice paddy a hundred feet below us. "It's OK, relax."

Actually I had been squirming around in my seat, fighting a primal urge to climb into his lap, throw my arms around his neck, and whimper. If it had not been for my seat belt and shoulder harness I probably would have. Abject terror had hold of my heart; I found it impossible to sit there and be cool.

At that point it would have been hard to convince me that I would ever fly in Vietnam again, much less volunteer for the risky job of Scout pilot. It would have shocked me to know that I would go on to be awarded the Distinguished Flying Cross, the Vietnamese Cross of Gallantry, the Bronze Star, and the Army Commendation Medal with a *V* for valor. On the other hand, the fact that I would receive two Purple Hearts for wounds in combat during my tour of duty seemed quite possible at the time.

The tracers stopped, the last few chasing the others slowly into the sky. Chief Warrant Officer Emet "Stoney" Parker, the pilot, looked at me, grinned his lopsided grin, and punched his microphone button. "Fix me another cracker sandwich, will you."

"Jesus Christ!" was all I could get out.

Taking peanut butter and jelly out of the C ration cans and spreading it on a C rat cracker for the nourishment of the aircraft commander was one of the primary duties of the copilot. Staying calm was another duty of the copilot, but as this was the first time I had been shot at, Stoney made allowances.

I had good reason to be surprised. We had been preparing to land at a major Army installation, and I had not expected the enemy to be that close. Stoney called the control tower for clearance to land and refuel.

"Tay Ninh, Stingray four-seven, one mile north for POL. And be advised we took small-arms fire just north of our position." He sounded so calm and collected.

"Roger that, Stingray four-seven. Third report today. You're clear to land POL," the tower came back. Stoney and the tower operator sounded so cool. It had to be an act.

Their composure, the fact that we had made it to the final leg of our approach, and the security of the base camp helped me to relax. Parts of my mind started functioning, and before long, control of my muscles returned. Muscle control's first job was convincing my butt to relax and let go of the fabric of the seat.

We landed at POL (petroleum, oil, and lubricants), the refueling area, and took on a thousand pounds of jet fuel before relocating the ship to one of the revetments in our compound. The ships were always parked or "shut down" in revetments, two parallel log-and-sandbag walls four feet high, spaced just wide enough apart to accommodate a helicopter. The revetments protected the aircraft from rocket and mortar attack, an almost nightly occurrence. Hovering just outside the revetment, Stoney said on the intercom, "You got it."

"Here? I mean, right now?" I peered down at the tight enclosure of the revetment below us. "Jesus, Stoney, this will take some practice. This is the first time. . . ." The stall to buy composure time was not working and my fear kept building. Stoney saw the panic in my eyes and smiled as parents do at frustrated children, a nice smile without pity.

Sweat from the ninety-degree heat stung my eyes. The controls in my hands felt too loose; the muscles in my arms and legs involuntarily tightened, paralyzing me. Relax, relax, I kept saying to myself, but the message just bounced around behind my eyeballs. Finally the ship started to settle to the ground, the tail slowly drifting to the right. I told my legs to push the pedals and bring it back to center. They refused. In desperation I took all the power out and we dropped to the ground, the tail rotor a few inches from the revetment wall. Still smiling, Stoney picked the machine back up to a hover and straightened it out. It was hotter than hell, I had just been shot at, and—to top it off—I could not even park the helicopter.

I was extremely unhappy. We had almost been shot down and could have been killed. It was becoming increasingly hard to keep a positive attitude.

This wasn't the first time I had had negative thoughts about the Army and Vietnam. In fact, I had been against joining the Army from the first day it was mentioned to me, many months before on a warm spring night in the Adirondack Mountains in Upstate New York. My oldest brother, Normand, was driving me back to school.

"Maybe you should join the Army, Tom," he said.

A response was unnecessary. This was the beginning of another one of his well-conceived plans to steer me away from my present preoccupations. Norm, an officer in the Navy, knew only one way of life—his—and thought I should follow along. I just looked out the car window at the green mountains cradling the valley.

"You know Judy's brother, Harry? He's flying helicopters in the Army. Having a great time." It was quite a change from his usual song and dance about responsibility and growing up. . . . How to handle this one?

"Norm! Helicopters? I don't think they let high school kids do that. . . . Do they?"

"You don't need a college education."

I wasn't sure why I did not want to fly helicopters, but I knew why I did not want to join the Army and go to Vietnam. People were dying over there.

"Look, Norm, I have seen those things on the news, in Vietnam. They are always getting shot down. Forget it, OK?"

His tone changed. Norm's temper, something to be feared, was taking off. "Can you tell me what the hell you are going to do when, or rather if, you graduate from Northwood? No college worth a damn would look at you with your record. The only thing you are accomplished at is getting in trouble. How long do you think you can keep that up?"

"OK, OK, I'll think about what you've said."

He began to calm down but then remembered something else I had done and turned on me again.

"What is this about, this memo Howard sent me?" He reached across me and pulled an envelope out of the glove box.

A handwritten note read, "Dear Norm, I hate to trouble you with this, but we could use any help you can give us with Tom." It was signed "John Howard, Headmaster." An attached, typed memo read, "For leaving the campus without permission last Friday night, you are on disciplinary probation through June 5th and restricted to campus for an indefinite period. . . . Any violation will result in permanent expulsion from school."

"What is this? The third note from Howard in as many months? How long do you think we are going to keep bailing you out of trouble, Tom?" Norm asked, exasperated.

No dodging that one, and it hurt. What hurt the most, though, was that I never intended to do anything wrong. One minute I would be having a good time hacking around with my friends, using my best judgment, and then suddenly I would be at the quiet end of a tongue-lashing. It always seemed to be my fault.

Norm could see that I was unhappy about the probation, so he went for the throat.

"You know, Tom, Mom and Dad really cared and worried about you. I do too." He stared through the windshield, his conviction turning to despair. "You know I'm just trying to help."

He was sincere and I appreciated that, but I did not know what he was talking about. It is hard to accept someone's help when you don't know what the problem is. Life seemed all right to me; I was just trying to get through it one day at a time. Sure, we didn't think about things the same way—but I still respected him. I knew his heart was in the right place.

I also knew why he wanted me to join the Army. It would solve the problem of who was going to be responsible for Tom.

Two years earlier our parents had been killed in a plane crash, leaving behind five kids. Norm, the oldest, took over as head of the family. My next older brother, Peter, was on his own in college. My younger brother, Nulsen, and sister, Tracy, ages thirteen and eleven respectively, had moved in with Uncle Pat and Aunt Kitty Merle-Smith, our legal guardians and close family friends, whom we had known and respected since we were children.

Uncle Pat and Aunt Kitty were nice, classy people. They were parents who held high standards for all their children, wards included. They had done what they could, at considerable inconvenience to themselves, to help me see the merits of responsibility. However, they had six children of their own, and with the added responsibility of Nulsen and Tracy they were glad to let Norm give me guidance.

Unfortunately Norm thought the Army was just the place for me—a little like prison, but not as tough on the reputation. He was tired of my impulsive behavior and my inability to follow his worthy example. What bothered him the most was my complete lack of concern about the future. Neither of us knew that this character trait was very desirable in combat helicopter pilots, Scout pilots in particular. Scout pilots had less than even odds of having a future.

After Norm dropped me off at school I thought about what he had said and realized that college was

the only way to get him off my back. If I didn't enroll
he could conceivably convince Uncle Pat that the
Army was the right place for me, and together they
could have forced me to join. Even my parents, who
had been much more understanding than my brother,
had been on the verge of subjecting me to military
discipline.

In the tenth grade I had been expelled for drinking
in school. It was not the first school I had been asked
to leave, and my parents were getting tired of wondering what I was going to do next. Our conversation
one day went something like this:

> "Well, Son, what are your plans?" Dad asked me.
> "I don't really have any, Dad."
> "Tommy, can't you see your atrocious academic
> record is limiting your options?" Mom put in, losing
> her patience with my indifference. "There is one
> school which we understand is willing to take you
> in the middle of the year, Culver Military Academy."
> "A military academy? I don't know, Mom."
> "Well then, what *do* you know? What do you want
> to do?" my mother demanded.
> "Maybe I should get a job or something" was the
> best I could offer.
> "As what? Who would hire you?"

Within a month my parents, who were living in
the Virgin Islands at the time, had enrolled me in
Colegio San Justo, a boarding school in Puerto Rico.
My enrollment there had been a last resort for them,
but in the long run it turned out to be a clever move.

San Justo was like a prison: damp concrete walls,
cockroaches in the seatless toilets, lizards eating their
hapless victims above my head during the night.
Breakfast was powdered eggs and powdered milk.

We broke our lunch bread into small pieces in order to find the *cucarachas* that had gone swimming in the batter. I adjusted to most of that, but I could not adjust to my classmates or their "Frog Races."

Several nights a week a significant portion of the student body, boys fourteen to eighteen years old, got together outside the dorms. They would bring with them several large frogs caught in the school pool. After they placed their bets, they would cover the frogs with lighter fluid, throw matches on them, and cheer and jeer as the balls of fire leapt about in agony. The frog that ended up farthest from the starting point won.

Clearly these were not guys I wanted to grow up with, and it did not take me long to change the direction my life was going in. By the end of the semester I had been readmitted to the same school in the Adirondacks that had expelled me. My grades and behavior at Colegio San Justo had been in the top one percent.

My parents appreciated this superb effort and let me go on with my life, but after they died my grades slipped again. My brother Norm got it stuck in his mind that the Army would help me get back on track and maybe even "make a man of me." As a last-ditch effort I applied to, and fortunately was accepted by, the University of Denver as a freshman for the fall of 1966.

Secure in the knowledge that I had derailed any plot that might have put me in the Army, it was back to life as usual, and a summer of fun in the Adirondacks.

North Creek, a back-road town of a few hundred residents in the southern Adirondacks, was taken over one weekend each May by hundreds of high school and college students. They gathered west of town, along the Hudson River, with a few being serious canoeists for the White Water Derby canoe races. The races go on for two days, but the drinking and parties last for three days and four nights, nonstop. It is on occasions such as this, with imaginations fired by cascading rapids and flowing Jim Beam, that the truth is occasionally bent. Life gets larger; egos speak. This happened to me.

It was obvious that the young lady I had cornered at the bar was bored and about to leave. No normal, mundane small talk was going to keep her around. "Well, I don't know if I will go to college next fall or fly helicopters," I said nonchalantly.

"You're a pilot?" She was interested.

"Yeah . . ." Even more nonchalantly.

"A helicopter pilot?" Even more interested.

"Yeah . . . well, sort of. I fly airplanes and I'm thinking about going to the Army flight school for helicopters."

As soon as this came out I felt a flash of pride. I am not sure whether it was the bourbon talking or my insatiable desire to be noticed. Most likely it was a desperate bid for sex, but I remember that night because now I know it is bad luck to lie about something that can happen. It usually does!

The good times of the summer had been everything a romantic ne'er-do-well could have asked for, and they did not end with the fall and my return to academic endeavors. The University of Denver was perfect. The open expanse of plains, mountains, and brilliant blue skies was a great place to be eighteen and on my own. How was I to know this lifestyle I found so free and full of fun was taking me another step closer to the Army and Vietnam?

One giant leap in that direction came when I encountered the skiing conditions in Colorado. I had skied all my life, but never on Rocky Mountain powder—my skis would float in the deep snow without resistance as I dropped down the mountain in a cloud of soft white crystals under the clear Colorado sky. Long, hard days of skiing were followed by nights full of camaraderie and bourbon. . . . It was heaven! One weekend during my sophomore year it snowed for five days in Vail; the skiing was just too much. Eighteen days later, when I got back to school, I found it necessary to go to the registrar to ask for a little help in remembering where my classes were. The registrar informed me I had been suspended for lack of attendance.

Suspension from college in the beginning of 1968 didn't upset me very much; I had wanted to see what was going on out in California with the "flower children" anyhow. But first I needed a tan. Without further ado I packed up my old VW bus and went to Mexico. The seventy-degree water and white sand beaches were great, but warm beer and diarrhea were no match for the wild stories from California. I headed back across the border, then up the coast of California.

Outside of Santa Barbara I picked up a young girl who wanted to see the Monterey coast. A week later we were holed up on Lime Kiln Creek outside of Big Sur with a retired bartender who had an inexhaustible supply of recreational drugs. It was true! Everything I had heard about California was true!

Occasionally I would drive the picturesque coast highway to Carmel to pick up my mail at the American Express office there. It was on one of those trips that I received the classic "Greetings" from the United States Armed Forces ordering me to report for an induction physical back in Denver. After a few weeks of deliberation, heavily influenced by the foreign chemicals filtering through my brain, I decided what the hell, let's see what's happening in Denver. I charged up the battery of my VW, kissed my flower child good-bye, and headed off to Denver again.

Not for a moment did I really think that the Army would take me: passing the physical seemed unlikely. At five-foot-five and one hundred and twenty pounds I did not consider myself the type of person anyone would be looking for to defend our country. Even if I did pass, my draft board was in the Virgin Islands, and I had been told that in the Caribbean the quota was usually filled with volunteers.

Just to be certain, I did my best at the physical to convince Uncle Sam's doctors that they did not want me. First came my near-fatal childhood diseases, and of course all the complications. Then there was the trouble with my kidneys and bad knees. I kept reciting until the doctor yelled "Next!"

The fact that they found me physically fit to serve reflects poorly on the standards set for our fighting forces; I was shocked. Thoroughly depressed and wanting to avoid the growing reality that I might be drafted, I moved in with some of my former classmates to start drinking in earnest. A week later, while I was still drowning my sorrows, Officer Gray from the Denver Police Department and four of his comrades in blue showed up at the front door with a search warrant.

It seems that several months before I moved in, a

former roommate had been selling drugs out of the house. When it was discovered that he was selling—not sharing—his roommates told him to leave. Months later that same dealer was busted. In an attempt to influence the police to drop the charges against him, and get a little revenge at the same time, he had turned in his former roommates as college student pushers.

The only thing Officer Gray hated more than drug dealers was college students. And so it was with divine vengeance that he tore the house apart until he came up with the damning evidence of a water pipe, three roaches, and a film canister full of marijuana seeds. Armed with these manifestations of depravity and his own righteous convictions, Officer Gray lined us up in front of him in the living room. With the water pipe in one hand and the roaches and seeds in the other he began his interrogation.

"Do these illegal drugs and paraphernalia belong to you?" he growled at the first of five scared college students.

"No, sir!" came the reply four times.

"Well then, this stuff must be yours." He glared at the last lad in line, me. I couldn't stand it, he looked so serious.

"No, sir," I responded just as seriously. "It must be yours!"

He had me in a squad car so fast I didn't even have time to grin.

It was a classic example of a well-intentioned desire to entertain being misconstrued, and a good example of bad timing. If this attempt to humor Officer Gray and the subsequent arrest for drug possession had occurred several weeks earlier, I probably would have failed my induction physical. The Army did not like people with drug arrests.

A few dreary months later a letter from my draft board in the Virgin Islands arrived and requested me to report for induction in, of all places, Puerto Rico. Horrible images of my old classmates at Colegio San Justo filled me with dread.

I beat a hasty retreat to Keene Valley, deep in the woods of the Adirondacks. Though my parents had spent the last years of their lives in the Caribbean, this town of five hundred people was where I had grown up. I loved it there, felt safe and secure, and even tried to convince myself that I could hide from the draft up in the mountains.

In reality this move proved to be another giant step toward Vietnam. My oldest brother, Norm—still convinced that I would be better off in the Army— was there when I got back.

It was the spring of 1968. The war in Vietnam was at its peak and young men were desperately needed. Draft dodging and card burning were being met with police action and long jail sentences. Nevertheless, the day to report for induction in Puerto Rico came and went without me; after all, I was a man of principle, I reasoned. Besides, there was no way in hell I was going to join my sadistic former classmates in a romp around some hot, stinking, punji stick-laced, leech-filled rice paddy. And was I really supposed to kill a bunch of guys I didn't even know or dislike?

However, as the month wore on, the probability of going to jail became more of a reality than the imagined fate of dying in Vietnam. Anyway, not everyone in the Army was in Vietnam, and as long as there was time I figured there was hope. It was in this weakened state that my brother Norm hit me once again with the helicopter trip.

"Look, Tom, right now you are in big trouble with the law. Draft dodging is a serious crime. Why not turn this thing around? Join up. They won't say anything. They need warm bodies." I wasn't arguing, so he went for it. "Go all the way; let the Army teach you to fly. Learn something that will guarantee you a job when you get out. See if you can get into helicopter flight school!"

I didn't want a job guarantee. I wanted to stay alive to have fun.

"Norm, flight school is a four-year obligation. Regular enlistment is only two. I don't want to be in the Army for four lousy years."

He had the answer, of course. "It's a four-year obligation only if you graduate from flight school. So if you don't like it, or they bounce you out, you're back to a two-year obligation. You can't lose."

At that time Norm was in the Navy flight school and was always telling me endless stories of flying and good times. They reminded me of my days at the University of Denver. Besides, if I didn't like it I could drop out, and if I did like it I would become a hotshot pilot. I liked the hotshot pilot part.

"Harry—you know, my brother-in-law—says you can get great deals on stereo equipment over there," he added. That did it. I finally had a good reason to join the Army.

I called the nearest recruitment center and asked what I had to do to join and fly helicopters. I was told to come by and take some aviation-related tests. Which I did, but it turned out that most of the questions had nothing at all to do with flying. It also seemed as if most of the answers had nothing to do with the questions. Nevertheless I did well on the tests. A few days later the center called to tell me the Army would guarantee me a place in helicopter flight school as a warrant officer candidate—just as soon as I signed their enlistment contract.

The enlistment contract read like something slaves might have put their Xs on. It read, "I swear that the foregoing statements have been read to me, that my statements have been correctly recorded and are true in all respects and that I fully understand the conditions under which I am enlisting." When I asked them what the contract meant where it read, "and certify no promise of any kind has been made to me," they explained that it was "just a formality."

My reporting date for oath of enlistment was set for 31 May 1968.

There was only one thing left for me to do: write a will. I solicited the aid of my brother Peter, a few nice girls, and a local barroom for this solemn task. A full bottle of tequila later, overlooking a few spelling errors, we had the text of my last will and testament composed.

I, Thomas Leming Smith, do hereby declare in sound mind and body on the 28th of May in our lord year 1968 that on my decease that I hereby do declare that I do will and decree all my earthly belongings to my brother, Peter Smith, my asshole brother, in that he may spend my GI insurance in all the drinking and good times that he can do in three days. If he doesn't he has to forfeit all he has left. This money he can spend on fast cars, fast women and anything that includes a fast life. If after my decease my body is in pieces that can be reconstructed then that Peter Smith must have my body

stuffed and mounted in Keene Valley. My Volks-
wagen will be left totaled in Keene Valley and left
where it sits.

A few days later Peter drove me the scenic, and
cruelly short, one hundred and forty-five miles from
Keene Valley to the enlistment center in Albany. My
brother thought it was all pretty funny. He was on
his way to a degree in nuclear engineering and had
no problem with the draft. Plus he was unfit for military service from a knee injury he received while
taking a ride on *my* motorcycle. Throughout the
whole trip I kept asking myself, "What have I done?"

As someone in a uniform read the oath of enlistment for us to repeat, I wondered if mumbling it
might be used as a defense later to prove that I had
not really joined. The oath ended with "so help me
God"; I added "Please?"

2

Silver Wings

Early June 1968

As the new recruits stepped off the old DC-3 into the hot funk of a Louisiana summer, a sergeant, all puffed up in his nice starched uniform and wearing a Smokey-the-Bear hat, marched up and started yelling, "Get your shit together, you worthless SHIT-birds! Keep your miserable mouths shut. FALL IN, goddamn it. Move your sorry asses, NOW!" His fists were clenched at his sides; little flecks of foam flew off his lips when he yelled.

Everyone started his career in the Army with basic combat training, but only an unlucky few were treated to basic training in Fort Polk in the summer: stuck in the hot, humid, stifling, stagnant Mississippi basin.

The sergeant lined us up in two lines and ordered us to follow him off the airfield. Everyone was doing a pretty good job of looking casual and unconcerned about the whole thing until some wise guy behind me cracked a joke about Louisiana. Without missing a step the sergeant whipped around, glared right at me, and screamed, "I said SHUT THE FUCK UP!" In the same pleasant demeanor he informed us that we were not there for "a goddamned vacation." He was right: Fort Polk was a pine barren, covered with a fine layer of red clay. The place was noted more for its deadly coral snakes and vicious pygmy rattlers than for its recreational facilities.

The principle of basic training was to instill a common mind in the young men who joined or were drafted into the Army. With one mind these men could function as a unit and better serve the designs of their commanding officers. But before the Army turned us over to the drill instructors to begin their insidious manipulations, we had three days of purgatory in the reception center. There our names were reduced to a nine-digit number; our heads were shaved and our clothes replaced with olive drab uniforms. The effects were impressive. It was hard to recognize anyone from the day before; except for the occasional pair of funny-looking ears, we were clones.

That was half of it, getting us all to look the same. The other half was left up to our drill instructors, getting us to act the same. To accomplish this they borrowed some of Pavlov's principles. When the bell rings—we wake up. Blow a whistle—we line up to eat, always in a group, always in unison. The past, the future, and any opportunities for independent thought were obscured in mindless, repetitious tasks. It surprised me how quickly so many young men with such diverse backgrounds were brought to one common denominator.

This approach kept life pretty easy: no work, physical or mental, was beyond the capabilities of the weakest in the group. Everything was according to Army regulations and on checklists so that we would not forget. For physical exercise we had the dodge, the jump-and-run, the one-mile run, the horizontal ladder, and the grenade throw. One weird kid from

New Jersey enjoyed it, kept saying it was like summer camp, but most of us were bored stiff.

Not long after we were assigned to our basic training companies our drill instructor appointed me to be the company driver, a job that got me out of marching around in the hot sun with the other trainees. I had to follow our company in a jeep and pick up the fat guys who passed out from heat exhaustion. A lapse in memory got me the job. I had forgotten what everyone had been saying in the reception center: "You're a fool if you volunteer for anything. No matter how good it looks, don't volunteer for it!" The first time our drill instructor called us together he asked, "Who knows how to drive a jeep?" Everyone knew he was asking for a volunteer except me: I thought he wanted to know if one of us knew how to drive a jeep. After this appointment basic seemed a lot better because it was obvious everyone around me had it worse.

Occasionally the Army even let us off base for a few hours. Of course, "on pass" we did what skin-headed trainees throughout time have done—we got drunk and tried to get laid. It was our only opportunity to pretend we were still civilians.

After a few trips up and down the main drag of Leesville in a red Ford Galaxie full of nerds, three of us jumped out at a bar, hoping we could do better on our own. For hours we sat around a table littered with beer bottles and cigarette butts, talking about the two things we thought about every day—Army life and girls.

It was close to a hundred degrees that afternoon; something that smelled a lot like urine rode on the thick air. Drinking was the only pastime that did not involve profuse sweating, so we drank a lot. As we

drank the stories grew. It was not long before someone started making suggestions about the lone
woman who had been sitting at the bar most of the
afternoon, the one with the sweaty mustache who
had been through the door beyond the men's rest
room three times in the last two hours, with four
different men.

The whiny kid from Decatur lost the draw, but
made it through ten minutes of insults before reluc-
tantly going up to sit beside her. The next thing I
remember was waiting my turn, watching Decatur's
butt going up and down on a middle-aged woman
who looked as if she was trying to remember her
grocery list.

Not quite the glorious return to civilian life I had
imagined. My first trip to town became my last. It
was easier to hang out in the small beer bar on
base—a dark cinder block box, a place where I could
be alone with my thoughts. I spent most of my free
time there working myself into the rhythm of the
pinball machine while the jukebox played "Put Silver
Wings on My Son's Chest" and "Earth to Major
Tom." When the pinball machines were tied up, I
daydreamed about home and the good times going
on without me.

Actually, what news I did get from home was
pretty depressing. One of the girls who had been
drinking with us the night I wrote my will had been
killed when a .22-caliber pistol fired accidentally, hitting her in the back. Another good drinking buddy
fell out of a convertible and had his head run over by
a following car. He almost died, but they managed to
piece his skull back together and stitch him up. I
heard that he looked pretty bad for a while with his
head shaved and covered with stitches, but he made

the best of it by responding to people's inquiries with "Cut myself shaving."

Basic was almost finished when the company commander called me into his office. I knocked twice (Army regulations) on the captain's door, stopped two paces in front of his desk (just as we had been taught), and saluted—with the wrong hand.

"Private Smith, it has come to the attention of the records department that you have a prior arrest for possession of marijuana." I just looked at him, obviously not getting his point. "You have been reassigned from the Warrant Officer Candidate program to Clerk Typists School."

Clerk Typists School flashed in my memory. I had wandered through it one afternoon. The building reminded me of high school—big, high-ceilinged classrooms, with yellow light filtering through dust and cobwebs, each room drearier than the last. Every classroom packed with orderly rows of fuzzy-headed kids in fatigues pecking away at typewriters. It looked like a prison work program. I did not want to go back.

The captain was waiting impatiently for a response. "But sir, I told them about that marijuana incident when I joined. They told me I had a waiver, sir."

"Take it up with records, Smith. Dismissed."

When I was halfway back to my barracks it dawned on me that I had missed a golden opportunity to save myself a trip to Vietnam. I cringed just thinking about going there. With a simple OK to the captain, I would have been out of flight school, safe from an infantry job, and out of the Army in less than two years—but a clerk typist? What would I say to everyone who thought I was going to be a pilot?

Later that same day, a day as gray as my mood, I

was walking along the railroad tracks past a company of trainees doing bayonet drills. I was watching the ties that kept tripping me up, my mind stuck on the thought that it would be smart to let them drop me out of flight school, when suddenly a flash of lightning and a loud clap of thunder split the air. Two awesome bands of sparkling light came dancing down the rails at me. Reflexively I tucked my head and turned my face away from the energy going by. When I opened my eyes I was looking at the trainees who were falling to the ground. I thought their drill instructor had given them the *Drop* command as part of the exercise.

When I got back to the company area everyone was talking about the trainees down by the railroad tracks who had been hit by a bolt of lightning; four of them had died. The same bolt of lightning had almost hit me.

The next day I went to the Judge Advocate's office, the Army's legal staff, and told a major there that if I was dropped from flight school I would sue the Army for breach of contract. He looked into the situation and found the waiver in my enlistment records. Once again I was on my way to becoming a pilot.

It seemed like the right thing to do, even though everyone knew that ninety-nine percent of all Army helicopter pilots went to Vietnam. Maybe one percent odds seemed good enough for me at the time, but my grandmother was not so optimistic. She wrote just before the end of basic training:

Dear Tom,

     It seems to me that we are losing a great many helicopters *and* pilots overseas in that crazy, idiotic

war. I wonder when it will ever end, and pray that
you won't get into it.

Basic training was over soon enough and ended
with the traditional parade and meaningless cere-
mony. Looking back, very little stood out about basic,
except boredom and the last rifle qualification course.
It surprised me how much I had liked that part. The
course was a walk through the woods with a loaded
M14 rifle: silhouettes of soldiers popped up, and we
scored by blasting them.

The day after graduation a group of us boarded a
bus to Fort Wolters, Texas, and Primary Flight School.
The Army had tried to warn us in our new orders
that life would be different in flight school. Special
Order Number 206 read:

> Individual is advised that if he takes his depen-
> dents to his training station it could work a severe
> hardship on his dependents and interfere with his
> training.

In spite of this warning we all felt life would im-
prove at Fort Wolters; a transformation came over
the group of short-haired young men as we rolled
through the gates of Fort Polk. For the first time in
months a little life, enthusiasm, and individualism
showed in the "sorry-assed trainees."

As the roadside clutter whipped by, the big, open
country rolled slowly on toward the horizon. Looking far away from the speeding bus, the world
slowed down, became focused, real to the mind but
not the touch, a nice vantage point for speculation.
In the big, sliding glass window a filmy reflection of
my unsmiling face stared back at me. There were

subtle but significant changes in my expression, and I did not know where they had come from.

It was odd that I was unable to understand how the Army was changing me. The system seemed so simple—Army regulations and chain of command, lead or be led. I was being led, and it felt lousy. Since leaving was out of the question, there was only one thing to do, the WOC (Warrant Officer Candidate) program, flight school and pilot's wings. It was common knowledge that a pilot in his aircraft was the final authority. As long as I was in the Army this would be my only chance of regaining control of my life. So, with few goals and a shortsighted view of the future, we rolled on into Texas and the world of Army aviation. The two helicopters mounted at the gate to Fort Wolters were impressive. Looking up at them I felt respect and, for one anxious moment, that mastering helicopter flight might be too tough for me.

After one look at our reception committee, a group of lean young officers in tight khaki uniforms and shiny helmets, I knew for certain it was not going to be easy. One dark little guy kept staring at me; every time I glanced in his direction he was looking straight at me. Another beady-eyed guy had a riding crop that he kept slapping into the palm of his hand. The whole scene was right out of the movies. Other officers were slithering around our formation, coming up to us, right in our faces, less than an inch away, with eyes flashing and lips curled, hissing horrible things in our ears. Then they would step back and order us: "Drop! Gimme twenty-five [push-ups]!"

Fort Polk may not have been a vacation spot, but it was a garden spot compared to Fort Wolters. The whole base, like most of Texas, sat on a great flat chunk of eroded, oven-baked dirt. It was so dry it made my nose ache; and the wind never stopped blowing. Even stranger than the natural elements were the crazy Bible-thumpers who lived out among the tumbleweeds. Anyone would be driven a little mad living where they did, but who could imagine outlawing beer in one of the hottest places in the country?

The purpose of the WOC program was to take enlisted men and turn them into officers and helicopter pilots in nine months. The Army wanted us to be officers first and pilots second, but with helicopter pilots dying at an alarming rate, the emphasis switched and the cadre responsible for training us (WOC company officers, class instructors, and instructor pilots) put all their efforts into making us competent pilots.

Quite a few of the cadre had done a tour in Vietnam and knew where we were going. All of them told us we would "have to have your shit together" if we did not want to come home in a body bag.

By the time we graduated we would have more than two hundred hours of flight time and thousands of hours of classroom study. We would know the aircraft almost as well as the engineers who had built them; our courses in weather, navigation, and gunnery would be more than adequate. But what would get us to work and make us excel was the feeling that we would need what we were learning.

The cadre included, in ranking order, the commanding officer, the executive officer, the company clerk, and the TAC officers. The TAC officers had been our reception committee, the guys in the shiny helmets. During the first month, which was designated preflight training, all we saw was our TAC officer—all day, most of the night, and in more than a few nightmares.

The TAC officers' assignment was to teach us discipline and see if we could take stress. The discipline revolved around attention to detail. Everything we did from sleep to sleep was directed by our TAC. The way we got up, washed, dressed, made our beds, and folded our clothes was criticized and corrected, even when it was not wrong. The stress test came with the slightest infraction of the many rules and standards; any inattention to detail brought punishment. Usually it was verbal abuse and humiliation along with something physical, such as doing push-ups or walking laps. The harassment never stopped. The classrooms were a welcome break, and learning a pleasant distraction.

My arrival date put me in the 8th WOC Company, class 69-11, and our TAC officer was CWO Jeff Henly. Henly was a pleasant-looking man, stout and covered with freckles, with an oval face and bushy head of red hair. He was a jolly guy, with an even disposition and an intermittent sense of humor, probably twenty-two or so. Young, but not inexperienced, Jeff could harass with the best of them. He would make us spit-shine our shoes for hours, and stand at attention in the corridors all night. For a nice guy he really made life miserable for us. Sometimes I thought he hated me, until one night when an irate major dragged a sorely intoxicated WOC into Henly's office.

"Mr. Henly [warrant officers are called "mister" by commissioned officers], is this candidate assigned to your company?"

"Yes, sir, Candidate Smith is."

"Is it customary for your students to flag down officers' cars for a ride home because they are too drunk to walk back to their company area? And just what the hell is this candidate doing drunk in the first place?"

Henly's expression did not change, but I could see his eyes lighten up a bit.

"Sir, this candidate has a lot of explaining to do, and I assure you his punishment will suit his actions."

"He should be washed out of the program."

"That will be a consideration, sir."

As the door closed Henly switched his glare from the major's back to me.

"Don't ever do that again or you are out of here, understood?"

"Yes, sir!"

I never heard another word about it. Everyone knew the major, the commanding officer of a rival company of WOCs, was a pain in the ass, and that Henly disliked him, but there was more to it than that. Watching my TAC officer as the major gave him a hard time, it was obvious that Henly was sticking up for me. It was my first taste of the camaraderie among pilots.

After the first month of primary flight training had been completed, the TACs backed off a bit and let us get into some real stress—learning to fly. It started out pleasantly enough. They issued us flight helmets, leather and Nomex gloves, real pilot sunglasses, and one-piece flight suits with zippers and pockets all over them. The first thing I did was go back to my room and put on the flight gear, like everyone else. Within half an hour the halls of the barracks were full of pilot impersonators.

Our professional pilot gear was accompanied by

printed material covering the spectrum of helicopter flight, navigation maps, and so on, but it was the schematics and descriptions of the TH-55A that became dog-eared with use first. The TH-55A was the helicopter we flew as a trainer. It looked like an undernourished dragonfly, carried two people side by side, was held up by three main rotor blades, and weighed thirteen hundred pounds. It was a responsive and stable machine, well suited as a trainer. Next we got into the study guide *Communication Procedures and Aviation Radio Phraseology*, consisting of pages of abbreviations, numbers, and select terms—with meanings of dire import that only pilots and their handlers understood. We were getting closer and closer to actually flying.

In September 1968, almost four months after my enlistment, we finally headed to the flight line. Even though I had taken my studies seriously, and had already been on several hundred fantasy flights, it was hard not to be a little nervous. We had recently received Special Order Number 228, which read:

Hazardous duty required to be performed as indicated for following individuals assigned 8th WOC Company. . . . Individuals are required to participate regularly and frequently in aerial flight.

There was no doubt about it, it was hazardous duty. In fact most of our training revolved around the many dangers of rotor-wing flight, and how to prevent and react to them.

The big day of our first flight arrived and off to the airfield we went. In the operations room we took care of our preflight paperwork: maintenance records, weather information, flight logs, and flight plans. Then we split into small groups to wait for our instructor pilots.

My instructor pilot, Phil Bensen, was a civilian and was nowhere near as excited about my first helicopter flight as I was. Without ever moving his face, he looked at me, looked at my paperwork, and said, "Let's go."

We walked in silence out to the TH-55As parked on the flight line. Hot Texas sun rose off the black asphalt apron, making the helicopters flow and dance on the heat waves; spilled oil and fuel vapors mixed and gave body to the surreal image. It felt great to be there.

Bensen showed me how to do a walk-around inspection of the helicopter and then climbed up on the side where he could get a closer look at the rotor head. In flight the helicopter hangs by the rotor mast from the rotor head and rotor blades. He tugged on the control arms running up the rotor mast, thumped on the rotor blades, and cast a suspicious eye on everything.

"This is a very important part of the helicopter. Check it before each flight," he mumbled to himself. We both knew he was supposed to be talking to me, but he was too engrossed in what he was doing.

"Goddamn it! They stop-drilled that crack yesterday and it's already cracked again.

"This pitch-change link rod end was tight at the beginning of the last flight." He looked at it with disbelief, pulled on it a few more times, and shook his head.

I recognized *rod end* from my readings and knew that all the spinning, sliding, pushing, and pulling parts were connected to the pilot's controls by cables, chains, levers, links, bell cranks, bearings, and control

tubes with rod ends. He had moved his hand to the
top of the rotor head.

"Know what this is, Smith?"

"No, sir."

"This is the Jesus nut. If this comes off you're
going to see Jesus." I gave him my best forced laugh.
It was a dumb joke and I had already heard it.

"It's a lot easier on the nerves to find out this machine won't fly down here." He said this into the
fuel tank. "Never trust the fuel gauges. Always take
off the filler cap and check the level visually if you
can."

The preflight check took about twenty minutes and
then we were in the cockpit, with sturdy lap belts
and shoulder harnesses holding us in. "Put your helmet on." Bensen watched me fumble with the big
plastic-and-Styrofoam flight helmet. "Can you hear
me?" A voice came over the earphones.

"Yes, sir!" I replied with a little too much enthusiasm.

"No, Smith, you have to put the microphone in
front of your mouth, and key the mike switch when
you want to talk." To avoid the you-sure-are-a-
dumb-shit look that accompanied this information, I
pulled out my cockpit checklist and started to go
through it.

While I read the first of the twenty-three steps to
start the helicopter, Bensen reached down, flipped a
switch, pushed a button, and the whole helicopter
exploded in noise. The hundred-horsepower Lycom-
ing engine located less than two feet behind us did
not have any mufflers. At first the ship just sat there
backfiring and shaking, but as Phil gave it more gas
the noise increased and the rotor blades started whip-

ping around above us. The whole aircraft started rocking and hopping around.

"It smooths out at operating rpm," Phil said in my ears.

He kept twisting the throttle until the engine peaked at a mind-numbing roar. The helicopter did feel a little more comfortable, but not because the vibrations had disappeared, as I had hoped. Actually, the cacophony and vibrations continued to grow as Bensen gave it more throttle. They kept building, but somehow, as the engine and rotor tachometer needles moved into the green arc of operating rpm, all the vibrations seemed to blend smoothly into one big, barely contained vibration. Bensen flipped a few more switches, turned a few knobs, and then said to me and the tower, "Downing, seven-six-eight-one, takeoff direction."

"Seven-six-eight-one, Downing, takeoff is one-six-zero, winds one-two-zero at one-five. How copy?"

God, it was really happening. The machine was roaring, lights were blinking, dials and gauges were indicating readings, and now we were even talking like pilots. The only trouble was, everything was happening just a little too fast for me to really know what was going on.

"Downing, seven-six-eight-one, I copy five by, how me?"

"You're broken seven-six-eight-one," the tower came back.

"Screw you," Bensen replied. My mouth fell open; I turned to look at him. I could not believe what Phil had said to the men in the control tower.

He looked at me and for the first time broke into a smile. "That was just over the intercom," and then to the tower he said, "Roger that, Downing. I'll write it up. Thanks."

Then back to me: "Now, I know that you have read a lot of stuff, and you think you know how to fly one of these, but you don't. You will, but you've got a lot to learn." Bensen waited for a reaction.

"Yes, sir." Damn! Key the mike switch, dummy. "Yes, sir."

Bensen shook his head. "OK, watch me," he said, and pulled up on the collective, the tubular lever in his left hand that was connected to the main rotor blades. "As I pull up on the collective and the rotor blade's pitch increases, we get lift. Right? But this is also creating more drag, so I've got to give it more gas with the throttle." The throttle on the end of the collective looked just like a motorcycle throttle. He made the helicopter jump up and down a few times with short jerks on the collective. "Got that?" He paused. "Look! Watch your engine tach. When you pull up and the rpm starts to drop, you give it more gas. After a while you can do it by ear, but you should always check your instruments every fifteen seconds or so. Cross-check, you know. Now I'm going to pick it up to a hover. Watch my feet."

Bensen pulled the collective up a few inches and the helicopter rolled left a little, then rose. With only the slightest sensation of movement we had risen above the ground, and there we sat—simply hanging there. If not for all the noise, it would have been magical. The roar of the engine had increased substantially and there were all kinds of noises coming from everywhere, but a few more of the vibrations had disappeared, and all in all it felt really comfortable.

"Did you see how much left pedal I had to put

in?" I was supposed to have been watching his feet resting on the pedals that controlled the pitch in the tail-rotor blades.

"It takes that much tail-rotor thrust to counteract the drag from the main rotor system."

Without warning the helicopter effortlessly rotated ninety degrees to the left, then swung back to the right while Bensen craned his neck around, looking behind and above us.

"Always clear yourself so you don't bump into things. And remember, the other guy probably has his head up his ass too."

With that we started to glide along about five feet above the asphalt, following a yellow line toward our takeoff panel. I knew he had moved his cyclic forward to get us going in that direction, but the move had been so small that I could not detect it. The cyclic, a tubular control rising between the pilot's knees from the floor, was held in his right hand. It controls which way the main rotor blades tilt and thus the direction we traveled.

"Feel that crosswind?" We were sashaying back and forth a bit in a fifteen-mile-an-hour crosswind. "You can keep control with the tail-rotor thrust, but if the wind picks up you'll have a hard time with it. So I'll show you how to ground taxi."

His left hand moved the collective down and, still gliding forward, we settled to the ground. "Keep it light on the skids with the collective." The skid gear, horizontal metal tubes that support the helicopter, slid along the asphalt, making a terrible sound. Then we rose back into the air. "Don't do it any more than you have to—hard on the skid shoes."

We stopped over a yellow square painted on the

asphalt and Bensen called the tower again, "Downing, seven-six-eight-one, panel two."

"Seven-six-eight-one, Downing, you're cleared for takeoff."

"Now, watch our engine manifold pressure as we take off." He pushed the cyclic forward; we dropped a little and started gliding toward the trees across the field. We moved faster and faster; the aircraft shuddered; and we began climbing into the sky.

"Did you see the change in manifold pressure, Smith?" I had completely forgotten to watch it, and could not stop looking around as the airfield slipped behind us and we rose above the trees. Birds leaped from limbs and tried to out-climb us, then dove, zig-zagging back toward the ground. The horizon grew, stretching into fields, gullies, homes, farms, on and on. Glimpses of a small town slipped through the trees off to our left. The highway to Fort Worth took off straight as an arrow. It was like my first trip on a Ferris wheel: I had to see everything.

"It takes less power to fly than it does to take off. Right?" Bensen was staring at me.

"Uh, Yes, sir."

"OK, look around some more and I'll tell you what you're supposed to have seen." An audible sigh over the intercom. "You saw the drop in engine manifold pressure because . . ." Everything I had learned in the nice quiet classroom was lost in the sights and sensations of rotor-wing flight. What I did remember was patchy and unrelated to what was happening, as though everything I had learned had stayed on the ground.

Bensen and I got along pretty well in spite of what happened when he let me have the controls for the first time. It seems he thought I was trying to kill him.

"You've got the pedals, Smith." (In flight school, whenever the controls are passed between pilot and copilot, the act is stated and acknowledged.)

"I've got the pedals, sir." No sweat—the two large metal pedals under my feet control the tail rotor. Piece of cake—push the left pedal to rotate left, push the right pedal and the helicopter rotates right.

"I've got the pedals, Smith."

"You've got the pedals, sir."

"You've got the collective, Smith."

"I've got the collective, sir." The old "up stick," the collective, took a little more concentration than the pedals. It was pretty sensitive and there was a slight delay before the machine reacted to the up or down movement of the control. It was beginning to get difficult, but I was still in control.

"Not bad, Smith. I've got the collective."

"You've got the collective, sir."

"You've got the cyclic. Don't overcontrol."

"I've got the cyclic, sir." I knew it was going to be supersensitive, but it was also loose. With arm muscles tensed I tried to hold the cyclic in center position so that the machine would hover in one spot, but slowly we started to drift to the right. I corrected to the left, overcorrected, and then overcorrected back to the right. Oops, going backward and then back to the left.

"I've got the cyclic, Smith."

Great! You can have it. "You've got the controls, sir."

"Not bad. Think you can handle all three of them at once?"

"Yes, sir."

"You've got the pedals, Smith."

"I've got the pedals, sir."

"You've got the collective, Smith."

"I've got the collective, sir."

"You've got the cyclic."

"I've got theeeeee aaaaaaaaaaaaaa!" The helicopter had suddenly assumed the flight characteristics of a yo-yo in a hurricane. We were dropping down, then jerking back up again, swinging from side to side, while the nose of the aircraft twitched spasmodically left and right.

There was a very logical explanation for what had happened. Not only are the controls extremely sensitive, but every control movement requires a corresponding adjustment of the other controls.

For instance, when he gave me the pedals, I knew that left pedal turns take more pitch in the tail-rotor blades, and subsequently more engine power than right turns because the blades bite more air. So it was not simply a matter of pushing the pedals to keep the aircraft pointed in the right direction at a hover.

Any move on the collective also influenced the other controls—a helicopter does not like to stay in one position in a hover and constantly requires up and down adjustments of the collective. This also requires more or less throttle, corresponding to the main blade pitch and power need. When I increased the pitch and bite of the main rotor blades the body of the helicopter wanted to turn in the opposite direction of the rotating blades, and this took more left tail-rotor pedal to keep the aircraft straight, which in turn took more power . . . About that time the sweat started to bead on my forehead and roll into my eyes.

When he gave me the cyclic, it was all over. Actually, it was all over before he gave me the cyclic, but trying to hold that cyclic in the neutral position was the final straw. All I could do was lock up on the controls and wait for the crash.

"I've got it, I've got it!" Bensen screamed at me, working hard to overpower me on the controls. Seconds later we were hanging smoothly at a hover. I was holding on to the sides of my seat and Bensen was shaking his head. We had been so out of control that he had gone white-knuckled, one of the many ways helicopter pilots express tension, trying to get us back to a hover. "You'd think I'd get used to you idiots trying to kill me, but I don't." When he glanced at me I could see he was tired, not angry. "I'm glad you're the last one I have to fly with today," he said.

Several weeks later I soloed. That day, as never before, I felt the strength of confidence and the feeling of independence that come with accomplishment. For a few moments the fantasy of unassisted flight was mine. Then an odd sound from the engine and a nagging doubt about being a little lost brought me back to reality.

Our instructor pilots turned us loose on solo time to go out to designated safe landing areas to practice the maneuvers and techniques they had taught us. By then we were qualified to do short field landings and takeoffs, steep approaches, maximum performance takeoffs, pinnacle and confined-area landings. Solo was also the time to practice the maneuvers our instructor pilots had told us never to do, such as herding cattle, flying under bridges, buzzing trains, and bombing church steeples with the apples from our lunches. All of this was a lot of fun, but nothing beat helicopter tag.

The exercise required a good friend, a wide, winding river, and two helicopters on solo time. The friend had to be a person who could fly a helicopter with abandon and not lose control of the machine. The object of helicopter tag was to close within a helicopter length of the other aircraft while he did everything he could to stay ahead of you. The rules were: Stay less than a hundred feet above the river, don't leave the confines of the riverbanks, and absolutely *no* sudden stops.

Helicopter tag was not something that one good WOC would suggest to another good WOC; it took a certain kind of relationship—a close and trusting friendship with a mutual appreciation of things more fun than safe.

When I first met Craig Fielding it would have been hard to imagine anything we might mutually appreciate, and he definitely did not know what he was doing. The first time he said anything to me was while we were walking punishment laps, not more than ten feet from a TAC officer who was looking around trying to catch people talking. I have no idea what he said—it came across as a mumble—but I gave a chuckle of understanding anyhow. We finished our laps at the same time and walked over to the WOC beer bar. He was not much of a conversationalist, but he was pretty good at pinball. A few beers and games of pinball later Craig and I were standing at the trough-type urinal with several other WOCs, everyone concentrating on keeping the splash-back to a minimum. Without warning Craig reached behind my back and crammed his thumb against the seat of my fatigue pants.

"Can't pee with a thumb up your butt," he said with an impish grin.

"What the hell are you doing? Jesus Christ! Craig, what . . . ? You're weird." And he was weird, but he was also right, I could not pee. But what an odd thing to do.

"Back home, call that a cob," he explained. "Pretty good one, huh?" I couldn't believe it; he actually wanted a critique on his "cob."

I just looked at him, trying to figure him out, which was not easy. Craig was a quiet guy, pretty inconspicuous except for his pale blue eyes and a pink scar that ran across his right temple. The way he mumbled while we were walking punishment laps was the way he talked all the time. Actually it was more of a strange speech pattern than a mumble. He talked in short clumps of words, started sentences in the middle, ended sentences in the middle, answered questions that had not been asked—all in a low Southern drawl.

"Do you ever smell your thumb after you do that?" I had to ask. We both cracked up, and so began one of the most interesting friendships of my life. Interesting, if for no other reason than that Craig was so hard to understand.

It was just a matter of time before we started playing helicopter tag. The raw material was there, the Brazos River, snaking across wide-open Texas, and almost every day we were in the air at the same time, both flying solo. One cool morning it all came together with a coded call on an unauthorized radio frequency.

"Phantom, this is the Shadow. Meet me at the OK Corral." Not very original, but it had the right elements. Ten minutes later I met Craig, a.k.a. Phantom, circling above the confluence of the Brazos and Kikapoo Rivers, our prearranged meeting spot.

Flight school was never the same after that. Every chance we got we took off for the OK Corral and raced up and down the rivers, engines screaming, skidding around corners, sliding up along the trees in nearly vertical turns, like riding a motorcycle in the air. We scared the poop right out of the little birds we almost ran over, and did a good job of scaring ourselves with near misses of birds, trees, and electrical wires. The necessity of using both hands and both feet to control the helicopter in the tight corridor of the river proved to be a direct link to the limits and incredible sensations of three-dimensional flight. We were learning the limits by feel and how to react by instinct. It was great fun, and that is why we did it, but those hours of illegal, low-level flight were also perfect training for flying Scouts in Vietnam.

The job of a Scout pilot in the 1st Cavalry Division in Vietnam in 1969 was much the same as any military scouting through history. He went out looking for the enemy. For a good scout anywhere, finding the enemy was usually easy; getting back home was the hard part. Later, when I was out hunting with the helicopter, my quarry knew I was after him and would hide. By the time I had him located, I was usually right on top of him, close enough to see him squeeze the trigger. He always got the first shot, so it was to my advantage to be proficient in erratic, high-speed, low-level turns, just as in helicopter tag. I was now also learning to fly while focusing on something else. In helicopter tag it was Craig; in Vietnam it would be the enemy.

My confidence in my flying ability and in myself grew. The system almost seemed to feed itself. My newfound flying ability fueled my confidence; my confidence allowed me to expand my flying abilities.

But even though we were having a great time learning to fly, it was hard to forget about what lay ahead for us in Southeast Asia.

A few weeks before we soloed, I had come up with another plan to keep me out of Vietnam. If I dropped out near the end of flight school there would be little more than a year left of my two-year obligation. There would be nowhere near enough time to retrain me as an infantryman, I reasoned. Most likely I would be stationed at Fort Wolters to hang around as a cook's assistant or something. After soloing, however, the dropout plan went on hold. Flying became the focus of my thoughts—a way of life. And as my interest in flying grew, the world outside flight school almost ceased to exist.

We tried to stay in touch with our peer group and the times. Off base we tried to be cool in our sandals, bell-bottom jeans, and tie-dyed shirts. Very few of my class actually supported the war in Vietnam; a number of us were openly opposed to it. There were even a few of us who smoked pot, but no matter what we did we were not accepted off base. None of the people our age wanted to associate with soldiers on their way to war in the midst of a popular peace movement. The worst part was trying to find someone to fall in love with. After a while we just gave up on any social life outside the Army and concentrated on being pilots.

The five months of Primary Flight School went by quickly, and it was time to move on to Savannah, Georgia, for advanced flight training. They gave us four days to travel from Texas to Georgia, which is normally a pretty easy trip, unless you decide to go via New York City. Craig and I turned an eleven-hundred-mile drive into a three-thousand-mile drink-

and-drive marathon. It was a noble mission, a party with old friends and girlfriends. Things went pretty well up to the last part of the trip. It seems that the massive amount of amphetamines we were taking to stay awake were covering up most of the signs of alcohol poisoning. The first hard evidence that we were losing it came when we stopped to get gas, only hours from Savannah. A mechanic noticed one of our tires was flat.

"Hey, y'all's rear tire's 'bout flat." He bent over and looked at it. "It's ruint. How long you been drivin' it laak that?" We had no idea.

A few beers later Craig lost his voice and began to turn a dull gray-blue color. Still, I think we would have made it to the base on time if that cop had not stopped us. It was one of those sleazy speed traps where they put a twenty-five-mile-an-hour sign on a straight stretch of road in the middle of nowhere, and wait for a car with out-of-state plates. The cop stuck his face in my window and asked, "You know how fast you was goin', son?"

As I looked at him, contemplating my answer, his face started moving out of focus, the way the moon does when you are real drunk. "No, sir." I was so tired it seemed plausible that he actually might not know. But he did know. And at a snail's pace he wrote up our ticket, took us to the justice of the peace, and took my money. We were forty-five minutes late reporting to our new WOC company at Hunter Army Airfield. Our new commanding officer, Major Warren, welcomed us personally.

"Candidates Smith and Fielding, I want you to give me at least one good reason why you are forty-seven minutes late reporting to your new duty station."

"Sir—Candidate Smith, sir—we are late because we were arrested in a speed trap just outside of town, sir."

"That is an excuse, Candidate Smith, not a reason."

"Sir—Candidate Smith, sir—yes, sir, well, the reason is that we had trouble coming up with the money to pay the fine, sir."

"That is an another *Excuse*, Candidate Smith, not a *Reason*."

As an Army pilot I should have understood that there was no reason, only excuses, but having so recently returned from four days of civilian life it was hard to see the difference.

"Candidate Fielding, what reason do you have?"

"Sir—Candidate Smith, sir—Candidate Fielding has temporarily lost his voice, sir."

"Well, Candidate Smith, can you give me a reason why Candidate Fielding has lost his voice, and why he looks like a three-day-old corpse?"

"Sir—Candidate Smith, sir—I think he has the flu, sir."

"Flu, my ass. Get him to the infirmary, and I am giving you twenty-four hours to come up with a *Reason* why you are late."

Craig went to the infirmary, where he was diagnosed as almost dead. A few days later, when he had fully recovered, the major suggested we think about the difference between reasons and excuses on our days off, while we painted the stairwells of all the barracks.

Major Warren was not much different from our preflight training officers, but Hunter Army Airfield was a lot different from Fort Wolters. Hunter was an operating military base, not a school. The disciplinary atmosphere was gone and the change was noticeable in everyone. The confidence and pride we felt inside rose to the surface. We had made it to advanced flight training, we had learned a lot along the way, and now we were at Hunter to finish the job. Also different from Fort Wolters was the aircraft we got to fly. At Hunter our training was in the Bell UH-1, the impressive "Huey," ninety-five hundred pounds gross weight and capable of carrying twelve passengers.

The TH-55 at Fort Wolters had been a "kick the tire, light the fire" kind of helicopter. Walk around, take a look, and start it up, similar to preflighting a motorcycle. The Huey was more like getting a large ship ready for sea. Hueys were more than forty-one feet long and at least four times the size of a TH-55.

The TH-55 had a metal tube about eight inches wide for a tail boom; I could climb inside the tail boom of the Huey. The Huey's fourteen-hundred-horsepower gas turbine engine, all covered in tubes and wires, sat in its own engine compartment above and behind the passenger compartment; it was quite a bit more elaborate than the hundred-horse piston engine sitting on some tubes behind the pilots of the TH-55. The rotor blades on the TH-55 were thirteen feet long; twenty-four feet on the Huey. The TH-55 had seemed like a toy from the first day; my first impression of the Huey told me it would need quite a bit of respect.

I could not see how I would ever learn to concentrate on all the instruments in the Huey. In front of the pilot and copilot were rows of gauges and dials; above them were banks of circuit breakers and switches, and between them were rows of radios and more circuit breakers. There was even a separate electrical system for starting the engine. It seemed that just preflighting and starting the Huey would take an hour or more.

Another big change from the TH-55 was the sound of the Huey. Instead of the customary cough, bang, and roar of the gas engine, the Huey's turbine started with a deep, resonant moan. In seconds the moan rapidly accelerated in pitch and tone until all sounds were drowned out by the roar of gases pouring out of the fourteen-inch exhaust cone. The only sound that rose above the turbine was the beat of the Huey's rotor blades, a truly beautiful sound.

At first it seemed that no matter how hard the big turbine whooshed away, it was not going to get those enormous rotor blades to turn. Several long seconds into the start, the blade sticking way out over the nose jerked up, fell down, and then slowly dragged itself off to the left. Just as it disappeared another great big blade swung overhead a little faster, then the next, faster and faster until they all but disappeared. As their speed increased, the rotor blades churned the air into a windstorm, and out of the rushing wind came a pounding sound, a muffled beat keeping time with each rotation of the blades.

There were other major differences at Hunter Army Airfield too. Anytime we were not involved with flight training we could leave the base. What a treat civilized Savannah was after the tacky sprawl of south Texas: Savannah, Georgia, a seaport wrapped in genteel Southern history and pride, shaded from the heat by the canopies of ancient trees and perfumed with flowers. The first chance we got, Craig and I headed downtown to the well-worn bars along the Savannah River.

This should have been a very untroubled time in our lives. The Army was treating us decently, Savannah was a comfortable town, and there were some great bars to frequent. But the looks we got as we walked in the door let us know we were not going to be making many friends in this town. Craig and I saw each other as two fairly cool, good-looking enough, fun-loving young men who were becoming damn good helicopter pilots. What they saw was two skinny nerds with shaved heads—military transients on their way to "who cares."

For the first three months of advanced flight training our free time was the least of our problems. There was still a lot to learn. But when we did get days when nothing was scheduled, Craig and I, tired of the social stigmas we felt, found new ways to entertain ourselves off base. We rented canoes to paddle the waterways and tidal marshes, most of the time just watching the wildlife. We also spent a lot of time out on the barrier island beaches, lying in the sun like lizards. And no matter where we went we took a cold twelve-pack of beer, our portable tape player, and the very worn-out soundtrack from the rock musical *Hair*.

One April day, on leave from our Army duties, Craig and I wandered off into the tall trees and dense undergrowth on the little barrier island surrounding Fort Pulaski, an old Civil War fort. We were just about to turn back when we came upon a clearing with an old decrepit house in it. Trees poked through the roof and vines hung out of empty windows. The old wood structure was dead, so new life was taking over. A tower rose straight up from the front door, twice the height of the house. It was the kind of place that spurs the imagination, just what we had been looking for. Minutes later we were perched thirty feet up in the air on the few remaining timbers of the tower porch, soaking up the sun and the character of our surroundings. Sparrows and warblers fluttered and chirped in the trees around us; big dark turkey buzzards floated high above us. It was a peaceful day.

"O'Connor told me Martin wants to fly medevac," I said.

Craig, as usual, did not respond. For months he had been doing his best to ignore the whole Vietnam issue, so I continued. "Absolutely no chance of not getting shot down. O'Connor's instructor pilot flew medevac. Got shot down; copilot and crew chief killed."

"Someone's got to do it," Craig said without opening his eyes.

"Sure, once or twice. But where there's wounded, there's enemy, and then it's just a matter of time. They shouldn't make guys fly those dangerous jobs day after day. That sucks," I said, getting more worked up than necessary.

"Shouldn't have to go at all. Stay right here and watch it on TV like everybody else," he replied. Craig sat up with a grunt, squinted at the sun, and slowly opened a warm Pabst Blue Ribbon.

"I've got to get a job like Judy's brother Harry flying generals around," I thought out loud.

"Vietnamese don't want us. It's on the news," Craig said, not even hearing my comment about Harry. "They're afraid of us. Treat us like big dumb kids."

"What do you want to fly over there, Craig?"

"Don't know. Maybe guns." Gunships flew around and shot rockets.

"That would be cool," I said, out of conditioned reflex. We watched a couple of birds fighting in a treetop across from us. "Jesus, Craig, do you realize how straight we've become? I mean, look at us, we are becoming model WOCs."

"Yeah."

"We're getting pretty close to goin' to Vietnam." Even to myself I sounded worried.

"Makes me have an erection." He smirked.

"What are you talking about, asshole?" I was not in the mood to figure out what he meant.

"Shut down?" He looked at me to see how angry I was and decided he had better continue before I started yelling at him for not finishing his thoughts. "You know, shut down. Gives me a hard-on."

"No kidding? That happens to you too?" It was a phenomenon created by the wide canvas-and-leather seat belts that lay across our laps. After shutting off the engine—"shut down"—we stayed at the controls until everything stopped turning. As the rotor blades slowed, the helicopter picked up a steady rocking motion, up and down. The rocking made the heavy seat belt buckle roll rhythmically in the crotch. On warm days an erection was almost inevitable.

"IP looks at me funny." Craig grinned. He was talking about his instructor pilot and the fact that our one-piece flight suits did nothing to cover up these untimely erections.

After a while Craig squinted at the sun again and said, "We're startin' to understand the system. . . . Means we think like them, act like them."

"What the hell does that mean, Craig?" I said, knowing exactly what he meant about our military indoctrination. I did not give him a chance to answer. "When I get back I might build a house like this one."

"*If* you come back."

"That's a really great thing to say, Craig."

"Yeah, you're right." He apologized by looking sheepish.

That night I wrote a letter to a family friend who had a summer home near ours in the Adirondacks—General Palmer, who was commanding general at Tripler Army Hospital, Hawaii. The purpose of the letter was to let him know that I was about to be sent to my death. I think he missed the point because he wrote back:

> You can be very proud of your accomplishments in becoming a pilot. The role you will play in Vietnam is an extremely important and necessary one.

We were all getting pretty nervous about the future, as well we should have. In fact, we should have been terrified. Flight school was almost over; Vietnam was inevitable. We had no idea where we were going or what we would be doing when we got there. More than two thousand helicopters had been shot down or crashed. More than a thousand pilots had been killed. I think I was even more worried than most, since I already had been through my first crash.

My instructor pilot and I were in a Huey, practicing autorotations. Performing an autorotation in a helicopter tests a pilot's reaction to an engine failure. Unless immediate action is taken when the engine quits, a fatal crash is inevitable.

"You've got to get that collective down fast. You're not pushing it down fast enough. Look how many rpm's you've lost. Do your instrument cross-check, but don't get hung up. Get it down," my IP said as he gave me a critique of my entry into autorotation.

When the engine quits, the lifting effect of the blades turns to drag. In seconds the rotor blades will slow to a stop and the helicopter becomes uncontrollable. To eliminate the drag, the pilot enters autorotation by bottoming the collective, reducing the lift and subsequently the drag—the helicopter then falls like a stone.

"OK! Now, see, your rpm is building again. That's good, but don't let it get too high." The helicopter's rapid descent had two effects: it forced all the blood to my head, making me dizzy, and it forced air back up through the spinning rotor blades. This flow of air kept the rotor blades rotating. In our autorotation it was even increasing the rotor rpm.

"OK! Pull up on the collective a bit. That's it, bring the rpm back down. . . . Watch that airspeed. You're below sixty knots. Nose it over, that's it. . . . Collective back down, your rpm is almost out of the green." The autorotation was starting to come together, but I was far from feeling comfortable. The ground was only two hundred feet below us and we were heading straight for it at the speed of fourteen hundred feet a minute.

"Start the flare now, sir?" Flare and cushion is the last step. At a hundred feet the pilot pulls back on the cyclic and holds it until forward speed drops to zero. Then he levels it and cushions the landing with the remaining rotor rpm.

"Nooo . . . Hold it! Keep it nosed over. Watch your rpm! OK, now!" I had just started to pull back on the cyclic when there was a loud bang. I was preoccupied with the flare and tried to ignore it, but my IP was yelling, "I've got it! I've got it!" and the helicopter started a sickening roll forward.

It did not take long to realize that we were out of

control. The more we rotated forward, the farther I retreated back in my seat, away from the ground coming at us. The helicopter was crashing; there was nothing I could do about it. It was the same terror I had felt as a kid the first time my brothers pushed me off the high dive, that same frozen panic as I hung suspended, knowing it was too late; I was already over the edge. We hit hard. The chin bubbles shattered and we bounced forward, hit again, and slid to a stop in a cloud of dust.

We had lost our ninety-degree tail-rotor gearbox and tail rotor. The gearbox had come apart and torn itself off the helicopter, taking with it the whole tail rotor. The loss of weight that far back on the tail (way past the center of gravity) left the nose too heavy and caused the machine to roll forward.

Three weeks earlier a student pilot and his instructor had died from the same mechanical failure. They had taken off from the airfield and were about five hundred feet up when they lost the ninety-degree gearbox and rotated into the runway. The helicopter burned before the crash crew could get them out.

We walked away from our crash because we had been in a nose-high attitude, only fifty feet above the ground. Fifty feet higher and we surely would have died.

For the rest of the day I kept sliding from the euphoria of great luck to the depression of a near-death experience, and back up again. But worse than the yo-yo effect was the memory of helplessness, of feeling doomed as we rotated toward the ground. It would have been worse if I had not stayed on the controls with my IP. After he said "I've got it," he had taken over, but I had forgotten to let go of the controls. The few simple moves I felt him make were flashes of hope. They had given me a feeling that something was being done to save us.

Other than almost dying in a crash and living with the fact that we were all going to Vietnam, life just got better and better those last few weeks. The cadre, our flight instructors, and other personnel let us know that flight school was over, that it was time for a break before the big test, Vietnam. They all wished us luck.

On 18 May 1969 I received my officer's bars and pilot's wings. That evening, at our graduation dinner, Uncle Pat gave the benediction and a little speech. It was a very proud day for me, having him there, having someone I respected see me finish a task as difficult and unique as mastering helicopter flight.

3

New Guy

Mid-June 1969

The ten months of flight training had left me mission-oriented and, as a new officer, I had developed, almost overnight, a sense of duty to the Army. My deeper conscience, however, had not been fooled and kept saying, "This is terrible. Run, you fool, run!" One side of me, the new officer and pilot, was willing to continue on to Vietnam as if it were another stage of flight training. But the other side of me, the rum-soaked sun sponge, on twenty days, leave in the Caribbean with his good buddy Craig, was very comfortable hanging out on the beaches and in the bars, and did not want to even think about, much less go to, Vietnam. The pleasures of civilian life in the Caribbean, along with a few nagging premonitions of doom, got me to rally for one last-ditch effort to avoid the inevitable trip to Vietnam.

After my appeal to General Palmer was ignored it was not easy to try again, but Craig and I flew back to Washington where a cousin, Colonel Owens (Uncle Bill), was stationed at the Pentagon. His secretary ushered us into his office and seated us on a big leather couch about fifteen feet in front of his desk. Uncle Bill sat there beaming at us for the longest time and then said, "You young men make me proud." For the better part of an hour he went on and on about young men like us going off to war, and how he wished he could be going with us. It was humiliating, sitting there like a ten year old, getting patted on the head, waiting for an opportunity to blurt out, "But Uncle Bill, we don't want to go. Save us!" But we never worked up the nerve.

The last few days before my flight left for Southeast Asia I spent in the Adirondack Mountains. Spring was turning to summer at our home on Johns Brook. Cool nights, soft flannel sheets and down quilts, the sound of the brook gurgling and drumming its song, brought with each night the dreamless sleep of a child. Mornings unfolded with the excited chatter of birds and the soft smell of pine needles warming in the sun. I spent the days lying on the warm boulders in the brook or sitting in the woods watching the new shoots and buds turn into leaves and flowers.

This environment did little to make me feel like jumping on a plane en route to a steamy jungle full of guys who were waiting around to blow my head off. I felt like someone caught in the suction of a whirlpool, or in a dream world where I was being chased but could only run in slow motion. My fears turned to depression on 16 June 1969, when my flight left New York for Saigon. Forty-eight hours later I was supposed to be in the Republic of Vietnam—and I would have made it, if we had not stopped in San Francisco.

There I was, last stop in the USA, on my way to what my heart knew was certain death. Well, one thing led to another, and before long I found myself wandering aimlessly, alone and quite intoxicated. My nose, caught by the rich and varied smells of the sea, led me to the waterfront and its seedy nocturnal patrons. There I found what I was looking for, a lady, as lovely and dark as the night itself. After our introductions were complete, I suggested we go somewhere for a drink.

"I don't drink when I'ze workin', and talk's goin' to cost you." She was a businesswoman and knew it. When I asked her what she charged for her time she looked down her nose at me and said, "I ain't cheap." I couldn't help correcting her: "You mean you're not inexpensive."

"You a smart-ass, or what?" She glared at me. That did it, I was in love. But not even love could solve our communication problems: even our good-bye suffered.

It was an awkward moment for me and all I could think of was, "Well, thanks. I don't know what to say."

She tried to make it easy and said, "You take care of youself, honey."

"Could I leave you a tip or something?" I was having a hard time walking away.

"Why, that's sweet of you, sugar, you don't have to." She was really being kind and I wanted to show her I appreciated it.

"Do you have a pen?" I asked.

"Somewhere, sugar. What you need a pen for?"

"To write you a check—all my cash is gone."

"I don't take no checks," she snorted, looking me up and down with disgust.

By then I was aware that she often took things out of context. "I understand that you don't accept checks in payment for your services, but this is a tip. You've already been paid and you can't lose by taking this tip." She still looked confused. "Even if it bounces, you won't have lost any income, and if it's good, you come out ahead," I reasoned.

"I don't take *no* checks." She was a woman of conviction.

I was more than a day late for my flight to Saigon, but when I reported no one even noticed—I was just a little part of a big machine. A sergeant directed us to the boarding area and the next flight to Saigon.

Less than twenty-four hours later we landed in Tan Son Nhut, just outside of Saigon. It was after midnight and still ninety degrees. Little skinny men in black pajamas, who looked a lot like the dreaded Vietcong we had seen on television, came out to service the plane as we unloaded. They were speaking to each other in what sounded like several different languages. Some of them drew out long, singsong sounds, high and low. Others spit sharp, short words at each other. Every one of them was talking and not one of them seemed to be listening.

The terminal was operating at maximum capacity. Civilians in suits and dresses, soldiers in stained jungle fatigues, sailors in their crisp whites, people of every shape, size, and color were going about their business as if it were twelve noon, not twelve midnight. My first impression of Vietnam was that everyone and anyone had been invited.

A gray Navy bus took us to the replacement center in Bien Hoa, an enormous green canvas tent camp where service personnel checked in and out. I liked the smell—it reminded me of the woods—but as far as accommodations went, they were less than adequate. It was a mess, dirty and dusty, with thirty of us in one tent, no one knowing where to go or what to do. I finally found a tent full of clerk typists who told me I was late and therefore no longer going to the 12th Aviation Group. "Where do I go, then?" I asked one of them.

"What's your name, sir?" he asked in answer to my question. "Tom Smith," I told him. "We'll take care of it, sir," he responded. This was fine with me, so I asked directions to the officers' club.

"The Army doesn't have one; Air Force does though. Down by the water tower. It's a wood building."

The Air Force Officers' Club was nice, by most standards. It was air-conditioned, dark, and cool, almost as fancy as some Mid-western Holiday Inn bars: a wood bar, brass rail, big high-backed leather bar stools, and dark velvet walls. One half of the building was for drinking, the other for dining and dancing. Food, entertainment, and twenty-five-cent drinks made it my kind of place.

Like any good bar, the officers' club was more than a place to eat and drink; it was a social center, a place where strangers could loosen up and feel at home. I had not seen one person I knew since leaving Hunter Army Airfield, but after three Jim Beams I was among friends. Army, Navy, and Air Force officers from one end of South Vietnam to the other filled the bar nightly. From the war stories I heard, it was obvious that Vietnam was a war of extremes. There were extremes in the weaponry. Square miles of dense jungle were churned to dirt in minutes by bombs dropped from invisible bombers. At the same time, supersonic jets were being shot down by small-arms fire. There were extremes in combat techniques. Some troops rode to the front line in helicopters while others tunneled through the earth below. And there were the usual extremes in job assignments. Some men crawled alone into enemy camps to kill their foes as they slept, while others tended bar.

Everyone had a war story except for a few guys who obviously wanted to be left alone. Most of the stories were full of gruesome details; some of them were pretty funny. The storytellers made it sound as if they were right there when the action was happening, had seen a lot of action themselves, but not one had been part of the action. Even the fighter pilots, just back from a mission, could relate only parts of the story. They would passionately describe every detail of how perfectly they executed their bombing run, but a major part of the story, what happened on the ground, was all speculation.

A number of particularly ugly war stories contradicted what we had heard in flight school: stories of American positions being overrun by the enemy, no survivors; and American prisoners having their skin peeled off, being left to die of exposure. In flight school we had been told that we were winning the war in Vietnam. Helicopters, infantrymen, and their supporting artillery were hopping around the jungle chasing the cowardly enemy. The hardest part, supposedly, was cornering the enemy long enough to kill them.

An infantry captain on his way home told me who he thought was winning the war. "Winning? You think we're winning this war? Who told you that?" was his response to my insinuation that helicopters were winning the war. "We're doing everything we can to *lose* this war. Who gives a shit, I'm outta here. One more wake-up and I'm gone, adios, back to the world."

The next day, 25 June 1969, my new orders were cut. MACV (Military Assistance Command Vietnam) had assigned me to the 1st Cavalry Division (Airmobile), Tay Ninh. Everyone had heard of the 1st

Cav—they were on a par with the Marines as far as stupidity went. One of the 1st Cav's proudest moments in Vietnam was the day they had had more men killed than the Marines. It was the worst assignment possible! Cav pilots were legendary assholes, gung-ho fools who reputedly paraded around in cavalry outfits, hats, swords, and spurs. Their commanding officers were always sending them out on suicide missions.

I went back to the clerk typists and argued, to no avail, that I had been assigned to the 12th Aviation Group, a comparatively easy assignment. Then I went back to the officers' club for a drink. John, the Filipino bartender, and I were the only ones there. We had come to know each other pretty well over the last four days, so I told him about my new orders.

"Uuuh, that no good," he said, shaking his head. "Tay Ninh, War Zone C, no good."

"War Zone C? Is that where Tay Ninh is? Goddamn, I heard about the fighting there all the way back home, on TV. It seemed as if every day the news started with, 'Today, in War Zone C, amidst heavy fighting . . .'" This was getting serious. "This really sucks," I whined to John.

"Maybe things be OK," John offered kindly, but he did not look me in the eye again until I changed the subject.

There were several small details to take care of before I left for my new outfit, a few more shots, dog tags, records. The process took on a dreamlike quality; this was really it, the end was near. When a sergeant asked me my religion for my dog tags I thought for a minute and told him "None." A lieutenant gave me a card that explained how to interact with the Vietnamese people without offending them.

As we flew over Tay Ninh at five thousand feet I remembered what John had said: *"Maybe things be OK."* However, things definitely did not look OK down there. The small circular base below us seemed like a wagon train drawn into a circle, outnumbered and cut off from support, making a last-ditch effort to save itself. Looking down on this circular cavalry outpost made me ache with loneliness. In a completely foreign world, full of hostile people, I was all alone, without even one of my buddies from flight school. A lot of my confidence and security had been built on the camaraderie that developed in flight school.

The small Vietnamese town of Tay Ninh and the U.S. Army base sat near the north bank of the Co Dong River, a few miles from the Cambodian border. The town covered the east side of the base, and the north and west sides were surrounded by rice paddies and banana groves. The dirt circle of the base, spotted with patches of concrete and asphalt and littered with machines, clashed with the pastoral scene of productive green fields and little thatched huts. Five miles to the northeast, Nui Ba Den, the Black Virgin Mountain, rose out of the fields and jungle. Like a mirage it loomed all alone in the ever-present haze, almost three thousand feet above everything else.

As the plane dipped a wing, turning to its final approach, I could see how the base was laid out. It looked like a high-security dump, surrounded by a hundred-foot apron of barbed-wire barriers. Immediately inside the barbed wire was the "green line," a wall of bulldozed dirt about five feet high and twenty feet wide. On top of that, about every thirty feet, bunkers were sunk in the dirt and covered with sandbags. Machine-gun barrels stuck out from the gun ports in the bunkers facing the barbed wire.

Inside the green line the place was trashed. The olive drab and camouflage paint on the tanks, trucks, artillery pieces, and aircraft gave them a neglected look. Oiled dirt roads full of potholes ran between tents, tin shacks, and storage yards. Sandbags piled around and on top of everything took away any semblance of the neat, organized military bases I was used to. As the plane came in to land I realized that the odd dark spots I had seen on the runway were mortar holes. Bulldozers were pushing dirt into them. We touched down with a squeal of tires, bounced back into the air, and landed again.

"Bad nerves or a hangover," the guy next to me said.

The hundred-degree heat and ninety-percent humidity rolled in through the open rear hatch, filling the cabin with the smell of turbine exhaust and the sickening odor of burned tires from the rough landing. The heat, combined with the noxious odors, became claustrophobic. It was hard to breathe; sweat beaded on my face and ran down my chest. As we taxied to the terminal, I could not help but consider the possibility of staying on the plane for its return flight to Long Binh. Then a helicopter hovered by, a Cobra gunship, with full rocket pods hanging from its stub wings and a minigun protruding from the nose turret below the forward pilot/gunner.

The Cobra stopped, then turned toward us. As it hung there motionless, watching us, a slow staccato beat coming from the blur of its rotating blades, my anxieties slowly disappeared. Sitting in front of me was my reason for being there. Slowly the lithe machine turned and moved off, trailing a wispy veil of turbine exhaust.

We rolled to a stop and the pilot cut the throttles. What little breeze there had been stopped. By the time I was halfway to the door of the plane the sweat stains from my armpits met in the center of my chest. None of the passengers talked or even looked at each other as we walked to the one-room terminal; it was too hot. The sergeant at the MACV counter said he would call for some transportation. Even if my new company had been right across the runway I would not have tried to walk there.

"Do people really fight in this heat, Sergeant?" I asked lightheartedly, trying to turn a depressing situation around.

"That's a dumb question, even for a new guy, . . . sir."

New guy. It seemed impossible for anyone to use that term with any kind of respect. A new guy was anybody who had arrived "in country" after you had, like the first day of flight school all over again.

"Jesus, Sergeant, I was just kidding. Take it easy," I assured him.

"Sorry, sir, can't handle it today. We were taking rockets and mortars for hours last night. Two of my buddies got blown away trying to get to a bunker. Fuckin' gooks!"

Waiting for my ride, I read a copy of *Stars and Stripes*, the Army's propaganda newspaper, and was once again assured we were winning the war.

A tired private in a dusty jeep took me to the operations office of my new company, right across the runway. It was impossible to miss. First came the big yellow sign hung over the road, NO. 1 BRIGADE IN VIETNAM, then a sign on the side proclaimed, ALL THE

WAY, FIRST TEAM. We came to a stop at another one that read, HEADQUARTERS, 1ST BRIGADE, 1ST CAVALRY DIVISION (AIRMOBILE), THE FIRST TEAM.

It was easy to get the message that the 1st Brigade was proud to be in Vietnam, but it was hard to understand why. The company area certainly wasn't anything to shout about. It looked like a refugee camp baking in the heat. There was not one thing green or alive on the hard-packed dirt that surrounded the rows of tin sheds. Next to one of the buildings some Vietnamese women, talking a mile a minute, were filling sandbags under a makeshift sunscreen. A shirtless soldier with an M16 rifle sat in the shade watching them.

"Over there, sir," the private said, pointing to one of many tin sheds behind the big FIRST TEAM sign. All the sheds were about the same size, twenty by forty feet. Some had sandbags stacked up to the screen windows. Others had sandbag shelters built beside them. The private had pointed to a shed with FLYING CIRCUS, OPERATIONS OFFICE painted above the door. As I passed the chattering sandbaggers they all fell silent, as if on cue, then watched me go by and started right back up again. One young girl gave me a cute, shy smile.

Inside the operations office was a solitary corporal sitting in front of his fan writing a letter. Corporal Wilson, the company clerk, was clearly a nice kid—he even put the fan on rotate so it would blow on me too. He took a copy of my orders, asked me a few questions, and filled out my paperwork for me. We were on the way out the door, Wilson showing me to my quarters, when a captain and a lieutenant walked in. "Captain Crane, Mr. Smith, new pilot from the replacement center, sir," Wilson told the short, round captain. I started to give him a salute, but he grabbed my hand to shake it.

"Smith, pleased to meet you; welcome aboard," the captain said. "This is Lieutenant Lonas." I exchanged greetings with the young lieutenant. "Come into my office if you're done with Wilson," the captain continued. It was reassuring to see that neither of them was wearing swords or spurs. With the possible exception of Captain Crane's skinny blond handlebar mustache, they did not fit the image of gung-ho Cav soldiers at all. The lieutenant looked like a college student at an ROTC drill; the captain, with his mustache and ruddy cheeks, looked more like a member of a barbershop quartet. The captain and I went into his office.

"Hot day," he said, turning on his fan.

"I haven't stopped sweating since I got here," I agreed.

"Gets worse when the monsoons come. So hot and wet, your skin starts to rot." We went through some friendly small talk about the weather and where we were from, and then he filled me in on what the aviation platoon did for the 1st Brigade's headquarters company.

"We have two missions here—Command and Control, and Scouts. Some Ash and Trash missions also," he started in.

"Ash and Trash?" I asked.

"Yeah, taking men out to the firebases, frequency changes, and stuff like that. We use the Hueys for Command and Control, LOHs [light observation helicopters; pronounced "loaches"] for Scouts and for Ash and Trash." He stopped in the middle of his prepared text and looked at me in a funny way. "You want to fly Scouts?"

"Scouts? I hadn't really thought about it, sir, but no. I don't think so." Scouts? No way. We had heard a few stories about flying Scouts from our IPs, none of them good. "Mark the target with a burning LOH," was a common joke about the mission of the LOHs and the Scout pilots who flew them. They were always getting shot down.

"Need some more Scout pilots," he said mostly to himself while he stared at a spot above my head. Then he began a one-hour narrative about why we were in Tay Ninh. "This aviation platoon supports the brigade commanders, the fire-support bases, and 1st Cavalry troops in our area of operations." While the captain was talking he started sorting through some files on his desk. This didn't seem rude, because even though he was obviously tired of the speech he continued to deliver it with feeling. My impression of him changed; he reminded me more of the pilots who had helped me through flight school than a baritone or a tenor.

"Our area of operations is about fifty miles on each side, with Cambodia to our north and west. We're in the middle of one of the major travel corridors for enemy troops and supplies moving south from Cambodia." He found what he was looking for and started to read it to himself while he continued his talk. "Tay Ninh and our fire-support bases are the heart of the 1st Cavalry's efforts to stop this traffic. We're accomplishing this by locating and controlling these routes with infantry and artillery." He lost stride for a moment when he caught me trying to look out the door. I could see Lonas and Wilson playing darts in the office outside. "You know, Search and Destroy missions." Seeing he had my attention again, he got back into his speech.

"It's a team effort. We locate the supply routes, move the troops in, and support them with artillery and air." The captain swiveled in his chair to face a bunch of maps tacked together on a piece of plywood behind his desk. He admired them for a moment. Then, with his back still to me, he said, "You see these here?" as he pointed to some flags on pins. "LZ [landing zone] White, LZ Grant, and LZ Jamie. See how the fields of fire from these fire-support bases [the LZs] overlap?" He drew some circles around the flags with his finger. "That's what makes it work—team effort." He turned to stare at me. "Where do we come in? Our brigade Scouts help the troops locate the supply routes and enemy locations. Our Command and Control ships provide liaison between troops, fire-support bases, and brigade commanders. We're in on it from beginning to end." He went on about how we could cover more area with fewer troops by using artillery to protect them, and how well our airmobile tactics were working. Then he swiveled back around to the map and started pointing to different places.

As he pointed to a location in Cambodia, slightly north of our area of operations, he explained, "The NVA have staging areas up here in the Parrot's Beak. Staging areas, R&R [rest and relaxation] camps, whole towns full of the regular North Vietnamese Army troops. So they cross the border and move into our AO [area of operations], south, like this. Most of our contact has been over here on these abandoned roads and trails to the east and northeast of Nui Ba Den. You probably saw Nui Ba Den on your way in, that big mountain to the northeast of Tay Ninh."

"Yes, sir, it was pretty hazy, but I saw it," I told him.

"One big mountain. It's full of Vietcong and NVA. Impregnable; one of their biggest complexes."

"Excuse me, sir, complex? You mean they have a base over there on that mountain?" I asked, amazed.

"Not on it, in it. Cut into the heart of the mountain," he said. "There are underground bunker complexes all over Vietnam, with mess halls, ammo supplies, hospitals, and everything else they need. Not too many large ones in our AO, mostly overnight stops for the NVA moving south."

Captain Crane gave me a pretty thorough briefing. He even took me over to the Tactical Operations Center, the exterior of which looked more like a roadside attraction than a military command center. The TOC was an enormous mound of sandbags, twenty-five feet high and fifty feet across. A sign reading LARGEST IGLOO SOUTH OF NOME would have been more appropriate than TACTICAL OPERATIONS CENTER. There were no windows, and the entrance was a sandbag tunnel leading to a solid steel door. Behind the misshapen lump were communication antennae of every shape and size. Inside, it did look more like a military command center, complete with maps on the walls, maps on tables, and banks of radios, but instead of a bunch of earnest generals making serious plans, there was a lone corporal sitting by the radios reading a book and drinking coffee. It was almost three o'clock and no one else had yet returned from lunch.

After the tour we went back to operations, and Captain Crane returned to his office. Corporal Wilson took me two sheds down from operations, to my new home. The whole setup, from the Tactical Operations Center to my room, seemed to be pretty slipshod. Wilson was a nice guy, and Captain Crane took his responsibilities seriously enough, but everything I had seen gave me the impression that no one really cared about anything.

There was no one in my new quarters, so I dropped my duffel bag on the empty cot and went looking for the bathroom. It was a short walk, but hardly worth it. The officers' latrine—THE SHITTER as the sign above the door read—was a bench with six holes cut in it, in—as usual—a tin shed. Under the bench were six tubs that were infrequently taken out to be burned clean with aviation fuel.

After a long discussion with myself about the hideous creatures that I might be exposed to from those dark round holes, I finally sat down. I was just beginning to relax for the first time when I realized all the holes in the tin wall in front of my face were shrapnel holes. I asked an infantry lieutenant who had joined me in the latrine where I could get a drink.

"Down that row of hooches and you'll see it on your left across from the mess hall." The row of hooches—the soldiers' living quarters—that he had referred to were just like all the others except one on the end that had *Wolf Den* and *Fred's Place* splashed across the outside walls and on the roof in drooling red paint.

I had no trouble finding the mess hall, since it was the largest building around, and just as the lieutenant had said, the officers' club was right across from it. I could tell it was going to be a classy place by the pig outside the door—a great big four-foot-long five-foot-around, black-and-white pig, sleeping in the shade near the front door. From a distance the pig's face looked exactly like *Zap Comic*'s rendition of President "Tricky Dick" Nixon. It was my first good laugh since arriving in Vietnam.

The officers' club was larger than the hooches, a nice-looking building with neat plywood walls and a boardwalk to the front door. It was the first thing I had seen that looked as if someone had put some effort and pride into the construction. Upon entering the building it was obvious that it was a bar for serious drinkers: there were no windows. Serious drinkers do not like a lot of sunlight.

Most of the pilots I knew loved to drink. They drank not only to relieve the pressures and tensions of flying and near-death experiences, but also for the camaraderie, storytelling, and laughs. A few pilots drank because they were scared silly. Those guys were frightening, alternating between high-energy good humor and totally despondent withdrawal. Whether they were happy or sad, they were always nervous. The emaciated pilot standing next to me at the bar was one of the scared types and he was in a manic state.

"Phil Skinner, how you doin'?" He shot out a bony hand and backed it up with a spring-loaded smile.

"Tom Smith." I shook his hand.

"Damn, this is great! Another new guy. We got two last week. Bet Crane is happy now. He was having a tough time getting anyone to replace Porpoise." Skinner talked too fast, and the way he used *new guy* raised my hackles. I was getting pretty tired of the pecking-order bullshit. Before he could finish what he was saying, I turned my back on him.

Someone farther down the bar said, "He's already got one, Linus," He was talking to Skinner. "One of the new guys, Foster. He's already been up with Stoney for a LOH transition. I'm taking him up this week for an area checkout."

"Mike Foster?" No one answered me. There had been a Mike Foster back in Texas: a pretty nice guy, hyperactive, a little straight, maybe. I had been so busy with Primary that I never really got to know

him and he had gone to another Army base for advanced flight training.

"That's Sharp," Skinner said, referring to the pilot
down the bar who had mentioned Foster's name.
"Flies Scouts with Cowboy."

"He's a Scout pilot?" I looked at the guy down the
bar. He was a little taller than me, probably five-
seven or so, and could not have weighed more than
a hundred and twenty pounds. He reminded me of
the kids in school that everyone picked on; he looked
like a wimp, not the macho wild man in a flowing
white scarf that was my vision of a suicidal Scout
pilot. Skinner misinterpreted my reaction.

"Yeah, only been here a month and he's starting
to look a little flaky." He gave Sharp a sympathetic
look. "He's been flyin' almost every day since Porpoise and Blue got blown up. Sharp and Cowboy
both; they're the only two Scout pilots left. Starting
to get to him."

"What happened to those two other guys?" I asked
Skinner. With a smile to the bartender, I asked for
some Jim Beam.

"Porpoise and Blue?" He took a cigarette out of
my pack and lit up. "Blown up by some NVA mortars. Freak thing, *ka-boom*, something went wrong."

"Killed them?" I asked, knowing it had.

"You bet, brains and pieces of them all over. It
was gross. The worst part was Porpoise lived for at
least five minutes. It was really a mess," Skinner said,
clearly upset by the memory of the incident.

"Jesus," I said, "that seems like a lousy way to
get killed."

Skinner let out a nervous laugh. "You can get
killed any way you want here, even sleeping."

"You fly the Hueys?" I asked, changing the subject.

"Yeah," Skinner said with little enthusiasm. "Been flying peter-pilot [copilot] for six months. What a drag! I'm supposed to be next in line for aircraft commander; almost went into Scouts just to do some flying—automatic AC [aircraft commander] in Scouts, no waiting," He laughed as he said *no waiting.* I had a hard time believing Sharp would fly Scouts, but Skinner was out of the question. I imagined Scouts would be pretty hard on the nerves, and Skinner was a nervous wreck already.

I still had not found out if it was Mike Foster who was getting into Scouts. It was weird, but I felt a little jealous, as if I were getting aced out by this guy—the same old syndrome that got me in trouble in boarding school. "So did Foster just get here? In the last week or so?" I asked Skinner.

"Yeah, seems like a nice kind of guy."

"Seems like a stupid turd to me," came from a warrant officer sitting at a table behind Skinner and me.

I laughed. One look at this short, pudgy pilot and I knew who he was—a wise guy.

"You mean stupid or dumb?" I asked.

He squinted his beady little eyes at me as his big smirk disappeared. When he did speak, it was more for the benefit of the others at the bar than to answer my question.

"We're dumb to be here getting our butts shot off while everyone else in the U.S. of A. is enjoying great drugs and getting laid. It's *stupid* to volunteer to fly Scouts," he said as he looked around for an argument or laughs. Getting neither, he continued, "Who the hell are you, smart-ass?" He was trying to read the name tag on my fatigues. Right then I knew it had been a mistake to have both my initials put on the tags. "What's that? 'T. L. Smith'? Two initials—that's got to be against Army regs. Throw the swine in jail! What does the *L* stand for, anyway?" he demanded.

"Leming," I told him.

"Leming, far out. Isn't that some kind of rat that throws itself into the sea in Ireland, or someplace, and swims till it drowns?" he said in wonderment.

"Those are lemmings, but that's spelled with two *m*'s, not one like my name," I calmly told him, feeling my ears start to burn.

He just laughed and said, "Beautiful! Crane is looking for new meat for Scouts, and here we have a suicidal rodent among us." The fat little wiseass got a big laugh out of that and retired the champ.

"Who's that guy?" I asked Skinner.

"He calls himself Evil Eye Fleagle. Gives everyone a hard time. I get real tired of his lip," he said, staring at his drink. "He and a couple of other guys are always causing trouble. Bad attitudes."

Evil Eye had overheard Skinner's comments and was not about to let them go without a rebuttal. "Yeah, well, you're a wimp, Skinner. My attitude will change when I get the hell out of here, but you will always be a wimp."

In most bars this kind of exchange would have caused bruised feelings, if not bruised knuckles, but these young men reacted with laughter. Everyone was laughing, even Skinner.

As I staggered back to my hooch in the wee hours of the morning I grinned, thinking that although I was with the infamous 1st Cavalry Division in a combat zone, things were not much different from a typical night at a local bar back in Keene.

"This ain't all that bad," I said to myself.

4

The Flying Circus

Late June 1969

The oppressive heat of Tay Ninh kept me on the verge of awakening all night, but it was the steady climb in temperature at sunrise that brought me to consciousness my first morning with the Flying Circus.

It seemed that in the short, painful time it had taken me to sit up on my cot, the mercury had climbed at least five degrees and on top of that the pain throbbing inside my skull had increased by a factor of fifty. My head hurt; there was something moving in my stomach. Twenty-five-cent drinks can kill. The cot on the other side of the hooch, only six feet from me, was empty. Someone in the bar the night before said he was my roommate, but I could not remember what he looked like.

First things first though—I had to find some water. No water was in sight, but there was a Coke under my roommate's cot. After chugging the warm, syrupy soda I laid back down again, but scenes from the night before kept me from falling asleep. The Foster that Sharp had been talking about was the same Foster I had known in Primary. Mike had appeared later that evening, so we had several drinks together. He was indeed going into Scouts and it seemed as if he had said his name was "Crab" or something. Crab, that was his call sign. Mike had informed me that the nicknames were really call signs, and that everyone—everyone who flew, that is—had to use call signs so that the enemy would not know our real names. Our real names could supposedly be used by the enemy for nefarious purposes.

"Crab? What kind of call sign is that?" I had asked. He seemed a little uncertain of the name himself.

"I'm a Cancer. You know the zodiac?" And then he forced a little chuckle. Somehow this guy in jungle fatigues, with a pistol on his hip, did not fit the astrological image.

Mike was a good-looking guy, about five-ten, tan and lean with a mop of curly blondish hair. He was from a small town in Pennsylvania, and he reeked of mom and apple pie. Except for that crazy smile and nutty laugh, he was a model for the all-American boy.

The officers' club had stayed packed until well after midnight. Excluding a nondescript meal at mess hall, I was at the officers' club for almost six hours. During that time I met most of the pilots and officers of our company, and like Mike, they all had nicknames. My roommate was "Luke." Once I remembered his name I could see him pretty clearly, with his round face and amiable expression. He looked like the kind of guy who could always stay out of an argument.

Most of the pilots and door gunners got their nicknames from some physical characteristic. Animal was a big man who would have looked like a fearful beast if he had not had that silly grin on his face. Cowboy had a handlebar mustache. The oldest pilot in the company, a guy in his thirties, naturally was called

Pop. Some of the nicknames reflected personalities. Snuffy seemed like a kicked-back sort of guy; he spent most of the night leaning back against the bar, chuckling at Evil Eye's nasty quips. Linus bore no physical resemblance to the Peanuts cartoon-strip character, but looked like the kind of guy who used a security blanket. Then there were the nicknames that were the antithesis of the character, like Stoney. Straight as an arrow, Stoney had probably never been stoned in his life. And then there were the nicknames that just seemed to suit the individual, like Scrotum.

Of all the nicknames, Evil Eye Fleagle's fit him the best. Evil Eye was about five-foot-six and pear-shaped, but you couldn't call him short or even fat. In fact you dared not call him anything at all. Any attempt to speak to him, or even to look at him, would give him an opportunity to fix you in a cocked, sidelong glance with his closest beady eye glaring from under a half-drawn eyelid. It felt like staring down the muzzle of a loaded gun. If you said anything at all he would ridicule you with his vile wit. That first night in the officers' club I got to see him perform; his victim, a hapless major from battalion headquarters, made the mistake of trying to engage Evil Eye in friendly conversation.

"Hey, Mr. Evil Eye, how you doing?" said the major, exuding camaraderie.

"Just fine, just fine and hunky-dory," Evil Eye replied with uncommon civility, waiting patiently for the major to say something stupid.

The major should have been able to smell the antagonism smoldering within, but like many field-grade officers, he felt secure because of his rank and assumed importance, and continued the conversation.

"Heard you took a few days' leave down in Saigon," the major said as he slumped into a chair, a little more intoxicated than he looked. "Have a good time? Get a little boom-boom?"

This unsolicited inquiry into Evil Eye's sex life along with the accompanying leer were just what Fleagle had been waiting for. He leaned over the table in his best conspiratorial manner, locked eyes with the grinning major, and smiled.

"Actually I'm glad you asked, Major. Not many of my friends like to talk to me about the fun I have in Saigon." His grin slowly changed into a wide-eyed smile and his lips started to tremble. "I mean, it's not as if it is illegal or anything."

He paused just long enough for the major to begin to suspect that this was not going to be a normal boom-boom story.

"After a few drinks we got a room. While I undressed, except for my socks, of course, she peeled the oranges," he said, then paused, savoring the moment. "I really like that." His laugh was high-pitched enough to make the major sit back in his chair. "Then she tied me up with that fuzzy rope I like, and, *Oh God*, she threw the orange peels at me and called me dirty names. I just knelt in the corner, whimpering and masturbating. It felt soooooooo good." By this time Evil Eye was half out of his chair and almost on top of his victim, breathing heavily in his face. The major sobered up quickly, started mumbling indignantly, and tried to get out of his chair.

That's when Evil Eye kissed him, right on the lips.

The major jumped up yelling and frantically wiped his mouth with his sleeve. It was impossible to understand what he was saying, but it kept everyone in the place on the floor with laughter. Realizing he'd been made a fool of, he pulled back his fist to take a swing at Evil Eye, but abruptly stopped, turned on his heel, and marched out of the club. The major must have known that there are more military regulations against striking a junior officer than there are regulations against kissing a senior officer.

The price for that show was a monster hangover. Fortunately I had only a few things to do that day— Captain Crane had told me in the bar that we usually took off by 0700, but I could use my first day to get organized.

Feed a hangover, they say, so I made my way to the mess hall. A sign on the door said OPEN 0500–0700, 1100–1300, AND 1800–2000 HOURS. NO EXCEPTIONS. It was 0900, so I decided to take a look at the Flying Circus's helicopters.

The Hueys were parked over by the maintenance hangar, past the operations office on the east side of our company area, and the LOHs were parked in revetments along the north side, past the hooch identified as the Wolf Den. To get to any of the helicopters, it was necessary to use one of the rickety bridges across a drainage ditch surrounding headquarters company's two-acre compound. It was a pretty impressive ditch, at least four feet across and three feet down to the putrid green slime that covered the bottom.

From a distance I could see that the company's Hueys were well used. None of our Hueys back at Hunter had been brand new; some of them had patches that were rumored to cover bullet holes, but at least they were all the same color. The first Huey I looked at was four different shades of green, owing to the number of parts that had been replaced. The interior was also different from the ones I had known in flight school. In the cargo compartment behind the pilots was a large console full of radios. The radios were set up so people sitting in the back could operate them. Upon closer inspection I saw that the Huey was actually very well maintained; it just needed a new paint job.

Over by the maintenance hangar there was another Huey, a total wreck. It was hard to tell which end had been the cockpit. As I looked at the twisted fuselage, I could not help wondering if the pilots had survived. Although it had obviously been a bad crash, the ship had not burned—very few pilots got out of burning wrecks alive. Ninety percent of the metal parts were made of magnesium-aluminum alloys, which burn hot and fast. Often the aircraft blew up when the fire got to the thousands of pounds of jet fuel in the fuel cells.

Looking the mangled aircraft over, it appeared to me that the pilot had dropped it on the ground—hard. The landing gear had been driven straight up into the belly of the aircraft. The slowly turning main rotor blades had cut the tail boom off, swept through the cockpit, rolled the machine over, and beat it to death. I figured the rotor blade had come through the cockpit just above the pilots' heads because there was no blood on the seat fabric. Maybe they lived. . . .

My morbid curiosity did not go unnoticed. Two scruffy-looking young men working on a LOH by the maintenance hangar stopped what they were doing and watched me, their stares almost hostile. "How's it going?" I offered, as friendly as I could. "Just joined the company, taking a look around." I paused and barely heard the shorter one say "no shit" to his companion.

"Be nice to the new pilot, Little Buddy," the taller,

redheaded kid said gently to his friend, not caring if I overheard him. Normally I would have been pretty offended, but the way they talked to each other, as if I were not there, made it my indiscretion for listening in on their private conversation. They were a sort of Mutt-and-Jeff team: the taller kid heavyset and jovial; his friend wiry and feisty. Both were in their late teens, with the classic enlisted-man slouch that stated they were in the Army against their will. The big redhead was also further out of uniform than anyone I had seen to date.

Being out of uniform in Vietnam was not quite the same as anywhere else. In flight school a soldier could be described as out of uniform for any one of a thousand reasons, from wearing the wrong outfit for the time of day to having a speck of dirt on a shoe. The typical uniform for Tay Ninh was anything that the Army issued, in any condition, dirty and soaked with sweat. The enlisted man in front of me, however, was wearing a striped, multicolored civilian T-shirt.

"You crew chiefs on these LOHs?" I asked. Each helicopter had its own mechanic, called a crew chief.

"Nope, I'm a Scout door gunner," said the guy in the T-shirt, adding, "Little Wolf Buddy here is a crew chief." He looked at his friend, who was frowning up at him. "Oh yeah, and sometimes a door gunner, but usually a crew chief 'cause he gets airsick and throws up on himself," he said, grinning at Little Buddy.

Little Buddy, actually D. Miles according to the name stenciled on his T-shirt, seemed gratified for the door gunner identification, maybe a little upset about the upchuck disclosure, but it was obvious Little Buddy thought the world of his big, smiling friend no matter what he said.

"Nice shirt," I said to the tall redheaded kid.

"Yeah, my wolfshirt," he said, smiling down at his chest.

"Wolfshirt . . . Little Wolf Buddy . . . Are you the guy who lives in that hooch with *Wolf Den* painted on it?" I asked.

"Yes, sir. That's me, Wolfman," he replied with a proud grin. Wolfman had a smile for everything he said.

"What happened to that Huey over there?" I nodded at the wreck.

"Got shot down landing at LZ Jamie. Pilot had to avoid some grunts and landed hard," Wolfman said.

"This the ship you fly in, Wolfman?" I asked, nodding toward the LOH behind him.

"Not *Worthington!*" he said, referring to the LOH behind him. "He's got like a thousand hours flying Scouts. Only flies Ash and Trash now, sort of like retirement. No way of knowing which one I'll be in, the way they keep getting wrecked," Wolfman went on, while relaxing against the sandbag and railroad-tie revetment.

"This helicopter only has a little over a thousand hours on it?" I said, looking at the green wreck behind them. "Wow!"

They both seemed a little hurt, but it was a rough-looking machine. From twenty feet away the "tin-canning" made the helicopter look as if it had, at least, a very hard three thousand hours on it.

Tin-canning is one of the side effects of an aircraft being overstressed. Helicopters are constructed a lot like sailing ships, with a skin attached to ribs and internal frames for support. If a helicopter is landed too hard, turned too sharply, or bent in any number of ways, the frames and ribs flex so much that the metal skin of the machine is stretched. While the rigid metal frames hold their original shape, the skin usually doesn't—it dents in, or bulges out, making the aircraft look like a beat-up tin can.

Getting closer I could also see that one of the front Plexiglas windows, or bubbles, was held together by tape. A regulation prohibiting this type of repair came to mind. . . . It seemed things were going to be different here.

"How long have you been flying Scouts?" I asked.

"Only for a couple weeks. Gotten shot at 'bout every time we've gone up," Wolfman answered, turning to his friend. "Right, Little Buddy?!"

"Yeah." Little Buddy nodded, a couple more times than he had to.

"What's your name, sir?" Wolfman asked.

"Tom."

"Don't have a call sign yet?" he asked.

"Nope. Well, see you later." With that I turned to walk away. New guys, call signs—it all seemed like a lot of bullshit to me.

As I walked back toward the company area I noticed a pilot who looked familiar doing a preflight on the other Huey. It was Luke, my roommate. I had been looking for someone to talk to about what was expected of headquarters company pilots, and to find out a little more about life in Tay Ninh. Luke would do fine. He had been "in country" two months, long enough to know what was going on, but he didn't have the disdain for new guys that pilots like Evil Eye and his pals had. Actually, Luke was one of the few pilots, besides Linus, who would even talk to new guys like Foster and me.

By the time I got over to my roommate's Huey, he was already strapped in the cockpit staring intently at his instrument panel as the whine of the starter motor rolled into high pitch. In my mind I could hear him saying to himself, "N1, twenty percent, oil pressure rising, watch the TOT [turbine outlet temperature] for hot start. . . ." With a twist of his wrist he dumped in the start fuel, and the igniter plug set the mixture ablaze. Within seconds the relative tranquility was lost to the whopping beat of the rotor blades and the hissing roar of the enormous gas turbine. A breath of burning turbine fuel blew over me; it smelled great, even with my hangover. Luke came to life as he threw switches, pushed circuit breakers, and twisted knobs. The whole machine was gently hopping and shaking to the beat of the rotor blades. I loved it—a symphony of discord and prelude to excitement.

A crew chief on a short ladder was bent over looking in the engine compartment, performing checks and making adjustments. He was almost lost in turbine fumes and noise, the rotor blades slicing the air a foot above his head. It was hard to believe he could concentrate in that chaotic setting. After a few minutes he got down off the ladder and walked up to the pilot's door. When he got the pilot's attention he drew his finger across his throat, signaling to shut down the engine. As the noise subsided, the crew chief came over to where I was standing. "How's it going, sir?" he said, offering me a cigarette. "Name's Rip."

"Tom; thanks for the smoke."

"You going to fly Scouts, sir?" It was more of a statement than a question.

"Jesus Christ, what makes you think I would want to do that?" I asked.

"Well, for one thing, I saw you over there talking to Wolfman and Little Buddy. You're a new guy—that's who they go after for Scouts—you don't know enough yet . . . and you're short," he said, looking over at Luke, who was getting out of the helicopter.

"What does being short have to do with anything?" I asked a little defensively.

"Those LOHs are pretty small, so short guys fit in them better," he said, still watching Luke, who was walking over toward us. "And there is less of you for bullets to hit." Rip looked at me and laughed.

"Hey, Tom, remember me from last night?" Luke stuck out his hand. "You were pretty loaded."

"I'm paying for it. Nice to meet you again, Luke," I said.

Luke wiped the sweat off his face with the sleeve of his Nomex flight suit. Only the most dedicated pilots wore Nomex, a fire-resistant material that looked like polyester and felt like wool, hot and itchy. Just what the doctor ordered for hundred-degree heat and ninety-percent humidity. The fact that he could wear something so uncomfortable made me wonder if he was rational.

"Could you find the leak?" Luke asked Rip. Luke's look of concern seemed more appropriate to a sick friend than a green machine.

"Nope, dry as a bone. As dry as it's ever been, anyhow," Rip replied.

Luke turned to me and explained, "My engine oil-pressure gauge is fluctuating; not electrical, can't figure it out." Then he turned back to Rip to ask, "What about trying a new gauge?"

"If we have one in parts." Rip crushed out his cigarette and walked off to the maintenance hangar.

"Probably won't be back for an hour. Go smoke some pot with his pals," Luke said, watching Rip walk away.

"Rip smokes pot?" I asked. Rip had seemed like a pretty straight young man.

Luke flashed me a disarming smile. "Maybe not Rip, but a lot of them do."

"How can you tell?" I was curious.

"They start disappearing. Can't find them anywhere. When they show up again it's real obvious. You know, they say stuff like 'Wow, man.' Gets a little ridiculous sometimes, but they get the job done, and that's what's important."

"Last night you told me you were flying Command and Control," I said, changing the subject.

"Sure do," he said, looking over at the Huey, obviously proud of the big aircraft.

"So what's Command and Control like, Luke?"

"Charlie Charlie?" (It was common practice to abbreviate names using the phonetic military alphabet: *Charlie* for C, etc.) "Most of the guys think it's a drag, but I kinda like it. There's a bit of emergency resupply, and a lot of miscellaneous bullshit pops up, but mostly we ferry the guys from the TOC back and forth so they can see what's going on in the field." He stopped and looked to see if I was listening. Satisfied, he continued, "We also pick up the commanding officers of the fire bases and take them around to their patrols. They check 'em out, talk it over, make plans, and then we all go home," Luke said.

"Sounds easy enough," I put in.

"Yeah, not bad. When the troops are in contact we do artillery adjusting for them, resupply, sometimes some medevac if we can. Makes for some really long days."

"Long, hot days, I bet. Crane said we're fighting the NVA, but he also said there are Vietcong in Nui Ba Den," I replied, hoping Luke would tell me we were not really fighting the NVA. The North Vietnamese Army was supposedly much better equipped and trained to shoot down helicopters. We had been told in flight school classes that the NVA even had surface-to-air missiles—nasty stuff.

"Yeah, we're fightin' the NVA. I guess there's some VC [Vietcong] in Tay Ninh; and Nui Ba Den is full of gooks. Most of the mortars and rockets we get here at night they say are from the VC. But anywhere north of here or north of Nui Ba Den is hard-core NVA. They kick some ass, especially with the ARVNs [Army of the Republic of Vietnam soldiers]." The ARVNs, our allies, were rumored to be pretty sorry soldiers.

"It's like a big game of hide-and-seek." Luke went on, explaining that planning how to catch the enemy was quite simple, but on the ground level it got complicated. One of the major problems was spreading our troops thin enough to search a wide area while maintaining sufficient strength to keep the enemy from overrunning them. That is what the fire-support bases were all about. The troops in the field could call in artillery from the LZs to back them up when they would go out on Search and Destroy missions. Close artillery support had saved a lot of lives. However, there were also many stories about friendly artillery taking a lot of U.S. lives.

"When I was down in Long Binh I heard that these firebases get overrun now and then," I said, trying to let Luke know that I did have a little knowledge of what was going on.

"Yeah," Luke said, but his face darkened as he looked toward his helicopter. "I said I liked Charlie Charlie, but going into an LZ that's just been blown away sucks. Guys all torn to pieces, screaming, bleeding. It's really a mess."

It was obvious Luke didn't like talking about overrun LZs, so I changed the subject. "Sounds like a bummer. Do you get shot at much in Charlie Charlie?"

"Not too bad," he said, relieved to be talking about something else. "Mostly when taking off and landing at the LZs. When we are flying around our area of operations we stay up at three thousand feet or more."

"They can't hit you at that altitude?" I was sure the NVA had .50-caliber machine guns that could shoot at least three thousand feet.

"They don't like to shoot at us unless they think they can score a hit. It's too easy for someone to see their tracers and call in an air strike. They hate those air strikes," Luke said.

"You can get air strikes just like that?" I asked.

"Usually have to wait a few hours. Depends on what's available. A Scout pilot who got killed the first week I got here took a little AK-47 fire and called for an air strike. They came back and told him there was a flight of B-52s right above him and he could have them. He brought an arc-light in on a couple gooks takin' pop shots at helicopters." He shook his head in amazement.

An arc-light was a flight of B-52 bombers flying so high that they were invisible to people on the ground. In their bellies each one carried up to sixty thousand pounds of high explosive bombs. When they got over their target all the planes unloaded at the same time—pretty impressive stuff, I had been told. In one long roll of man-made thunder, acre after acre of prime triple-canopy jungle would disappear in a cloud of smoke, dust, and splinters. The people hanging around that part of the jungle wouldn't even hear the planes arrive—or the bombs fall.

"But that's really rare," Luke went on. "Most of the time it's our Air Force in F-105s based out of Tan Son Nhut Airfield. The ARVNs fly these old propeller-driven jobs; they're supposed to be lousy pilots, but I haven't worked with them. Sometimes we get the Navy. They're pretty good."

"Doesn't sound like the ARVNs are popular on the ground or in the air," I said. Luke frowned, looking down at the ground. Everything Luke thought showed on his face. He didn't like criticizing people very much.

"The Navy, where the hell are they from?" I asked.

"They fly all the way in from their carriers, I guess." He looked toward Nui Ba Den. "That would be the way to go, wouldn't it? Live on a nice, big, safe boat, eat fresh food in an air-conditioned stateroom, then jump in your jet and go blow away a few gooks," Luke said.

"Living in this stinking heat is not going to be easy," I agreed. It wasn't quite noon, and already the sun was turning the ninety-percent humidity into a steam bath. Just the effort of breathing was making me sweat.

From the cockpit of the Huey, Rip's voice called, "Got a new gauge in it, sir. Let's run her up again."

"Luke, I appreciate the information," I said, and turned to leave. "See you later."

Luke walked over to the helicopter; I went back to the mess hall for some lunch. The meal was standard Army fare: potatoes, canned vegetables, and some unidentifiable meat, but I lost my appetite after swallowing a gulp of milk that had turned. As I threw up behind the mess hall, I could not believe that my tour was just beginning, that I had an entire year left.

I had almost made it back to the shade of my hooch when I saw Corporal Wilson walking toward me. "Mr. Smith, you're scheduled to go on an orientation ride with Mr. Parker tomorrow at 0700 hours, sir."

"Mr. Parker, who's that?" I asked.

"You know, the little warrant officer with the big .45 automatic, Stoney," the corporal answered.

My heart sank. "Wait a minute, Corporal—Stoney, the one who transitions guys to LOHs?" I asked, more than a little agitated.

"Yeah, that's him, but he also does orientation and in-country checkouts in the Hueys. That's what you're scheduled for tomorrow, sir," Wilson said, chuckling at my response.

There was no denying it. When he had said *Parker*, I thought he meant *Scouts*, and the floor dropped out on me. As Wilson walked away I felt a little embarrassed by my overreaction. Thoroughly depressed, I went back to my hooch and tried to fall asleep. An hour later I gave up and peeled the sweaty synthetic poncho liner off my back; without a fan survival was doubtful.

"Mr. Smith." It was Corporal Wilson again. "Captain Crane told me to give you this list of things you are supposed to do as part of checking into the company," he said, staying respectfully outside the hooch.

"Come on in, Wilson." He came in and sat on

Luke's cot. "Was I supposed to go to operations and pick this stuff up?" I asked. Holding my head in both hands, I started moaning. "I can't remember anything, Corporal. Where am I? This isn't Kansas, Toto. Auntie Em, Auntie Em, I want to come home, I want to come home." Wilson thought my imitation of Dorothy from *The Wizard of Oz* was pretty funny.

"It could be worse, sir. This company's pretty cool compared to the infantry company I was with. That was a drag. Talk about uptight! Crane is Army all the way, but he doesn't hassle too many people. Anyway, he's leaving in December. Lieutenant Lonas doesn't hassle anyone," the corporal explained.

"Yeah, they're OK," I agreed.

Wilson looked at his watch. "You'd better get to the supply clerk to pick up your weapon, chicken plate, and other stuff before you go up with Stoney tomorrow. Supply closes at 1600 hours."

Off to the supply room I went. First they gave me a survival vest, loaded with things that I didn't want to think about using. The mosquito netting was a reasonable idea, but the hooked needles for sewing up skin were too much, and the knife with the long blade for hand-to-hand combat—out of the question. I preferred the run-and-hide tactic.

As I was standing there contemplating the chances of needing to use that stuff, another pilot walked in. It was Fred Gordon, also from Primary at Fort Wolters. Fred was a gung-ho, brownnose jerk. He walked up to the counter, cutting in front of everyone in line, and told the sergeant he was there to pick up his Nomex flight suits. It was the same old Fred: he was so preoccupied he had not even seen me or the rest of the line. In flight school Fred was always in a frenzy trying to please the TACs or anyone else in authority.

"Gordon, you dirt-bag, there's a line here," I told him as politely as I could.

He turned around and looked at the line of men. "Sorry."

I was glad to see he did not recognize me. It would have been embarrassing to be associated with him in front of the other men in the supply room. Gordon got in line and when it was my turn the supply sergeant issued me a flight helmet, Nomex flight suit, leather gloves, and some instruments and maps for navigation around Tay Ninh. They also gave me a "chicken plate," a solid steel chest protector that slipped over the head like a life vest, with straps to hold it snug at the waist. Since only Plexiglas windows were there to stop bullets aimed from in front of and below us, the chicken plate seemed like a pretty good idea.

"Do they work?" I asked the supply sergeant.

"You're the very first person to ask that question, sir," he said, reaching below the counter. The sergeant lifted up a mangled sheet of metal. "Check it out." I did. It was indeed a chicken plate, bent almost in half and all torn up. "Fifty-caliber. Blew him right out the other side of the Huey. Lucky the door was open and they were on the ground," the sergeant said.

Yeah, sure buddy. The supply sergeant probably shot it himself. I picked up my new chicken plate and tapped on it. "Hey, this one's hollow," I complained. It did have a hollow sort of thunk to it. The surprised-looking sergeant grabbed it from me to give it a thunk. "Yeah, it does sound sort of hollow, but that's just the fiberglass coating they put on them."

"What's the fiberglass coating for?" I asked.

"It catches fragments from the slugs so they don't hit you in the face," he said. Last, they issued me a pistol. The choices were a .45 automatic or a .38 revolver. The .45 was a lot better for shooting people, but the revolver looked better on me, so I went with that.

Back at the hooch, trying everything on again, was almost like going through the same ritual at the beginning of flight school. Rituals, the most pleasant and effective method for conditioning behavior . . . It seemed like yesterday, playing with my new toys, all excited about getting into a helicopter. The toys still turned me on, but it was hard to get excited about using a chicken plate to stop bullets or fish-hooks to sew myself up.

When Luke returned around 1700 hours we went down to the officers' club and drank until they closed the place. Luke's appearance and mannerisms had led me to suspect he was a little too straight for me, and he was, but five hours of drinking uncovered a lot of common interests. Luke would never be a fun friend, but he was a good friend. I don't remember much of what we talked about, war stories mostly, but I do remember that his tales about life in Vietnam did nothing to comfort my growing depression.

Wilson shook me awake at daylight, but it felt as if I had never gone to sleep. After a quick powdered-egg-and-Kool-Aid breakfast in the mess hall, we headed to company operations for a 0600 briefing. Evil Eye, Snuffy, Animal, and the dissident group of pilots were lounging around outside Operations. Some of them had not completed the process of getting dressed, and most were still half asleep. I felt really stupid walking past those grubby, grumpy combat veterans decked out in my new double-knit flight suit. Inside Operations, the rest of the pilots—the gung-ho group—Pokey, Linus, Scrotum, Captain Crane, and Lieutenant Lonas were talking about the day's missions. Crab and "Cletus" (Gordon wanted to be called Cletus) were standing off to one side, watching.

"What's happening, Crab?" I asked.

"Crane wants to fly the new H model Huey we just got, and that guy who's flying the colonel says the colonel wants it."

Mike was in his jungle fatigues. Only Cletus, Sharp, and I were wearing Nomex. "I thought we had to wear this goddamned Nomex," I said. The itchy material was twice as hot as the cotton fatigues and already driving me nuts.

Crab looked at me and laughed. "What? Are you a dumb shit, fuckin' new guy or something? Nobody cool wears that stuff." Then we both looked at Cletus. Cletus had heard but did not react to that kind of talk.

"You men want to listen up here?" Captain Crane said, looking straight at me. "This is a briefing. Evil Eye, the rest of you, come on in here." Snuffy came in rubbing a red welt on the back of his arm.

"Goddamned centipede bit me," he moaned pathetically.

"Bummer," Animal consoled him. "Watch out for those sandbags. Watch out for everything." The sandbags piled everywhere made great homes for the centipedes, along with scores of other crawling, biting vermin.

The missions were assigned. Stoney and I paired

up and walked off to preflight our aircraft. He was short, sandy-haired, and pleasantly intense. When Stoney talked he would stare into my eyes, as if what he was saying was the most important information in the world. He would keep staring at me until I gave him a response, and then he would flash a big, friendly smile and slap me on the back if he could.

In his mid-twenties, Stoney was older than most of us and noticeably more mature. He was on his second tour in Vietnam, but he didn't have to tell me—he had that certain self-confidence that seemed to prevail among men who had extended their tour of duty. We preflighted one of the older UH-1-D model Hueys and took off for a trip around our area of operations.

First we headed east out of Tay Ninh, straight toward that great lonely mountain, Nui Ba Den. Stoney's voice came over the intercom, "Nice thing about flying around here is you always got the old Black Virgin Mountain to get yourself un-lost. We do most of our navigating by using rough compass headings and mostly knowing where we are. When you screw up you can always get back to Nui Ba Den and start over." Then to the door gunners he said, "Ready to check your weapons back there? We got an open field coming up."

The Hueys had two door gunners, one on each side at the end of the cargo bay behind the pilots. They sat facing out the open cargo doors, with their backs to the main transmission housing. Sitting right in the middle of the helicopter gave them a nice, clear field of fire from one end of the machine to the other. They were armed with 7.62mm M60 machine guns, which rode on mounts in front of them. It was standard procedure to test-fire them after takeoff. I was mentally prepared for the rapid explosions but still jumped when they fired.

A few miles from Tay Ninh the orderly sequence of rice paddies, dirt roads, and thatched huts thinned out and finally disappeared among low bamboo and shoulder-high grasses that led to the edge of the jungle. We cruised northeast around the big enigmatic mountain at an altitude of three thousand feet, following the only road still in sight.

"That little stream down there, we call them 'blues' 'cause that's the color they are on the maps," Stoney said. "They should call them 'browns' 'cause that's the color they really are. That road below us turns east up there, on the north side of the mountain, then goes straight up north to Katum, about thirty klicks," he said.

More troublesome for me than deciphering the military clock was converting feet and miles into meters and kilometers, "klicks."

"Used to be a small town, but not much more than an outpost of special forces and ARVN troops now. Only five klicks south of the Cambodian border. Spooky place up there. NVA own the place at night. Up the same road—you can almost see the clearing from here—is LZ Barbara. Halfway between Barbara and Katum is LZ Christine." Stoney looked relaxed surrounded by the steel plates of his armored seat. The aircraft controls were loose in his grip; the Huey just chugged along. It was cooler up here at altitude, and it felt great.

Past the mountain, the jungle began. The scattered fields and thickets disappeared under a canopy of green. We turned east past Nui Ba Den, still following the road. Off to our eleven o'clock, a few miles away, was a large clearing with smoke rising from it, LZ Barbara. Stoney saw me staring past him. "Barbara's got a couple of those 175mm self-propelled howitzers. They shoot a 170-pound shell twenty miles or so. Not very accurate, but they're good for prepping LZs and scaring the shit out of Charlie [another epithet for the Vietcong]. You can get fuel over there if you need it."

· "Do all the LZs have fuel?" I asked.

"Nope, Barbara's the only one. Got to be pretty damn secure before they will sling in any fuel. Dinks just love to blow up fuel dumps." A mile later the road turned north, but we kept heading east, into the middle of a sea of green.

What a trip it was, seeing the jungle from the front seat of the helicopter. The scale was enormous. Below us, the tops of trees a hundred or more feet across mushroomed up, jostling for position in the canopy. Larger trees rose together in clusters, high enough to be mistaken for small hills. The earth was completely concealed in the turbulent mass of green, and so was the enemy.

The knowledge that there were men under those trees who wanted to kill us did a lot to spoil the natural beauty. Just the thought of an NVA soldier sighting on our aircraft made me squirm. Not only that, there was no place to go but straight down into those enormous trees if they did shoot us down or we had an engine failure. The only ones who could find us down there would be the NVA. Thankfully, Stoney distracted me.

"We're going to fly east to LZ Grant and then northwest to Outlaw, halfway up the road to Katum. Then maybe west to the Cambodian border, by LZ Jay, then back southeast to Tay Ninh. That will make a circle around the center part and cover about half of our area."

At a cruising speed of a hundred and ten knots we were over LZ Grant in less than ten minutes. It looked like a miniature Tay Ninh base camp, except dirtier—a little trashed-out island cut in the middle of the jungle. The only discernable objects inside the barbed-wire perimeter were a bunch of howitzers: several circles of the big guns surrounded by dirt, with three howitzers in each circle. The defensive positions, command post, and living quarters were buried.

Stoney came on the intercom; "See that road there, it runs almost straight back to Tay Ninh, around the south side of the mountain. It used to run past here up to An Loc and over to Phuoc Vinh, but that part of it's only trail now, used mostly by little yellow guys in black pajamas." He turned and winked at me.

"OK, I'm going to show you the standard 'high overhead' approach that we use for these LZs when someone might want to try and shoot us down," Stoney said. Then he turned and gave me a serious look. "You learn any of this stuff in flight school?" I told him I had, so he continued, "The landing pad is just about always near the command post. Which is just about always under the antenna farm. The trick is to stay inside the circle of the green line, right down to the pad." Then over the FM radio, he said, "Grant, Stingray four-seven, landing in zero-one minutes."

Stoney pushed the collective all the way down and rolled the machine over on its right side. As the bottom dropped out we fell like a rock, spiraling down toward the ground at two thousand feet a minute.

We definitely were a hard target to track as we twisted and dove at the same time. Also working in our favor was the suppressive fire we could expect from the LZ if the enemy started shooting at us. Plus, if we did get hit we could crash on the LZ. It was pretty much the same thing we had learned in flight school except the control movements were a little more extreme. However, in flight school they had taught us to spiral left, increasing the pilot's visibility of the landing area. "Stoney, wouldn't it be easier to see to the left?"

For the first time Stoney did not stare intently at me when he answered. He just said, "Uh-huh." Then it dawned on me that this was a particularly good defensive move on his behalf. The whole helicopter was between him and the enemy, with me as part of his shield. Well, at least I had a great view and nothing to do, so I could think about all the trees full of sharpshooters. A hundred feet above the ground Stoney leveled the ship, pulling back hard on the cyclic, putting the ship into a radical flare. As we slowed on a cushion of air, Stoney spun the ship in an arc around its tail. We settled to a hover right beside the antenna farm. It was a great maneuver and a great feeling, the rush of the spinning descent, the radical turns at the bottom, then rolling out in a precision landing right on the spot he had picked from three thousand feet above.

I looked around grinning at Stoney. Off to my right a trench led to a crude door buried under three feet of sandbags and dirt-filled ammo boxes. Above the door CP (Command Post) was painted on a splintered board. The whole place was made of sandbags and howitzer ammo boxes filled with dirt; nothing rose higher than several feet above the ground. Infan-

trymen were scattered around lounging in what
shade they could find or rig. In their sweat-stained
T-shirts they looked like laborers from a prison camp
taking a break from turning the jungle into piles of
dirt. So much for the alert troops ready to put down
suppressive fire for us.

"Makes Tay Ninh look mighty nice, don't it?"
Stoney said, following my gaze around the LZ. He
punched his radio microphone button. "Grant, four-
seven, departing." Then, over the intercom: "There's
two types of departures. One is you climb back up
the way we came down, or you can do the kind I'm
gonna show you now." As we lifted off, our rotor
wash kicked up a cloud of dust that washed over
several soldiers. A few reflexively tried to cover their
eyes, but most of them just sat there.

As we reached a ten-foot hover Stoney pushed the
cyclic forward and pulled in all the available power.
Gauges jumped up to their red lines as we shot over
the defensive berm and its surrounding barbed-wire
beach, no more than three feet above the ground. We
cleared the edge of the jungle with less than that.
When the airspeed indicator was up around one hundred and twenty knots Stoney smoothly pulled the
cyclic all the way back. The Huey's nose came up
slowly at first, then rose rapidly to near vertical as
the airspeed dropped to sixty knots. By that time we
had climbed to almost five hundred feet, and Stoney
began a climbing turn to the right. "Less exposure
time down low, see; but try not to fly right over the
dinks when you do that." He leveled the aircraft and
continued the climb to three thousand feet.

Ten minutes later we cruised over LZ Outlaw. It
looked just like Grant except that it straddled the
road to Katum. Good thinking, I reasoned, why move

more than one inch from the road? It reminded me of my first solo camping trip, when I set up my tent outside my bedroom and left the window open. Fifteen minutes after Outlaw passed under us Stoney came back on the intercom.

"There's the border up there."

"Where?" I asked.

"Where the jungle gets thicker up there. Where the bomb craters stop and the trees have not been stripped by Agent Orange," Stoney replied.

"Jesus, you really can see a difference, can't you? What's Agent Orange?" I asked.

"That's this stuff they spray out of C-130s that kills all the leaves on trees, mostly here along the border and along NVA trotters [trails] in the heavy jungle. People in the TOC think it makes the gooks easier to see, but it don't. The jungle grows back as quick as they spray it," he said. It was easy to pick out the break between the ravaged jungle of Vietnam and undisturbed Cambodia.

"Amazing how an imaginary line stops the war," I said.

"You wouldn't believe what they've got a couple of klicks from here. Big base camps of houses above ground, hospitals, playing fields, and even a stage for NVA USO shows. Yeah, they are real confident we will not cross that border to get them. Dumbest damn thing," he said.

"Stoney, how much of the jungle down there is in the hands of the NVA?" I asked as we cruised above the deep green canopy.

"All of it," he said with a big grin. "They're real mobile. Move in and out of the area a lot. Hard to say how much they actually control at any one time.

They got bunkers and tunnels strung out all over the place."

"Luke said they don't shoot at you very often at this altitude." I wanted to hear again that it was perfectly safe where we were.

"Yeah, mostly on landing and takeoff, but every once in a while a dink will get a wild hair up his ass and take a few shots at us up here."

"Berger took a round in his elbow up here. Put him in a world of hurt," one of the door gunners said over the intercom.

The jungle came to an end; soon the rice paddies resumed as Tay Ninh came into view. We started our descent through a little smog layer that spread out from Tay Ninh base and Tay Ninh city.

Just below two thousand feet the show-and-tell cruise ended abruptly. There was no noise, just two or three blips of orange passing the helicopter—the glow from the tracer rounds almost looked friendly. Then, as Stoney put the aircraft in a dive and the door gunners opened up, it dawned on me that we were being shot at. When one of the next tracer rounds flashed by a few inches from my window, every muscle in my body jumped. I could not believe someone was shooting at us! My next reaction was a total body cringe.

When I opened my eyes I found myself looking at a rice paddy and a little farmer in a straw hat. The farmer was waving his arms, splashing through the water, running away from us as fast as he could. It appeared to both the farmer and me that we were going to fly straight into the middle of his crop. A few more tracers flashed by, and I jerked away from them so hard that the impact with my armored seat forced out a little grunt. Stoney rolled the machine on its side. We fell even faster, then he rolled it straight, then back on its side again. Just before hitting the paddy, about twenty feet above the rice stalks, he pulled out of the dive and turned back to Tay Ninh for another approach.

Back at the company area the crew did a postflight on the aircraft to be certain the Huey was still in flying condition. We did not find any bullet holes, so we closed out the flight logs—the flying day was over.

Later that night I sat nursing another glass of Jim Beam and felt my blues lift a bit. When Stoney came in for a drink I told him about the feeling. "That's what happens to you when you get shot at," he said. "First thing is have a couple drinks to forget how bad it scared you. Next you realize that you were pretty damn lucky not gettin' killed—that's worth feelin' good about. Then you start thinkin' it wasn't all that bad. But don't forget, in a helicopter you're always a sittin' duck."

"Thanks for the advice." We drank a bit, and then I asked, "How come you train guys in the LOH but don't fly Scouts, Stoney?"

" 'Cause it's too damn dangerous. I train them because I'm the only LOH pilot who doesn't go out and get himself killed." He lit up a cigarette. "Tell you the truth, I'm not good Scout material. I can do the flying OK, but I just don't have that desire it takes to get down in there and mix it up with those NVA dudes." He thought a while. "My survival instincts beat out my curiosity every time."

"I'll drink to that," I put in. "We almost died today just taking a look at the place."

"Nah, you didn't almost die. You just got shot at. When you almost die you get real calm-like. You sort of almost stop breathin' and it's just as good you stop because your pants stink real bad from where you shit in them." He laughed and slapped me on the back. It was probably pretty funny, but I just couldn't laugh. Stoney continued, "Anyway, look at the bright side, this is one day done, and you only have three hundred and sixty-four more." I felt like crying. The way he drew out *three . . . hundred . . . and . . . sixty . . . four* made it sound like an eternity.

It was another hot, miserable night when I finally made it back to my hooch. After hours of sweating and listening to Luke snore, I fell into a fitful sleep. Sometime later an enemy rocket landed sixty feet from our hooch. The explosion was so loud it was unidentifiable at first. My reaction was to throw myself off my cot and whimper "Mom" into the dusty bamboo mat on the floor.

Then the second rocket roared like a freight train right over the roof, landing between our hooch and the Huey revetments. My chicken plate was close at hand, so I pulled it over my head. The sound of the rocket's passage still filled the air when the concussion of the explosion shook the hooch. Shrapnel ripped through tin six feet above me. Seconds after the last debris fell on the roof, it was calm. Just as my hearing started to return, the next one came over.

5

Command and Control

Mid-July 1969

The weeks rolled by and before long I got used to the routine of life in Tay Ninh: get up early, bitch and complain, go fly, hang around with the other pilots, drink until the bar closed, then try to get some sleep. Except for the heat, living conditions, and the occasional rocket or mortar, life in War Zone C was not all that bad. Flying Command and Control was easy and a lot safer than my first flight with Stoney had led me to believe. In fact, getting shot at on the orientation flight and the rocket attack later that night turned out to be the most exciting events of the entire month.

Tay Ninh had changed a lot in the short time I had been there. Before I arrived, rocket and mortar attacks were a nightly occurrence, according to the war stories in the officers' club, and the company had been losing Hueys and LOHs to enemy ground fire on a regular basis. During my first weeks with the Flying Circus the pilots and door gunners were paranoid and reclusive. Conversations were short, often cold; some of the pilots seemed to be at the breaking point. A month later, toward the end of July, the lull in fighting brought life in the company area back to normal. Part of normal life was hanging out in cliques.

The easiest group to join was Sharp, Scrotum, and friends, the operations office clique. Requirements for membership were an irrational, undying respect for anyone of superior rank coupled with a love of competitive brownnosing. The hardest group to fraternize with was Evil Eye, Snuffy, and the gang of malcontents and misfits. Their club was Evil Eye and Snuffy's hooch. Most of the time they lounged around outside in the shade of the roof overhang, relaxing in ratty old canvas beach chairs. Other than moving from one side of the porch to the other to stay out of the sun, the only activity Evil Eye and company participated in was insulting everyone who walked by. When it got too hot, they moved inside to play Bob Dylan's *Nashville Skyline* over and over again. Occasionally the tunes would be drowned out by fits of bawdy laughter.

The first time I heard Bob croaking out his songs in their hooch it occurred to me it was the first music I had heard, short of the muzak in the officers' club, since I left home. I really missed hearing contemporary music. Dylan was not my favorite, but he was better than nothing. So there was little doubt in my mind which group of pilots I would rather be hanging around. But for reasons I had not fathomed, Evil Eye and company never invited anyone, not even fellow warrant officers, into their tin clubhouse.

One day, after many attempts, I made it through a merciless barrage of insults all the way to where Evil Eye and Snuffy were slouched in their chairs. "Why are you guys so nasty?" I asked. "I mean, I like sarcasm, but you guys are brutal."

"What's it to you, *new guy*?" Snuffy returned with a scowl.

"It's just that we don't want to have to attend any

asshole Army award ceremonies for nice guy of the month," Evil Eye added.

"Well, I was just wondering," I said and started to walk away.

"Hey, if you're going to the PX pick up a six-pack of Heineken, and we'll help you drink it, Smith," Snuffy said to my back.

The PX was not that far, so I picked up the beer and returned to their hooch. They had moved inside by the time I got back, so I knocked on the red sign nailed to the door that said RAP! and they invited me in. As the door closed behind me the harsh glare of the midday sun disappeared; the walls, floor, windows, everything, were covered with bamboo mats. Normally, covering the windows would have been suicide. Trapping the insufferable heat and humidity under a tin roof in the sun would have been torture, but they had a fan, the first one I had seen in a hooch.

"Jesus Christ, you guys have a fan!" I exclaimed. "How the hell do I get one of those?"

"The easiest way to get one is to be good buddies with someone who has one and then wait for him to DEROS [date of expected return from overseas] or get blown away," Evil Eye explained.

"Can't you just buy one somewhere?" It seemed like a reasonable question, but Snuffy and Evil Eye cracked up.

"Yeah, maybe on the black market in Saigon for a couple hundred bucks. That's where the sorry mothers in the PX system sell them." They both laughed again.

As my eyes adjusted to the dark, I noticed another rarity. "Amazing, a refrigerator—you guys even have a refrigerator." It was a small, sweaty contraption with peace decals and sloppy hand-done psychedelic paintings all over it, but it was humming away, making everything cold.

"It works OK, but keeps me up at night." As he said this, Snuffy opened the door and a wave of cold air spilled out, rolling across the floor and up over my sandal-clad feet. My toes squirmed in pleasure.

Something else that I could not miss upon entering this well-concealed home of hedonism was the unmistakable smell of incense. In a flash I understood why they were so selective in choosing friends. They were smoking pot. And it was barely noon. These guys knew how to take a day off.

"Sit down, Smith, you're making me nervous. You look like a goddamned inspector general."

The only space available, a cot, had a flight helmet on it that I had to move. The back had *Snuffy* and *Peace* written on it, and on the front of the helmet was a beautiful rendition of a psychedelic butterfly. It was the same creature that graced the cover of one of Iron Butterfly's albums, and it was a great job, perfect in detail and color. "Far out! Nice paint job. Nothing wrong with Iron Butterfly," I remarked, holding up the helmet—trying to let the guys know I was cool. "Snuffy, if you like Iron Butterfly so much, how come you are always playing that Bob Dylan music?"

"My mom. I wrote her for a tape deck. She sent me the deck and *one* tape. Wanna smoke some dope, get stupid, and listen to it?" he answered.

"Nothing I'd rather do," I said, feeling more at home than I had for months. We had a lot of laughs in that hooch getting stoned, drinking beer, and avoiding the realities of the military system. But no matter how far we went, we never really escaped.

We always had to return for war the next day, a war in which helicopter pilots were major players.

Never before had the helicopter been used so extensively in combat, and with so many functions. The lethal Cobra and UH-1 "Charlie" model gunships, the life-saving UH-1 medevac helicopters, troop-carrying and equipment-carrying UH-1s and CH-47s, heavy-lift CH-54 Sky Cranes capable of lifting ten tons, nimble OH-6 LOHs perfectly suited for ferreting out the enemy, and UH-1 Command and Control helicopter communication centers capable of transporting high-ranking commanders to the front lines only moments after initial contact with the enemy. Of all these jobs, Command and Control was by far the easiest and safest.

It was safe because we were under strict orders not to do anything foolish—like getting shot down—so we flew around at three thousand feet, far out of harm's way. These orders came from our passengers, the commanding officers of the ground troops. Command and Control was easy because we did not have to do a whole lot of flying. From my first day with the Cav, 27 June to 28 July, I flew C&C fourteen days for a total of only 60.3 hours: an average of 4.3 hours a day with every other day off—nice, easy work.

As Luke had mentioned, our job was to ferry the COs around so they could keep tabs on their troops in the jungle and help them out when they came in contact with the enemy. There were two types of commanding officers we carried in the back of our Hueys, good and bad. What determined if they were good or bad was whether they truly helped, or just interfered with, the troops on the ground.

From three thousand feet the COs and their aides had a bird's-eye view of the area and a better overall picture of maneuvering potential than the ground commanders down below. Often this vantage point provided the troops with valuable information. The COs also had radio contact with Tay Ninh base, the Air Force, ground troops, and fire-support bases in the area. This, coupled with the authority of their rank, could expedite whatever support was available when the troops got into a fight. The good COs helped where they could but let the troops and ground commanders fight their own battles. The bad COs insisted on running the whole battle from the air, more of an ego trip than a sincere desire to help.

The commanders usually arrived shortly after the fighting had begun, when the soldiers below were locked in battle. These were wild scenes with everyone shooting at everyone else from very close distances, a lot of confusion. Situations developed so fast that life-and-death decisions had to be made instantly on the basis of what was happening right in front of, and all around, the soldiers. Even though our passengers had good visibility of the whole area, they couldn't see down through the thick jungle canopy. Logic would dictate that the men on the ground should make their own decisions in these cases, but some of the colonels and majors in the air would jump right in, giving orders to anyone they could get on the radio.

It disgusted me to hear pompous commanding officers cursing men who were fighting for their lives, men who did not have time to follow ridiculous orders. How could those COs possibly expect the GIs below to allow someone circling above them, with nothing to lose, play war games and take chances with their lives? No doubt some of those COs were good soldiers and decent men, but it was impossible not to question their judgment when they had nothing to lose and everything to gain. How many of their plans would have changed had we dropped them on the ground in the middle of one of those firefights?

Flying around in boring circles at three thousand feet, listening to the company and battalion commanders in the back trying to direct battles below, was a heavy price to pay for the safe and easy job of Command and Control. At the end of the day, back in the officers' club, I would have to listen to the same commanding officers complaining about how *their* COs in Saigon and Washington were screwing up the war by overcontrolling.

It was odd, but Evil Eye actually seemed to enjoy Command and Control. He always seemed to be having fun—sick, disgusting fun. One day we were turning circles at three thousand feet, the COs in a huddle in the back, when I started telling Evil Eye that one of the CO's aides, a young lieutenant with big ears, looked like Howdy Doody. Evil Eye came over the intercom with, "You know they can hear everything you say in the back, don't you?" I looked down at the console between us, certain I had left my intercom switch in the *off* position. Sure enough, someone—it could only have been Evil Eye—had moved my intercom switch to the *on* position. Just to make sure, I turned around and looked at the lieutenant. No doubt about it, he had heard everything I said.

Evil Eye finished his malicious little chuckle and reached down to turn my intercom switch off. "Close your window halfway." I slid the Plexiglas half closed and looked back at Evil Eye. His face was contracted, straining. As he rolled up on one cheek of his butt, it became obvious what he was doing.

The fart he let rip was loud enough to be heard throughout the whole helicopter, even above the noise of the turbine engine and pounding rotor blades.

Sure enough, the lieutenant heard it because now his wicked stare was fixed on Evil Eye. I watched as the lieutenant's expression changed from hate to distress and then to loathing as that nasty fart got to him. Evil Eye sure knew his air currents: that blast had gone straight into the cargo area where the COs sat. With my oil-soaked flight glove over my mouth and nose it never got to me.

As far as I was concerned he could do whatever he wanted with the helimobile commanders in the back of Hueys. They were not men we could easily respect. They lied too much. Little things like, "Charlie Company, can you estimate the size of your opposition, over?" from the backseat.

"Roger that, sir, maybe a couple dozen ahead of us and ten or fifteen on our left flank, over," came the reply from the ground troops.

"Make it an estimated force of one hundred-plus enemy, Lieutenant." This on the intercom in the back.

"How many enemy kills?" back to the ground commander.

"No body count yet, sir," from below.

"Twenty NVA KIA, Lieutenant," in back.

There were many factors involved in this kind of irresponsible behavior. The COs had the pressure of performing in our country's first televised war, playing to a disinterested and often hostile audience back home. Those who did support the war, and the soldiers in it, wanted to see results for their efforts. Since the advent of TV, the viewing audience had become used to entertainment larger than life, and Vietnam had to be competitive.

Another factor in the problem was that the COs we flew around faced the same problem as every combat soldier in Vietnam. They had been thrown into the middle of a jungle war with no practical experience, taking over from someone else in midstream, learning through mistakes, while all the time knowing it was only a one-year job. A number of them had never been closer to combat than the backseat of a Huey. But all of them wanted to look good, and one way to do that was by reporting back with high body counts.

It went on all the time, officers losing control to their egos, lying. Being their pilot made me an accomplice. Worse than an accomplice, I was there because it was safe and easy, an impotent witness to other people's misery, more useless than the worst textbook commander in the back. On the rare occasions I could have proven my worth by actually doing something other than flying in circles, the aircraft commander—not me, the peter-pilot—was on the controls. Those rare occasions were the few times we got shot at, on landings and takeoffs at the LZs; often by the time we realized that we were taking fire, the enemy had quit shooting.

I tried to salvage what pride I had left by becoming as proficient as I could on the controls of the Huey. Surprisingly enough, the best teacher in the company was Animal—surprising because he was a genuine pothead. Snuffy and Evil Eye got stoned at the end of the day or when they had time off, but Animal's first waking breath was full of cannabis smoke, yet Animal was the steadiest pilot of the lot. He had the most coordinated technique in the company.

A normal Army aviation approach to landing required a downwind leg, a base leg, a final leg, and termination to a hover. This involved flying a pattern a mile long with two ninety-degree right turns, a descent from four hundred feet to the ground, and a decrease in airspeed from a hundred and ten to zero knots. Animal had such a feeling for the aircraft and was so smooth on the controls that he could complete the entire maneuver with just four movements of the cyclic and one adjustment of the collective. Most pilots made a normal approach to a hover a physical workout.

Vietnam was also the first test, the proving ground, for the many new and different types of helicopters. The less inhibited pilots were creative, spontaneous, always developing new techniques for expanding the helicopters' effectiveness. The more normal pilots were so hung up on military regulations and procedures that they had trouble learning from experience. Their ability to respond to atypical situations was restricted and usually less successful.

All through July of 1969 the lull in fighting around Tay Ninh continued and so did the relatively relaxed times. Some pilots and door gunners were complaining that it was too quiet, that the NVA were building up for an offensive. Some of the COs were saying the war was over. Most of the pilots who knew the area well felt that the enemy was just taking a break and would continue along at a normal pace when they felt like it. The men out in the firebases were just glad there was a quiet spell.

When I started flying Command and Control, the firebases were getting attacked so often they could not even send men out on Search and Destroy patrols. They had to keep everyone on the firebases to keep the enemy from overrunning the place. Usually when we landed at the LZs the only sign of life would be machine gun barrels sticking out of the gun slots facing the green line. The men would scurry, heads down, holding on to their helmets, from one dirt-covered shelter to the next. Three weeks later they were lying out on the same bunkers, in their underwear, getting suntans, with rock-and-roll music blasting from the gun ports of the green-line bunkers.

Maybe it was too peaceful, or maybe I thought there was more to flying than being a peter-pilot who made good peanut-butter-and-jelly cracker sandwiches, but after two weeks of flying Command and Control, boredom set in. Occasionally, as I performed my duties as a chauffeur, I would catch a few minutes of the Scouts in action—skimming across the treetops at high speed, then whipping around in sharp turns to come to a hover. They would circle an area for a while and then zip off, while I continued to turn in monotonous circles high in the sky.

Our company Scout helicopters always flew in pairs, with one pilot in each machine and one door gunner. From up above, the two Scout ships darting around the jungle canopy looked like two dogs checking out a big field.

On the radio in my C&C ship I could listen in on their chatter. "White two-one, two-zero, let's go check out that trotter over by the swamp. See if there're any gooks hanging out today." The Scouts really seemed to know what was happening down in the jungle.

"I'm right behind you, Cowboy," replied Crab, who was White 21.

And off they would go on an adventure of their own, no one telling them what to do. It reminded me of days gone by in flight school when Craig and I would take off to run wild over the baked landscape of Texas. The Scouts were having a good time doing a job that was greatly appreciated by the guys who did ninety percent of the dirty work of the war, the soldiers in the jungle, the "grunts."

Scouts would fly ahead and all around the troops in the field, looking for signs of trouble. When the troops got in firefights the Scouts were right there putting down machine gun fire, throwing grenades, giving the enemy something else to worry about. All of this support was done at treetop level, where the Scouts could see both the friendlies and the enemy.

Jet pilots liked Scouts because the Scout pilots knew exactly where the enemy was and could get in to drop a Willy Pete (a white phosphorus grenade that sent up a highly visible white cloud of smoke) on them. This set the jet pilots up with an excellent mark, right on the target.

The Air Force had its own target markers, FACs (Forward Air Controllers), but their fast-moving airplanes could not accomplish the mission with the accuracy of a Scout helicopter. The jet pilots also appreciated the BDAs (bomb damage assessments) the Scout pilots could give them. After the smoke and falling debris from the bombs had cleared, Scouts would fly right into the middle of the bombed area, at ground level, and give the jet pilots a detailed picture of what their efforts had accomplished.

Commanders were extremely fond of the Scouts because they took a lot of the guesswork out of the tactical side of the job. Just like the original cavalry scouts of the Wild West, the Army Scouts operated independently, and therefore could move fast, covering lots of ground. Scouts brought back a large and very detailed picture of what was going on in their area of operations. It seemed everybody liked the Scouts, and because of the high risk involved, respected them, even if they did think they were totally insane. Scout pilots had the highest fatality rate, by far, of the different jobs that were available to helicopter pilots in Vietnam. Every day they went out looking for armed men who wanted to shoot them down.

It was about this time that I received a letter from my good buddy Craig. He was about forty miles away in Cu Chi, flying gunships—not the sleek Cobra gunships, but the old slow C model Hueys. They looked the same as our Command and Control D and H model Hueys, except they were a little shorter and seemed a lot wider because of the machine guns and rocket pods hanging on their sides. Craig wrote that he was having a great time and loved the Charlie model gunships.

During my third week in Command and Control the last experienced Scout pilot remaining, Cowboy, was shot down. The aircraft burned after crashing and Cowboy's face, arms, legs, and feet had third-degree burns; his fingers were cooked down to stumps. The only place he was not severely burned was behind his chicken plate. Later I heard from another pilot that Cowboy died from his wounds back in Texas or somewhere. His door gunner, Thompson, never got out of the wreck. Sharp, flying wingman for Cowboy, got his aircraft shot up when he made a heroic attempt to rescue the downed crew.

That left Sharp and Crab, with Crab still in training, as the only Scout pilots. Because they flew two LOHs together, neither of them could take a day off. The pressure was on to find some new Scout pilots.

Since I was definitely on the list of possibilities, I decided to talk to Foster to see what he thought about Scouting. I found him working on the minigun of one of the LOHs.

"This communist minigun is giving me a hard time. The cowling doesn't fit right and it keeps jamming. What a Mickey Mouse setup," Crab complained. The minigun was mounted on the floor in the backseat section of the helicopter and stuck out of the left side, facing forward. It was a six-barreled Gatling type of machine gun, driven by an electric motor, and could shoot up to four thousand rounds a minute. Because it shot so many shells so fast, the shell casings and links had to be ejected with forced air from the cowling. They were always jamming.

"Hey, Mr. Smith, how's it going?" Little Buddy called out as he walked up to us from the maintenance tent with a couple of seat belts in his hands.

"Not bad. How come so many seat belts?" I asked.

"Puttin' them together and making a monkey strap. Wolfman won't wear a seat belt. Says he can't move around enough with one on. I figured I'd put two together so he can hang out the back and still be strapped in." Then he climbed into the back of the helicopter.

"You having a good time flyin' Scouts, Crab?" I asked.

"It's a gas. Bet you'd dig it, Smith." He looked at me and smiled his crazy smile. I couldn't tell if Crab was serious or not.

"You don't even know me. What makes you say that?" I asked.

"Well, I got to find someone to fly with. Think old Sharp is losing it." He looked up and laughed a short, nutty laugh. "Don't think it was a good idea for him to see Cowboy and Thompson get all messed up like that. He's getting pretty squirrelly." Crab worked for a while in silence; he was enjoying tinkering with the machinery, something I could not bring myself to do. My suspicions were that if you messed with anything in a helicopter, the whole thing would come apart.

"It's a great job, Smith, you'll love it. These LOHs are unbelievable. They can do anything." He kept working on the minigun. "It's the most fun flying you can get into. And trying to find the gooks is pretty wild. Best of all, no one tells you what to do in Scouts. No sitting in the right seat of a fat Huey getting bored to death. No working at night . . . That should do it," he said. Crab admired his handiwork, then walked around to get in the pilot's seat on the right side of the LOH. Little Buddy was still working on the seat belt in the back right seat. Both the door gunner and the pilot sat on the right side of the LOH because most of the work of locating the enemy, trying to read signs on the ground through the tops of the trees, was done by flying in tight right-hand circles.

"One thing I'm having trouble with is talking on three radios at one time." Crab was fooling around with the radio switches on the instrument panel in front of him. From flying Command and Control I was accustomed to listening to two radios, air-to-ground FM for the troops we were working with and air-to-base UHF. A Scout pilot had to listen to, and talk on, three radios—air-to-ground FM for the troops, air-to-air UHF for his wingman, and air-to-air VHF for the Air Force pilots.

"Well, what do you think of the getting killed part, Crab?" I persisted.

Crab flipped on the battery and armed the mini-gun, its red warning lights indicating it was opera-tive. "The chances of getting killed in Scouts are higher. Big deal. At least I do the flying and get to kill myself," he reasoned. This was logic I under-stood. Ever since my parents had died in that air-plane crash four years earlier, I had been making my own decisions. I liked it that way.

Wolfman had joined us and was trying on the elongated seat belt Little Buddy had put together for him. I asked, "What do you think about getting blown away in Scouts, Wolfman?" Wolfman was standing on the skid with his M60 machine gun, test-ing his new monkey strap. The strap was almost three feet long, and by standing out on the skid he could bend around and shoot under the helicopter from one end to the other. He had almost a 360-degree field of fire.

"Wolf-luck, got to have it or that's it. You're his-tory, sayonara, adios, motha-fucker." Wolfman made some machine gun sounds as he played on his mon-key strap, pretending he had someone in his sights under the helicopter. "Only trouble is I may have used it all up when Cowboy and Thompson got shot down." He looked at us with mock concern. "I flipped with Thompson to see who was going to fly with Cowboy the other day." Wolfman slumped down on the metal floor of the LOH and looked off at Nui Ba Den. "What a drag." Wolfman had a sad-ness in his eyes, a resigned look, and for the first time since I had known him he seemed to be drained of energy.

I knew how he felt, and I knew I was going to be flying Scouts with them. There really was no choice; I did not belong in Command and Control. There was the self-image problem, being identified with the authority figures of the commanding officers, and having to be a subordinate witness to their incompetence. The COs' incompetence was not something that happened on a daily basis but their indiscretions were numerous, and of such a magnitude that it was hard to forget them. And there was the feeling that I could be doing more for whatever it was I was doing there; but most of all I wanted to get into Scouts because the flying looked like so much fun.

My last straw for Command and Control came in the middle of July. We had a battalion commander sitting in the back who had a lieutenant right out of Officer Candidate School as an aide. Frequently the officers in the Command and Control helicopters or their aides called in artillery from the firebases in an effort to help the soldiers below. This usually worked out pretty well, and was appreciated, but when they made a mistake it was an expensive one, especially for the young men who got hit by shells called "errors" and who then became casualties of "friendly fire."

The lieutenant had little more than a textbook education, no field experience at all, but the colonel decided to let him direct the firebase artillery for a platoon of men involved in a close-contact firefight below us. It was a complicated situation—the artillery had to shoot over, and close to, the friendly troops to hit the enemy. The jungle was so thick that even the friendlies' smoke grenades were not making it through the trees; it was almost impossible to tell where the troops were. "Fire mission," the lieutenant radioed LZ Jay's howitzer crews. "Grid coordinates 395984 North and 688672 East," he said, marking a spot for the gun crews that was near, but not on, the friendly troops.

"Give me one Willy Pete," he said, asking for a marking round to check his grid coordinates. Moments later a white mushroom blossomed below us, a few hundred yards from the troops. After three repetitions he had the Willy Pete rounds landing as close as one hundred yards from the friendly troops and very near the enemy. He made one final range correction and then said, "Load HE [high explosives] and fire for effect."

The lieutenant instructed the gun crews to switch from marking rounds to shells that were used against enemy troops and their fortifications. The jungle erupted in a gray-brown cloud right above the friendly position. In the same instant the FM radio screamed the frantic pleas of the ground commander to "Check fire!" The lieutenant's last adjustment had moved the guns to the right and dropped nine thirty-pound 105mm rounds on his own troops. All the way back to Tay Ninh the lieutenant kept offering lame excuses to his CO.

The next day I told Captain Crane that I wanted to fly Scouts. He was nice enough to remind me that it was a voluntary assignment and then asked, "You're not married, right?" The captain did not like letting married men fly Scouts because he hated writing your-husband's-coming-home-in-a-box letters.

On 19 July I wrote my first letter home, to my brother Peter.

Dear Peter,
    Well let me tell you about Vietnam. It is right down here in the middle of heat, humidity, big spiders, snakes, monkeys, tigers, elephants, and all kinds

of animals. It is a pretty colorful war. But I am not sure I really like it.

The incoming mortars wake me up a lot. Another problem is all the trips to the laundry to get the excrement out of my pants after some one shoots at me while I am flying. The social life is really very pleasant.

Anyway I am stationed in Tay Ninh with the infamous 1st Cavalry Division. They are a bunch of hard core fighting mother fuckers. One good thing about the Cav is we have the best equipment and air assistance. Also the morale and guts of the people are pretty high. This helps to make for a smooth war, if you happen to like smooth wars.

I have been assigned to fly Scouts; our last Scout pilot was shot down the other day and he had to go home for a new face, hands, feet, and legs. He got a little burned. When he got shot down he went bullshit and attacked the two twin fifty cal. machine guns that had screwed him up and killed his door gunner, with only his pistol. He fell over before he got to the positions, and the other Scout bird came in and picked him up. So now we are in the process of starting a new Scout team.

A lot of people getting killed, but I think if I am cool, know what I am doing, and am really lucky I should be able to make it home.

Please write.

Love,
   Tom

I wrote to my brother that I had been assigned to Scouts; I didn't want him to know I had volunteered for something so risky and foolhardy. On 28 July, five weeks after I had joined the Cav, I started flying wingman for Crab. One of the first things he did was give me a new call sign. The Scouts did not use the same call sign, Stingray, that Command and Control did. Crab was White 21 and I became White 24.

6

Scouts

Early August 1969

My transition into Scouts had to be brief; the NVA decided to get back into the war, and Crab and I were the only Scout pilots left. Sharp had gone slowly downhill and was starting to develop some worrisome nervous habits—little things like a twitch in the corner of his mouth during mission assignments, constantly checking his watch, laughing out loud at things that were not funny. The final straw for him came when a .51-caliber machine gun round hit the bottom of his aircraft, went through the armor plating of his seat, and tore a hole in his fatigue shirt where it hung lose under his armpit. Sharp never flew below three thousand feet again.

After a two-week lull in the fighting, patrols were constantly engaging the enemy; fire-support bases were being hit on a daily basis. The commanding officers wanted as much information on enemy positions and strengths as the Scouts could provide. Consequently I was given only three days to train as a Scout pilot. In that time we flew around some of the areas Crab knew well, and he showed me the basics.

Crab taught me how to fly cover for the lead ship. We flew two LOHs with the wing ship covering the lead. When the lead ship, flying a couple of hundred feet in front of his wingman, found something interesting in the jungle, he would slow down and make tight right turns to keep the object in sight. The slower the lead ship got, the easier it was for the NVA to shoot it down. Crab showed me how to position myself so that my door gunner could always put down cover fire if the enemy opened up on him.

I had to learn to be in the right place; things happened in a hurry. As Crab put it during one of our first training flights, "It's a bummer, but they always get to shoot first." He explained that as we tracked the enemy they could hear us coming and conceal themselves in the dense lower canopy of the jungle. "They hang out, waiting until we're right on top of them. Then they let loose with everything they got—gets ugly. If I'm low and slow when the shootin' starts, you're the only one who can get me the time I need to get my airspeed up and get my young ass out of there. You've got to have your door gunner where he can shoot back. Make them duck, miss their shot. Killing them, of course, is best," Crab said. After teaching me how to keep him alive, Crab showed me some tricks that I might use to keep *myself* alive.

One basic trick was kicking the ship out of trim. When the shooting started we used our tail-rotor pedals to twist the nose of the ship off to the right or left of its true heading. We would still be flying in the same direction, but to the enemy it appeared we were turning. A lot of them would adjust for this and miss.

We also practiced flying in the treetops. The best way to get out of their sights was to disappear. The trees were the closest cover, and the quicker you got there, the better. The trick, of course, was to get down among the branches without hitting them.

"You won't have any problem with it when fifty little guys in black pajamas are trying to fill your LOH full of holes," Crab assured me.

Of special importance to me was mastering the use of the minigun. At four thousand rounds a minute, it put out bullets five times as fast as conventional machine guns. Visions of mowing down a screaming wave of NVA, John Wayne style, helped me feel confident that I could shoot my way out of any difficult situation. After two exasperating days of working with my minigun I realized that if the NVA had me surrounded, I was dead; it was impossible to aim the damn thing effectively.

The 7.62mm minigun was on a fixed mount and the only built-in movement it had was up and down, at a slow crawl. Also, no efficient sight had been developed for it, so we used a rather primitive method for getting the rounds on target. We pulled the trigger and watched where the tracers went, then moved the tracers to the target by turning the helicopter.

It was actually easier than it sounds. I had a general idea where the gun was pointed and every fifth round was a tracer. At four thousand rounds a minute the tracers formed a solid ribbon of red in front of the LOH. Unfortunately, the only way to move the gun from side to side was by pushing on the tail-rotor pedals and twisting the entire helicopter. The torque was tough on the machine and moved the minigun only a short distance. This pedal-pushing also threw off the door gunner's aim. Unless the NVA were sitting right out in front of me, or I had lots of time, the minigun was pretty ineffective as a quick-response weapon.

Another part of Scout training involved working out with my door gunner. Whether we were getting into a fight, or trying to get out of one, we had to be a team working at its best. The most important part of the teamwork was communication. Unless he was hanging out of the aircraft, the door gunner could see only along the right side of the helicopter. The pilot could see out in front, so it was the pilot's responsibility to let the door gunner know when and where a target was coming up. The door gunner had to let the pilot know if he had the target and if anything else was happening behind him—if there were people shooting at him, for example. My door gunner for training was a corporal named Slater.

Most of our door gunners were infantry soldiers who had transferred in order to fly, pretty regular guys who wondered what it would be like to buzz around in a LOH. Slater came from the infantry, but he was not a regular guy. He looked and talked like a panhandler straight from Haight-Ashbury. A scrawny guy about five-foot-ten, he looked as if he slept in his clothes and had just that minute gotten out of bed. When he talked, Slater had a not-so-fetching habit of tilting his head back so he could see out from under his filthy glasses. Every time he did this, his mouth would hang open about two inches. Slater was an odd young man, and the second-best full-time door gunner we had at the time.

The first thing to do was find out how Slater handled his M60. No two door gunners had the same field of fire. Some shot better to the left, some to the right, others could also shoot under and behind the helicopter. It was important to know how wide a field of fire each door gunner had—no sense in giving him a target he couldn't hit. I picked out a stump in the middle of a field and flew up, down, and all around it trying to throw Slater's aim off. He never missed the stump by more than two feet and usually had the tracers going right into it. Next we made a few passes throwing grenades. Slater loved it, but it made me nervous having live grenades lying around where they might get hit by an enemy round or have a pin fall out.

Another weapon the door gunners liked to use was the M79. This was a little single-shot cannon, shaped like a short rifle. The projectile it discharged was about five inches long and two inches wide. When it hit, it exploded like a grenade, which was very effective at killing people who had good cover, and unlike with the grenade, we did not have to be right over the target. All the door gunner had to do was lob one of those shells on the enemy's exposed side and the shrapnel would get them. I had been told that a good door gunner could put one in the small openings of bunkers and blow up everyone inside.

One day we were out practicing with the M79, flying as low as we could over a small forest of bamboo, approaching the target Slater had picked out. I was having a good time watching out my door as he took aim and fired. Just as the shell should have exploded on target, there was a loud *crunch* as the helicopter jumped and bucked. I had been so intent on seeing the shell impact that I had flown right into the bamboo thicket. Fortunately we just bounced off it and continued to fly, but both chin bubbles—the Plexiglas windows in the bottom of the helicopter's nose—were broken, and my ego was shattered. When I got back to the base, people I had never even seen before were coming up to me to give me a hard time about it. Evil Eye smirked at me for a week.

Crab and I also spent a lot of time talking about different ways we thought we should fly Scouts. As

I had mentioned in the letter to my brother, we were in the process of starting a new Scout team. Crab had been in Scouts only a few weeks, and he had already seen a door gunner die, a pilot burned up, and another pilot quit. I had absolutely no experience, but I did have a strong desire to stay alive, so we decided to be smart and start out with some safety rules. Every mission would have two armed LOHs; it was just too dangerous without a wingman's cover fire. We would also not fly into an area of known enemy activity without a high bird, a gunship flying a couple of thousand feet above us for cover. There would be no letting our airspeed get under twenty knots while circling in the trees, since slow targets are easy targets. Flying out into the middle of fields was prohibited—it takes too long to get to cover. It was also agreed that we should not circle with less than fifty pounds of fuel, as continuous banked turns could starve an engine. Finally, there would be absolutely no missions scheduled after five—cocktail hour.

One of our safety rules, no acrobatics, we borrowed from the only other Scout platoon in Tay Ninh, the 1st of the 9th Cav, who were losing pilots twice as fast as we were. "They're out of their heads," Crab screamed one night, totally wasted on Canadian Club. "Did you hear about that idiot? Went up and tried to do a loop from ground level. Hit the goddamned ground with his door gunner and two passengers. Straight in. No possible way you can do a loop from ground level. What an asshole."

So, relying on Crab's limited expertise and a little common sense on both our parts, we went out on our first Scout mission. I was not only short on experience, but also on sleep. The VC around Tay Ninh had been mortaring Tay Ninh base every night for over a week—blew up our latrine again.

We had breakfast before sunup. A glass of Kool-Aid was all I could get down. The same wicked butterflies that had visited me before every high school wrestling match were flitting around in my stomach. Gruesome images of Scout tragedies dragged themselves into my mind and had to be forcibly evicted. The self-confidence that had played such a major role in getting me into Scouts was letting me down. After breakfast we went to the Tactical Operations Center for a briefing from Major Sorenson. Sorenson was an aide to the brigade commander and was responsible for giving the Scouts their missions. His orders were "Go out to Grant and get me an estimate on what size enemy force we are dealing with out there. They took a few mortar rounds last night. When you get done there, go to LZ Christine and see if they can use you." We picked up our maps and left for the flight line.

"Remember, our whole area of operations is a 'free-fire zone,'" Crab said as we walked away from the TOC, reminding me to shoot first and ask questions later. Anyone we saw in the jungle was presumed to be enemy; we were supposed to have our door gunners shoot them. The townspeople had been told to stay out of the jungle or they would be mistaken for NVA.

"Something else I should've told you. Fly with your right earphone pushed back off your ear. It'll make it easier to tell when you are taking fire," Crab added. I went back to my hooch to pick up my flight gear. As I strapped on my pistol I was excited and anxious, with emphasis on the anxious side; I knew the pretending part was over. "Just be cool, don't do anything stupid," I said as I picked up my chicken plate, helmet, and gloves.

Crab, Wolfman, and Slater were already on the flight line loading the LOHs with minigun ammunition, grenades, and smoke bombs. Wolfman was flying with me and Slater with Crab. Just the sight of Wolfman relieved a few of my anxieties; he was so relaxed, smiling and joking with Slater. Neither Wolfman nor Crab had a chicken plate. All Wolfman had on were combat boots, fatigue pants, and his wolfshirt. When I asked him why he didn't have a chest protector or a pistol, he replied with a big grin, "I use my M60. Everything else just gets in my way."

Crab said he didn't wear a chicken plate because it made him sweat. I think he chose not to wear it because it made him look fat.

I asked Crab if operations had assigned us a high bird. "Not this morning," he said. "They're off covering some Slicks [Hueys used on troop insertions], but we'll get a Cobra from the Tigers in Phuoc Vinh for the afternoon."

I told Wolfman I would feel more comfortable on my first mission if we had a high bird for cover. He said, "Don't worry, that's what me and my M60 are here for. We'll take care of things." Seeing I was not convinced, he twisted his face in an effort to think about it some more and finally said, "If it gets too bad we'll come home." The sun and heat were rising, so we did an abbreviated preflight and got our little green LOHs running.

"Tay Ninh, White two-one, flight of two LOHs, Stingray pad for northeast departure," Crab called to the tower for clearance to take off.

"Roger two-one, be advised that smoke is covering the base north and northwest of you and we have patchy haze to the east and northeast from ground level to five hundred feet," the tower came back. As we lifted off we could see the whole west side of Tay Ninh covered in smoke. The night before, a rocket had hit one of the fuel tanks at the refueling area, and it was still burning.

We took off toward Nui Ba Den and circled north around the Vietnamese town of Tay Ninh in loose trail formation (one helicopter following a couple of hundred feet behind the other), twenty feet above the patchwork of rice paddies and the men working in them. Besides a few sandbag girls and PX employees, those farmers were the only Vietnamese I had seen since arriving in Tay Ninh. It felt great buzzing past them, heavily armed, on our way to look for the enemy in the jungle. I half expected them to stop what they were doing and wave as we flew by, but they didn't even look up. No big deal; it felt great to be flying, with the moist haze from a light night rain blowing in the open door, rich and cool. Through the mist we could see the spires of the large Cao Dai temple. A surreal vision in the morning fog.

A few miles out of town, in a vacant field, we tested our weapons, a chore we had to perform every day on the first flight. Wolfman ran a few rounds through his M60. "Everything A-OK back here, sir," his cheerful voice came over the intercom. I flipped my minigun switch to *armed* and squeezed the cyclic-mounted trigger. The gun roared like a runaway chain saw—I could not see how anyone would ever get used to that awful noise.

As soon as we reached the edge of the jungle we went to work. Our mission actually started at LZ Grant, but Crab wanted to check a few things on the way there. We agreed that the more we knew about overall enemy activity in our area, the fewer surprises we would have. In a few minutes we picked up the road leading to Grant. Crab dropped down to a few feet above the road and slowed down from a hundred and ten to twenty knots. "Two-four, two-one, I'm looking for signs of bicycle or foot traffic here," Crab's voice came over the UHF radio. "Stay up above me in the tree line and watch for gooks."

I flew along the treetops on the left side of the road, looking down, trying to see the jungle floor through the layers of branches. It was hard to focus in the short time the ground was exposed at fifty knots, so I pulled it back to thirty. "Keep your airspeed up, Smith! If you get slow they'll nail you. I'll have to come pick up your sorry ass." Crab sounded pissed. When I looked back to check on him he was nowhere in sight.

He had stopped right in the middle of the road, hovering one foot above the ground, and was hanging out the right side of his helicopter. We never flew with the doors on, which left the two-foot-by-four-foot oval door hole open for ventilation and leaning out to take a closer look. "There're motorbike tracks here. They weren't here yesterday!" His voice leaped over the airwaves. "The goddamned dinks are riding to Tay Ninh for some boom-boom. Must be twenty of them went by here."

"Crab's afraid they're coming in and screwing Tu," Wolfman said over the intercom. Tu was one of the Vietnamese sandbag girls Crab said he loved.

"Probably going to get it on with our sandbag girls," Crab said over the radio. "This is supposed to be our road, goddamn it!" With that he nosed his ship over and popped up above the opposite tree line.

We flew along on the edge of the road, skimming the tops of the trees at a hundred knots. I rolled the aircraft left, then right, looking down into the jungle flying by. Large, long-tailed, resplendent birds leaped from their islands of trees. As their brilliant colors flashed in flight, I imagined their exotic cries, drownd by my engine noise, in the thick jungle morning. An amazing world slipped by me. At that moment there was no place I would rather have been—I felt so alive.

The fact that every man below us was the enemy no longer bothered me. Going looking for them put it all in a new perspective, a feeling of control. Flying Command and Control had left me with the impression we were fighting a phantom. In those days I kept asking myself, where are they now, how many are there, what are they going to do next? It was their game, they were calling the shots. Down in the jungle I knew we would find out where they were and what they were doing.

The morning haze was starting to burn off and Nui Ba Den rose into a blue sky between two towering cumulus clouds. At the intersection with the dirt road that ran along the east side of the mountain, Crab dropped down and hovered while Wolfman and I patrolled the tree lines. I felt as if I was getting the hang of it and took a left into the jungle. A small stream with smooth grassy banks flashed under us. Just before the clearing slipped by I saw a small trail on the far bank.

Five seconds later it occurred to me that it was probably not ours. With a surge of excitement I pulled the cyclic back and laid the helicopter over in a hard turn to the right. The rotor blades popped and the helicopter bucked as we pivoted around the top of a large tree just ten feet below us. The near-ninety-degree bank and coordinated turn felt so good; it seemed the aircraft and I were welded together. At the same time, though, a subtle fear was working on my enthusiasm. Someone might be waiting in the trees to blow me away—maybe I was not doing the right thing. I nosed it over for the security of more airspeed, then crossed the stream even faster than the first time, making the trail nothing but a blur.

"Pardon me, sir, but what was that all about?" Wolfman asked in a slightly mocking tone.

"Two-four, two-one, where the hell are you, Smith?" Crab's voice startled me.

"Over here, up the road to Barbara. A little north of you. Got a trotter along this little blue here," I told him.

"How about getting back over here? You're supposed to be covering me," Crab said. Feeling a bit hurt I popped up fifty feet above the trees to get a heading back to the intersection, but Crab was already heading our way, a bubble scooting across the tops of the trees. "Where's the trotter?" he asked. We dropped back down to the treetops, and Wolfman and I led the way back to the little trail we had found. At a hundred-plus knots, ten feet above the treetops, it was hard to be sure exactly where it was, so I used a general compass heading. We came in fast over the tree line, and I had to pull a radical turn to start a circle around the trail.

"If you think it's safe, drop down and take a look. I'll cover you," Crab was saying as I rolled her over a little more and dropped down into the clearing. The helicopter did exactly what I wanted it to do. From a ten-foot hover I looked at the trail, expecting to see some of the obvious signs of activity Crab had seen back on the road. There were tracks of some kind on the trail, little ridges here and there in the light-colored dirt, but I could not tell if they were footprints. "Can you make anything out, Wolfman?" I asked over the intercom.

"Not from up here, I can't," Wolfman came back politely. We dropped down to a three-foot hover. "Lower," said Wolfman. The noise and motion of the helicopter made it hard to concentrate. Maybe there were footprints, but I could not tell how many, how old they were, or even which way they were going. We settled a little lower, only inches above the trail. Rotor wash whipped up dust devils and flattened the grass on both sides of the trail. Suddenly it dawned on me that we had been hovering there for what seemed like hours. I jerked my head up to see if we were being watched from the tree line just as a loud popping sound let loose behind us. "What's that?" I yelled over the intercom.

"Think you stuck your tail rotor into a bush, sir," Wolfman answered in his usual calm manner.

"Come on up and cover me for a minute, Tom," Crab called, as he slid off the tree line to a hover behind me. We went back up and started circling Crab. "Hard to read," he called a moment later. "If you can't figure it out right away, leave it. Check out a different spot, keep movin'. These tracks are too old to make much of anyhow." We continued on toward LZ Grant, checking the trails Crab knew, but not coming up with any sign of recent use by the enemy.

"Grant, White two-one, two LOHs. Landing one minute," Crab called on his FM radio.

Even though I had been to Grant several times, I had no idea we were even near it. Nui Ba Den was out of sight, and we had made so many circles and turns it was impossible to even make a guess where we were. But a minute after Crab's call, we shot over the tree line surrounding Fire-Support Base Grant. We landed outside of the wire, leaving the main landing pad inside the fire-base open for Command and Control and other air traffic. After we shut down the helicopters we walked through the wire on a path they kept open for the infantry going out on patrols.

It made me a little nervous walking up to the break in the barbed wire. Bunkers along the green line bristled with machine gun barrels, and claymore antipersonnel mines were scattered in the wire, with the business side facing us. Even the big howitzers were leveled straight at us; I pictured one of those big cannons going off accidentally and discharging its flechet round at me. Flechets were steel darts a couple of inches long, thousands of which were loaded into shells. When fired from the big guns, they spread out in a broad pattern to rip through anything in their way. At night, if the 105mm howitzers were not on a fire mission, the big cannons were pointed at the surrounding jungle edge to ward off a surprise attack.

The sun was already hot enough to fry brains. The two grunts doing sentry duty at the wire looked tired, but were friendly, offering us cigarettes when we slowed down to say hello. "Seen any dinks on the way in?" one of them asked. "Blew the crap out of us last night."

"So we heard. Anyone hurt?" Crab asked.

The guy looked at Crab for a second and started chuckling, "Yeah, lots of hurt."

"Well, we're here to check and see if we can find

those mortars for you boys," Crab said cheerfully, almost condescendingly.

"You find 'em, we'll grease 'em," the chuckler bragged.

His partner looked at him and said, "You go right ahead, shit-bird." Then he turned to Crab. "Better'n that, how 'bout you find 'em, and you grease 'em for us." They thought that was really funny and were still laughing to each other as we headed through the wire to the Tactical Operations Center.

Inside the TOC, a cool, dark hole in the ground, my rivers of sweat instantly turned into trickles of cold water. The floors were dirt, the walls were dirt, even the roof was sandbagged dirt held up by steel sections of prefabricated road. The small room was full of officers and enlisted men, with twice the amount of activity as the last time I had been there. Some were talking on radios, others drawing on maps; they looked like mad moles fretting around in their dark dirt hole. Crab introduced me to Captain Lasell, who looked just like every other soldier there, officer or enlisted man—dirty, tired, and hassled. Everyone in there looked as if they were college age or younger. In the month I had been with the Cav, the only men I saw who were over twenty were the commanders back in Tay Ninh.

"Glad you're here, men. Want some coffee?" Lasell said with a handshake instead of a salute. "They hit us hard last night, heading zero-two-zero degrees, approximately two klicks, and zero-five-zero degrees, about the same distance. It was all mortar fire, maybe fifty rounds from 2000 to 0300 hours. . . . Cocksuckers!" He talked to Crab as if they had been friends for years. "We returned fire with mortars and the 105 howitzers all night, but they never missed a beat.

We got two KIA and six wounded. This shit's gettin' old!" the captain concluded.

"Have you had any patrols out there recently?" Crab asked, studying the map Lasell had spread out on an ammo-box table.

"Last one came back a couple hours before they unloaded on us. They found some old trotters, a few blown-up abandoned bunkers. Nothing newer than a couple weeks," the captain said as he frowned into a cup of something that may have been coffee. "It's always the same; they're never there when we are."

"We'll go check it out. Anything else you want us to do while we're out here?" Crab asked.

"Yeah, check in with Bravo Company. They are at grid coordinates three-five-nine-eight-six-five North and six-zero-eight-five-two-five East. Their frequency is four-three-point-eight, call sign 'Hector.' They had some movement last night, sounded big." As we started to leave he called across the TOC, "If there's anything we can do for you here, give us a call, appreciate the help. Good luck."

We woke up our door gunners, got the blades turning, and headed out to find where the mortars had come from. Crab told me to take the lead. After we had flown what I considered to be two kilometers on a heading of 020 degrees I started a slow right turn, looking down into the trees. "Coming right." I warned Crab over the UHF that I was starting my turn.

"Two-four, two-one, looking for the mortars, Smith?" Crab came back.

"Roger that," I responded.

"Won't find them in these thick trees. Look for a clearing. They need a hole to shoot through. We're about three klicks—start some S turns until we find an opening. I'm off to your left." We found a little stream and checked it out pretty well, but no signs of enemy activity. We covered the area out to four kilometers and saw nothing. "Two-four, two-one, let's go back to the LZ, try again," Crab suggested.

Wolfman had an even better idea. "Let's go back and take a little nap," he said over the intercom. Back at Grant we took up a new heading a little to the right of 020 degrees. This time, about three kilometers out, we found a small field. We circled, checking for signs of trails, bunkers, freshly cut trees, or any other signs of activity. On the far side of the clearing was an old road. Crab covered me while I dropped down to take a closer look at it. The bike and foot traffic on it was so clear and fresh it made the fur stand up on the back of my neck.

"Two-one, two-four, Jesus Christ, Crab, looks like the whole NVA army went by here minutes ago," I called on the UHF. "Bicycles and Ho Chi Minhs heading south. The dirt's beat to mud." Ho Chi Minhs were the sandals made of worn-out tires that some of the NVA, and all of the VC, wore.

"Getting warm, two-four," Crab called back. "Probably resupply. If they're wearin' Ho Chi Minhs and pushing bikes they're in the resupply business. Most of the infantry I've seen around here wear boots. Probably movin' a bunch of rockets and mortars to Tay Ninh. Keep looking for the mortar site, two-four."

Searching the ground from the tree line was not all that easy. Anything and everything caught my eye, but only for a second at thirty knots, then it was gone, and I had to try to catch up with a quick scan of the area I had missed. We had been around the clearing several times and were just about ready to give up, when Wolfman said, "Right there." I rolled the machine over in a sharp left turn to go back to check out what Wolfman had seen. Too late, I realized Crab was behind me on the left. There he was a hundred feet away, coming straight at us. I dropped the collective and dove between two trees at the same time Crab yanked back on his cyclic and climbed up over us. "Asshole!" Crab said over the UHF as he came back around behind me again. "Call your turns!"

Wolfman had found the mortar site. He pointed it out to me with the barrel of his M60, and said, "Right there, sir." I still could not see it. Then my eyes caught one piece, a slit trench, and the scene quickly came into focus. The slit trench had caught my eye because it had been cut in a straight line and was only partially concealed by a few limbs. Everything else they had built was in a series of curves and much harder to recognize. We found where they had set up the mortar tubes, a couple more slit trenches, two hastily built bunkers, a fire pit, and a small lean-to deeper in the trees. "An overnight job," Crab told me later. They had not bothered to camouflage the site very well, which probably meant they weren't planning to come back in the near future. We looked all around, but could not see any signs of where the return fire from LZ Grant had hit.

When we got back to Grant and told Captain Lasell what we had found, he was not surprised. "Should've told you men about the heavy use we've been getting on that road. Makes sense, but usually they just keep on going along that one. It's a main supply route. Been a real pain in the ass. Every time we send a recon patrol out there they get the shit kicked out of them. So then we send out a whole company, but the gooks just go around them." The captain was still drinking that black mud.

"Doesn't look like they'll be there tonight either," Crab told the captain. "We'll go refuel and check in with Hector."

Instead of going all the way back to Tay Ninh, we went to LZ Barbara for fuel. I had never landed at Barbara, which was different from the other firebases. Square instead of round, it looked more like a small town. There were trailer-mounted radio rooms and all kinds of sophisticated equipment parked around, but the most impressive pieces of equipment were the 175mm cannons. The barrels looked like factory chimneys lying down on tracked carriages the size of small train-cars. As we let the aircraft engines cool down, one of the barrels started a slow climb to thirty-five degrees or so. When it went off I could feel the ground shake even in the helicopter; the sound of the explosion blocked out the noise of my screaming turbine engine. After we shut down, Crab came over to my LOH.

"If you stand a little off to one side, you can see the shells leave the barrel. They're that big around," he said as he made a circle with his arms that was twice the size of the barrels.

"How come this place is so secure?" I asked him.

He turned and looked at the enormous clearing that surrounded the big guns, half a mile to the nearest tree. "Would you attack across that field into those guns and a mess of quad fifties?" Quad fifties were four .50-caliber machine guns mounted and operated together—a scary weapon. The NVA sometimes put two .50- or .51-calibers together and turned them on helicopters. They were also pretty effective, as Cowboy and Thompson could have told us.

After we topped off with fuel we went looking for Bravo Company. When we got in the general vicinity of the coordinates Lasell had given us, which turned out to be a solid ocean of two-hundred-foot trees, Crab gave Bravo a call on his FM radio. "Hector, White two-one, two LOHs on our way to your location. Could you put your CO on?"

"Roger that, two-one. This is Hector six, glad you're on your way. Afraid we got beaucoup dinks out there somewhere. Sounded like a company went by last night. Over there at one-six-zero through one-eight-zero degrees."

"Hector six, two-one, when's the last time you heard anything?" Crab called on the FM.

"Say again two-one, batteries weak, you're broken." We could hear them fine, but they were having trouble hearing Crab.

"Roger that, six, I say again. Last contact, last contact and which way did they go?" Crab called him back.

"OK, two-one, I got a solid copy that time. Last contact about 0400 hours and heading northeast to southwest."

"Hector six, two-one, when you hear us, pop smoke." A minute later yellow smoke seeped out of a thick carpet of jungle a hundred meters off to our right. The air was so thick the smoke could barely rise through it. "Hector six, I got yellow smoke."

This system of "popping smoke" was the only way we could locate friendly troops through the thick jungle cover. When the soldiers heard the helicopter they would set off a smoke grenade. The smoke would filter up through the trees, and we would have them. It worked pretty well, except for one pilot who was immortalized in folklore for new guys. The story went that the hapless pilot told the troops to pop red smoke. He flew to the red smoke he saw rising through the trees and got shot down—the enemy also had red smoke. "Roger, two-one. From the smoke they should be one-six-zero through one-eight-zero degrees, maybe fifty yards."

We flew off on the 160-degree compass heading Hector 6 had given us. Crab started circling at about thirty knots. He radioed that he could not see a thing through the trees and brought his airspeed back even more. "Two-four, two-one, close in tight. Keep me covered." Crab's voice was stressed. "I'm going to hover here. Gotta blow apart the limbs if I'm going to see anything," he said as he brought his ship to a hover. The giant tree limbs below him danced madly in the downwash from his rotor blades. Enormous brightly colored birds dropped from the trees to seek cover in the jungle below, as monkeys gracefully leaped from limb to limb.

"Little more right pedal," Wolfman said on the intercom, letting me know that the rotor blades limited his field of fire under Crab's aircraft. "That's good, hold it like that," he said. Crab hovered there for about a minute and then stood the machine on its nose and sped back up to thirty knots or so.

"I thought we weren't supposed to do that," I said over the radio, but got no response. Crab repeated the slow circles, but did not hover again.

We must have covered a couple acres that way before Crab said, "Got something here." He was drifting along at a sideways angle, following something on the ground. "Definitely a heavy-use trail down there," he said as his helicopter jumped up and nosed over, spinning to the right. "Thought I saw something move." Crab's voice was pretty excited.

"White two-one, Hector six," came back on the FM radio.

"Two-four, two-one, you wanna talk to Hector," Crab said on the UHF. Our helicopters were equipped with a UHF, a VHF, and an FM radio. We could listen to all three at once, but could talk on only one at a time. If Crab got shot at he would call me on the UHF radio we used between helicopters. He wanted to keep his transmit-selector switch set on the UHF, so I switched to my FM radio and took Hector 6's call.

"Hector six, White two-four for two-one, what's up?" I called the infantry CO back.

"Two-four, six, can't hear you anymore. Thought we would check up on you. Find anything?" he asked.

"Found one trotter, still lookin'. Thanks for checking. We'll give you a call before we leave your area." After traveling a hundred circular air miles we had uncovered only two kilometers of trail. About half a klick away, in the direction the trail seemed to be heading, was a depression in the trees that indicated a field. The enemy, like most rational people, liked to go through open fields. They usually stuck along the tree line in case they had to make a hasty retreat into the jungle, but they liked the easy walking in the open area. "Two-one, two-four, Crab, I'm going to fly up to that field ahead of us real quick and see if I can pick up the trail there."

"Roger that. We'll stay here and mark this spot in case you can't," Crab answered. He picked up his speed and widened his circles a bit, and I nosed it over to a hundred and ten knots, aiming the aircraft at what appeared to be the left side of the field. My guess was about twenty yards off and we shot over the tree line, and out into the open field. "Whoops," I said to Wolfman on the intercom as I rolled the machine over in a sharp left turn, to pick up the cover of the trees again.

"Gooks in the open!" Wolfman yelled back at me. At the same time rapid explosions from his M60 tore the air around us. For a split second I did not understand what he was talking about, or why he was shooting. As it registered, my hand wobbled on the cyclic, and I felt unsure of my controls, out of touch with the aircraft. My only conscious move was to try to slip down into the protection of my armored seat. Within seconds, however, the trees were in front of us, and I instinctively rolled it out straight, giving Wolfman an easier angle for shooting. Then I threw a glance back over my right shoulder.

Wolfman was leaning out behind me shooting back at our left rear. Over his bucking shoulder, and through the gray smoke of his M60, I saw the little fireballs of the tracers flying away. They were heading in a haphazard pattern toward bouncing dark figures in NVA uniforms, about three hundred feet behind us on the opposite side of the clearing. My heart did a flip-flop. Were they going to shoot?

Panic rose quickly in my chest, spreading to my arms; the tree line was not getting any closer. We were suspended out in the middle of the field. Long seconds later we dashed between the mushroom tops of two giant trees and dropped as low as I could, zigzagging along the leafy valleys, out of their sights. Finally Wolfman's M60 fell silent. We climbed up twenty feet, rolled out level, and then looked at each other over the bulkhead between our seats. Wolfman was grinning, probably at my saucer-shaped eyes and surprised expression. "How many were there? Were they NVA, VC?"

"Not too many," he said, and started messing around with his M60. Not really knowing what to do next, I headed back to the area where Crab was still circling. As I began to relax, a strange popping sound worked its way up from my memory. At first I tried to relate it to something in the helicopter or perhaps in my mind, then I realized it had been the sound of light machine guns, Russian AK-47s. It had been hard to pick it up over the noise of our LOH, Wolfman's M60, and the blood pounding in my ears. "Wolfman, did they shoot at us?"

"Yep, the little shits," he said, sounding as relaxed as ever.

The fear and confusion of the moment started to fade as a nervous excitement took their place. Getting shot at did not scare me as much as it had before— this time it seemed to be more of a game. We had tracked them down, exchanged fire, and gotten away. We made it back out. Maybe this was a fight we could win, I thought to myself. Then tinges of fear crept back in as I remembered that for a few seconds, when Wolfman yelled "Gooks in the open!" no one had been flying the helicopter.

"Two-four, two-one," I heard Crab say. "What's up? Were those tracers I saw? What're you guys doin'?"

"Yeah. Goddamned gooks in the trees!" I answered, unable to disguise the tension in my voice. "In the field, I mean. I think I messed my pants." Crab was heading at me, and I turned and fell in behind him. "The trail is on the left side of the field. At least five gooks are in the tree line on the south side," I told him as we closed on the left side of the field.

"More than that," Wolfman interjected on the intercom.

"Crab, what're we doing? We know they're there. Shouldn't we just call in an air strike or something, maybe sic the grunts on them?" I tried to reason with him.

He came back over the UHF with, "Just a quick pass." I had not really figured out what had happened the last time we ran into those guys. But Crab was going back for another look, and I couldn't let him go alone. We stuck to the left tree line and seconds later were in the area where Wolfman said he saw the NVA soldiers dive into the jungle. "This's it, Crab," I relayed from Wolfman.

"Roger that. If they jumped off the trail here . . . probably hiding in those trees down there." As if on cue a light veil of tracers surrounded his ship. "Taking fire! Taking fire, goddamn it!" Crab yelled as he rolled his LOH onto its left side. I heard the now familiar pops of the AK-47s, immediately followed by Slater's and Wolfman's M60s and Crab's minigun. Not to be left out, I pulled the trigger of my minigun and broke a little left, putting the bad guys off to the right where Wolfman could hose them down. My minigun roared as a solid stream of tracers disappeared into the trees a hundred feet behind Crab's LOH, making some people on the ground very nervous, I hoped.

"You OK, Crab?"

"Yeah. Let's see if the grunts can get us an air strike," Crab answered, his voice an octave higher than usual. We found Hector 6 again, briefed him on the enemy's location, and what we had seen, and told the infantry captain that we were going back to the TOC to try to dig up an air strike. He thanked us, and said they would be moving toward the field as soon as possible.

We landed at LZ Grant, asked Captain Lasell to request an air strike for Bravo Company, and went back to our LOHs to wait for a response. Within half an hour the captain came out to the helicopters and awakened us with, "No jets yet, but the Air Force promised us something around 1400 hours. Can you hang around?"

"We'll come back," Crab told him. To me and the door gunners he said, "Let's go get some lunch." We flew twenty minutes back to Tay Ninh to grab a quick lunch and even quicker nap. We had logged only two and a half flight hours, and I was exhausted. When we had taken off that morning, the sweat stains on my fatigue shirt were mere dark accents on the armpits. When we returned for lunch, the same stains had joined on my chest; now my whole shirt was drenched.

At 1200 hours we took off again, and flew out to Hector's new position. We had given the ground commander a compass heading to the field, so they were almost halfway there when we found them. After checking in with Hector 6, we left them to see if the enemy was still in the field where we had been shot at. Crab and I flew up and down the tree line at a hundred-plus knots, going slower with each subsequent pass, until Crab dropped down on the trail on the south edge of the clearing, way past the spot where he had taken fire. He was back up in a second. "They kept going," he said. "Let's try to follow the trail. Keep the airspeed above sixty. If we find them they're going to be real pissed."

We spent a frustrating hour trying to pick up the trail at high speed, but the jungle was just too thick. At 1300 hours we broke off and refueled, ensuring we would have plenty of fuel when the jets arrived. While we were shut down at LZ Barbara we discussed what we should do with our air strike. There really wasn't anything worth dropping a bomb on. "Look at it this way," Crab said. "Do we want these gooks around here thinking they can shoot at us and get away with it?"

"No, man. Right on, let's blow 'em away!" Slater chipped in.

"Slater, you dufus turd, we don't know where they are," Wolfman scolded his friend.

"We'll put the bombs where we last saw them. Leave a message," Crab finalized the idea. I agreed with him wholeheartedly.

We got back before the Air Force arrived and ended up circling one particularly large treetop off to the side of the NVA trail. The tree was crawling with monkeys, lanky brown creatures with really long forearms. The noise of the helicopters upset them, so they were leaping from limb to limb, agitated.

Slater fired the first shot, then Wolfman let a few rounds go into the tree. Not to be outdone, I rolled in with the minigun to hose down a corner. To my horror, a couple of little hairy bodies fell through the limbs. Seconds later we heard our air strike arrive "White Scouts, Dragon four. Do you copy?" came the casual, and very practiced, radio call from an Air Force pilot. He called us on the VHF, using the standard Air Force frequency for ground-support operations. Crab called him back, gave him a compass vector from LZ Grant. A few minutes later we spot-

ted the two F-100 Super Sabres up above us at four
or five thousand feet, the sun glinting off their silver bodies.

"White two-one, Dragon four, we've got two LOHs
at our one o'clock, on the deck." The Air Force pilot
sounded so cool, and the muffled roar of his jet engine gave his astral presence great authority.

"Roger that, Dragon four, that's us down here,"
Crab called back. "Took fire along the eastern side
of this field this morning. We think there may be
some bunkers they're protecting."

"White two-one, Dragon four, OK, good buddy.
Can you mark the target for us today? Our FAC
never got off the runway." The Air Force usually
sent along their own spotter plane, FAC or Forward
Air Control, to mark the target with a Willy Pete
rocket.

"Can do Dragon four. We'll make a pass, mark
with Willy Pete, and hold northwest over the friendlies," Crab said on the VHF, then said on UHF to
me, "Let's go in, two-four. Call Hector six and let
him know what's up." I switched to FM as I briefed
Wolfman on the intercom and told the infantry CO
we would be hitting some suspected bunkers in three
minutes. At the same time I monitored the plan of
attack that the Air Force pilot was explaining to Crab
over the VHF. Crab had been right; it was hard trying to work on three radios and the intercom simultaneously.

We raced down the tree line, ready for anything,
feeling quite safe at a hundred knots. Slater threw
out a white phosphorus grenade as we passed the
site where Crab had taken fire, and then we moved
over to fly slow circles around the friendly troops.
The jets rolled in from north to south in near-vertical

dives. They were moving fast, but in such a straight line that they looked vulnerable. Around three hundred feet, they slowly lifted away from the bombs they had released and pulled their aircraft back up into a climb. Seconds behind them black and brown clouds rose above the jungle's roof.

They each made two runs, dropping a total of sixteen five-hundred-pound bombs. "Two-one, Dragon four, we've expended all our ordinance. We took negative, repeat negative, ground-to-air fire on either pass. How about a BDA?" the fighter pilot called.

While they held up above us almost out of sight, Crab and I flew back into the settling cloud of dirt and smoke to give him the requested bomb damage assessment. We looked around, found nothing, faked it a little longer, and then Crab made the prearranged call. "Dragon four, two-one, sorry, but we got a big goose egg this time. We were pretty sure they were holed up here."

"Understand zip on the zips," the jet pilot said, obviously disappointed. "Thanks for the help, two-one. We'll get them next time. We're heading back to the barn." Crab told Hector 6 that the air strike had not turned anything up, but the field looked like a major route that might be worth staking out for a day or so. We flew back to within FM radio range of LZ Grant and told them we were going back to base.

The hard day was almost over. We raced back, two feet off the tops of the trees at a hundred knots, rolling into banked turns, dropping down into the holes, sliding up the other side, in the most natural sequence of reactions, like the best of dreams. Slater leaned out, looked back at us, and flashed us a peace sign. Miles from Tay Ninh, still in the treetops north of Nui Ba Den, we could pick out our base. Smoke was billowing up from something else there the enemy had hit. We refueled, parked the aircraft in their revetments, gave them a postflight check, and went to the TOC for a debriefing with Major Sorenson. Next stop was the officers' club.

While we had been flying no one had talked much about our contact with the enemy. Slater had muttered something about the tracers looking "groovy," and Wolfman had said the NVA fire had been "way off" to our right. Way off to our right, he admitted, was "at least twenty feet." In fact, it all didn't seem like much to me until the whiskey made the muscles in my neck relax and let the spring between my shoulders unwind. Then I couldn't get my mind off trying to remember exactly what had happened.

"You weren't kidding about airspeed," I said, trying to drag Crab into the conversation. "That's the only thing that saved my ass today. Jesus Christ, I was hanging out in the middle of that field like a clay pigeon. Felt terrible."

"Why didn't you go after them?" Crab laughed. He was making a real effort not to talk about the incident. Sometimes Crab was a hard guy to figure out. He liked to talk about sending anti-war demonstrators frag grenades, but did not like to talk about killing the enemy. He would say, "I like them. The North Vietnamese are hard-working people," and then let out a short, humorless laugh. I could never tell when he was serious.

We were just about to order another drink when a message came from Wolfman—there was a party at the Wolf Den, and we were invited. We bought a couple of six-packs and went over. After several hours of drinking, a little pot smoking, and a lot of war stories, I found myself outside with Wolfman, enjoying a rare star-filled night. The pot and booze had really loosened me up, and I wanted to tell him about being confused when they shot at us, maybe even apologize. "Definitely screwed me up when they shot at us today, Wolfman. Felt pretty stupid out there."

"Ain't no big thing," he said reassuringly. He was right, I could barely remember it. "I'm just glad I didn't waste any of those little furry buggers," he said softly. I had completely forgotten about the monkeys.

"Yeah," I mumbled, "that was a pretty weird thing to do. Why the hell did I?" It hurt physically to think of the monkeys. As I sat there with my head in my hands, the ghost of another murder crept into my memory. I was twelve or thirteen, walking down a dirt road in Keene Valley with my new .22-caliber rifle. About thirty feet ahead of me a lithe brown form scurried along a fallen limb. Without a second's hesitation I cocked the rifle and shot from the hip. The chipmunk stopped, suddenly awkward, and slowly rolled off the far side of the limb, clinging with one small paw for a second before dying. He was so cute, and so still—my heart ached. Even the Christian burial I gave him did not ease the pain.

Wolfman understood when I told him about the chipmunk, but when I suggested we go out and bury the dead monkeys, he just laughed and passed me another beer. Later that night, as I found out the next morning, someone gave me my nickname, Atom Ant.

7

Tempting Fate

Mid-August 1969

Like homicidal hummingbirds, we furiously worked the jungle's dense canopy until we found signs of recent enemy activity. Every day we methodically tracked and pursued them, usually to find them anxiously awaiting us.

One day Slater asked me, "Atom, don't you think it's a little weird how we bust our butts just to let some dinks shoot us up?" He was a little upset about the racket made by the new bullet holes in our rotor blades. Upset or not, Slater had a point—the NVA fought hard when we caught up to them, which, in itself, was not all that easy. They had a lot of tricks and were masters of camouflage.

One stunt that was hard to beat was the NVA/VC method of crossing the many meandering jungle streams. They strung their footbridges just below the surface of the slow-moving brown water, making them undetectable except for the lines used to secure the bridge to the bank.

Their permanent bunkers were so well concealed below ground that soldiers would sometimes fall through the doors without even knowing they were in a bunker complex. Finding enemy bunkers from the air at any speed was an art form or more likely a gift from a sixth sense. Regardless of the effort re-

quired, finding them was critical. By locating and de-
stroying the bunkers, their only fixed bases, we
greatly reduced their ability to maneuver. If we
played our cards right, we got the Air Force bombs
to drop on the bunkers when they were full of NVA.

After a while Wolfman and I got pretty good at
finding bunkers and bunker complexes. Sometimes
the clue was a roofline rising a little above ground
level, or a chance sighting of the butt ends of logs
sticking out of a dirt mound, anything that seemed
unnatural or otherwise caught the eye. Straight lines
were always something to check out, since there
weren't too many truly straight lines in nature. Vegetation was a good indicator of activity in the area. If
the usual litter of sticks and twigs was missing, they
could have gone into cooking fires. Grass and brush
flattened in different directions meant heavy local
foot traffic between bunkers. Sometimes there was
something obvious, like a trail that ended too suddenly. No matter what we found, the most important
thing to determine was if there had been recent use.
Were they there now, in that bunker, slowly squeez-
ing a trigger?

We usually worked our way into a complex, following a trail, but invariably we would not see the
bunkers until we were right on top of them. The next
move generally was to pull out and circle, locating
all the trails in the area. Checking the trails leading
into the bunkers was the safest way to find out if
there were people and potential danger there. If the
dirt or vegetation on the trails was disturbed at all,
we knew there could be trouble. If that was the case
we would go back into the complex fast, shooting it
up, dropping grenades. We wanted to draw the
enemy out, to get them to shoot at us while we were

prepared to take fire. If it looked as if no one was around we moved in slower, trying to get as much information as we could about how big the complex was and its likelihood of being used in the future.

Whether the bunkers we found were U.S. or NVA was understandably important. If they were large, well-made, well-concealed bunkers, they were most likely NVA, but if they were just slit trenches, mortar sites, and overnight bunkers, it was often hard to tell who had been there.

Surprisingly, the sense of smell worked well from a helicopter in helping us determine whose bunkers they were. Cooking fires left evidence in still air for a long time. If the residual odor was only wood smoke, it meant NVA cooking. They only boiled water over their fires. Our grunts' fires stank of all kinds of things, most noticeably the smell of burned rubbish. Another readable smell that lingered was fecal matter. We could not pick out the NVAs'; the rice and whatever else they ate was undetectable, but the GIs' poorly digested diet of canned goods left behind an unmistakable odor.

August went by quickly. Every day we worked with the grunts in the jungle, checking their perimeters, scouting the area they planned to move into, helping them out in firefights, marking air strikes, doing BDAs and, of course, looking for bunker complexes.

Working with the infantry was my best excuse for going up each day. As Scouts we did a job no one else could do for them, and they loved us for it; however, there was a price. Our LOHs made such inviting targets, buzzing obnoxiously in the tops of the trees. It was more than the average gook could resist. In the beginning I kept score of the number of times we were shot at, but after twelve consecutive days of taking fire I quit counting.

Taking fire was something Scouts had to expect and usually we had a good idea when the fight would start. It was weird, like slowly working our way into the *Twilight Zone*—anything could happen.

We knew they were going to open fire on us when we found them. They had to—it was shoot or be shot at. We learned to expect it and did everything that we could to minimize our chances of getting hit. Maintaining high airspeed while staying low in the tops of the trees was our best bet, since it kept our exposure time to seconds.

When we had to slow down to get a good look at something I could usually convince myself that we were not going to get shot at. I would keep saying to myself, "Nobody here. This is cool. We'll split in just a minute. Keep going; just a little more," and every time they opened up on us, it scared me silly. To make it worse they only shot at us when we were low and slow, easy targets.

Taking hits, with bullets ripping through the helicopter, was more than a shock, it was immediate, total terror. Instincts screamed, "We're caught! This is it, we're gonna die!" as confidence evaporated and panic filled the void. The first time, not too long after I started flying Scouts, was the worst.

My door gunner—a new guy I had never seen before—and I had found a small bunker complex. There was no sign of movement on the trails leading in or anywhere around. The bunkers themselves were falling apart, apparently abandoned. Reasonably certain no one was home, I brought my LOH back in a slow turn, at about ten knots, right down in the trees.

My attention was focused on a bunker opening, trying to see inside, and I was thinking we should go back for fuel soon, when the first shots hit the door frame and the Plexiglas skylight on the left side of the cockpit. Pieces of metal and plastic peppered my face; the calm of my mind shattered like a thin sheet of glass. The report of AK-47s filled the air as tracers sped past the cockpit in every direction—we were obviously surrounded. Worst of all, we were moving so slowly, with no momentum, no options; we had lost the fight before it started.

The force of the impacting rounds came to me through every sense, hitting me like electrical shocks, sending my body into spasm after spasm. "Taking fire, taking fire," I yelled over the UHF radio to Crab who, I hoped, was covering us.

Adding to the confusion was my door gunner, who kept yelling over the intercom, "I can't see 'em, god-damn it, I can't see 'em!" I was not helping much either, because I kept yelling over the UHF radio that we were hit and going down, even though I had no idea whether that was true. In a state of sensory overload, I could not even find my engine instruments, much less interpret them. No training in the world could have prepared me for that. The only thing that kept us from oblivion was the M60 fire Wolfman put down. Crab was flying close cover, and Wolfman started shooting as soon as the NVA opened up on us.

The main problem was that I had not made an emergency plan to follow. I had been thinking about the bunker and fuel, not what I would do if we took fire. When they started shooting, I had no control of the situation. If it had not been for Wolfman's cover fire, they would have had no reason to stop shooting.

As it was, they only got to shoot at us for a few seconds.

Without knowing what I was doing, reacting more like a bee-stung dog than a pilot, I spun the LOH around to the right, so hard it almost flipped and yanked on the collective. We did a kind of uncoordinated roll over the treetops to safety.

The popping of enemy fire disappeared, my door gunner's M60 stopped, and my mind started working again. A quick scan of the instrument panel gauges revealed everything was still operating normally. I could not feel or hear any radical sounds or vibrations, yet tremors of fear and the hollow feeling of being beaten made me sick. I felt so vulnerable, as if those bullets had ripped into my body as well as my aircraft. Even worse was the sense of betrayal that slowly floated to the top of the hodgepodge of my emotions—self-betrayal. I had set us up by flying low and slow.

Back in Tay Ninh, examining the bullet holes, I masked my fears with anger at the enemy. "Goddamned asshole gooks," I cursed as I cut my finger exploring one of the bullet holes back by the engine compartment. "Almost had my young ass."

Our new executive officer, Captain Brisa, a new guy from Hawaii, was also looking over my shot-up machine. He seemed really impressed with the damage the NVA soldiers had done. "Wow, Smith, bet your pucker factor went to ten when this happened," he said, ogling the bullet holes. Brisa reminded me of a mongoose, with his ferret face and darting dark eyes.

"No doubt about it, Scouts is good exercise for the sphincter muscles, Captain," I said, finding it hard to be civil to him. "How about going out with us

tomorrow? You might like it, sir." Brisa was so insecure that we had to call him "sir" or he got worried.

"Negative, not me. I'm too chicken," he said with
mock humility, looking around for someone to give
him an argument. In fact Brisa was a coward of the
worst order, the kind that hid from danger by using
his rank. His job as operations officer allowed him
to schedule himself on all the easy, safe missions.

Brisa was not the only pilot in our aviation platoon
who did not want to fly Scouts. A lot of the guys
talked about doing it, but usually thought better of
it the next morning, when they had sobered up.

Consequently Crab and I remained the only pilots
for brigade Scouts, flying almost every day. Wolfman
never missed a flight, and Slater usually completed
the foursome. However, every so often Slater would
become incoherent and disappear into the darkness
of his hooch for a few days.

When Slater took a break we normally had no
trouble finding a replacement for him, but we did
have trouble finding replacements who would come
back for more than one flight. The few who did try
out usually did so because it looked like fun. When
it came to the important part—information gathering,
where we had to get in low and slow—they quit.
Nobody sane felt comfortable letting himself become
a target.

We lost a lot of would-be door gunners because
the tight right turns made them throw up. Little
Buddy held the record for trying. He had been a door
gunner on Slicks up north in I Corps (northern South
Vietnam, near the demilitarized zone); he had liked
that, so he extended his tour another year to be a
Scout door gunner. He must have tried fifty times,
and every time he threw up.

Then there were door gunner recruits who could not handle their M60 well enough. They either had it or they didn't. If they were off more than a foot or two with their first burst, I figured the novelty of shooting from a helicopter was throwing off their aim a bit. If they missed by the same amount on the second burst, we went home. One candidate, Norris, never even got a round off before we dumped him. He tried out three times, but each time his gun jammed. When he came back for a fourth try, Crab told him to go talk to the guys flying Command and Control.

Crab had the best technique for getting volunteers. He would approach his prey while they were in the midst of their peer group. "You can't possibly get hurt," he would start in on them. Then he would tell them how safe it was, never giving the intended recruit a chance to argue the point. When he finally gave the victim a chance to reply, he would cut him off every other word with, "You wouldn't want your buddies here to think you're a wimp, would you?" It worked quite well.

We had a few regular part-time door gunners like "Short Round," a bunker guard, but even the regulars were unreliable. They would fly a couple of days, get freaked out, and quit. Sometimes it was weeks before they forgot how scared they had been and would let us talk them into going up again.

If there weren't any volunteers around and we really got desperate, we would corner a bored mechanic or a Command and Control door gunner. We did not really like to take either of them up because it pissed off the C&C pilots if their door gunners got hurt, and good mechanics were hard to find.

Point men, the men who lead other infantrymen

through the jungle, had the best potential—they didn't panic. However, just as we would start to notice a particular grunt was good at point, he would get killed. What we were always looking for was another Wolfman.

Wolfman was the best—reliable, and could handle an M60 better than anyone in Tay Ninh, maybe all of Vietnam—and it was always a pleasure to fly with him. He was so mellow, just sitting back there with a big grin on his face, enjoying the breeze. But no matter how relaxed he seemed, he was always right on top of the situation. When it came to a shoot-out, he never faltered and his gun never jammed. It didn't matter to me whether Wolfman was riding in my LOH or Crab's, I knew that he would get the enemy off my back.

He was near perfect, but even Wolfman could screw up. It was the end of a long, hot August day and nothing had been going right. A good day is a day with no surprises, but that day was full of them—dinks where they weren't supposed to be, getting shot at without warning, mechanical troubles, and no lunch—a tiresome kind of day.

Even the microphone cord on my helmet tried to get me. As I brought the airspeed back on short final approach, Wolfman dropped something, and I turned my head back to see what had made the noise. When I tried to look back at our landing spot, only feet away, I could not turn my head forward again. I was so tired I couldn't even panic, which made it easier for Wolfman to unhook my microphone cord from the protruding inertia reel on the back of my seat.

When we got to the revetment, I could not make the fine control movements necessary to land a hover. "The hell with it," I said to myself and dropped the collective. It was a pretty rough landing, one that would normally have brought a response from Wolfman. But when I looked behind me, I could see that he, too, was so tired he had not even noticed. He just went about unloading his M60, as he usually did, throwing the gun and the ammo belts on top of the revetment beside the helicopter.

That's when he blew it. The M60 went a little higher than usual this time, right into the spinning rotor blades—two blades were destroyed. Within seconds Captain Brisa was at the scene, having heard the sound of crunching metal all the way from the operations office. He arrived just as our fatigue-numbed brains started to see the humorous side of the situation. Brisa looked from the broken blades to our smiling faces and, as usual, lost it. In the past few weeks Brisa had unceremoniously taken on the role of company disciplinarian; he hated to see us enjoying ourselves.

Most of us recognized it for the major identity crisis it was—the slippery little captain was suffering from a lack of respect from his officer peers. Nobody would listen to him. As an operations officer he was not needed—we all knew more about our jobs than he did—and he was not respected as an individual because he couldn't be trusted. What hurt him the most was his lack of control over junior officers, especially junior warrant officers. So every chance he got he jumped on our cases. It invariably started off with, "*Mr.* Smith, I've got a problem with . . ."

Brisa had a problem with the unauthorized Vietnamese jungle fatigues we wore, with the haircuts we would not get, with his petty rules we broke constantly, and with our attitude in general. Actually it was our attitude in general that got to him the most; we looked down on him.

Brisa also didn't like our drinking on our time off, or the jokes we made about him. And he didn't like the way we used the helicopters for noncombat-related activities, such as flying our door gunners a few miles over to the river for a swim, or even better, to the deep, cool water of the enormous bomb craters out by LZ Jess.

The captain had a lot of problems with the Scouts, but fortunately there was little he could really do about us; his complaints fell on deaf ears. Captain Crane and all of Brisa's superior officers, right up to the battalion commander, didn't care what the Scouts did as long as the job got done. They knew it was a nasty assignment.

Even though it was hot, horrible work, most of the time I loved flying Scouts. We were blind to most of the dangers, owing to a catch-22 phenomenon. We needed so much confidence to fly such a dangerous job that our confidence kept us unaware of the dangers. That confidence failed when we were getting shot up or when we arrived at an overrun LZ, where the disgusting reality of the Vietnam War was laid out for all to see.

My first taste of that reality came one mid-August morning when the company clerk got us up a little earlier than usual. The Tactical Operation Center had lost communication with Fire-Support Base Jamie in the midst of heavy fighting. Crab and I took off before daylight.

When we arrived we made a turn to hug the tree line around the firebase, checking for NVA. The sun was still struggling with the dark, mixing with the damp air, pulling at the shadows left in the jungle.

The breeze coming through my door was thick with the unmistakable stench of combat. My nose was getting pretty good at differentiating smells, and on the wind were most of the scents I had learned in my two months of combat: acrid odor of rifle and cannon smoke; mustier smells from grenade, claymore, and mortar explosions; and pungent stink of burning canvas, wood, and petroleum products. Wispy columns of smoke curled up from the firebase and merged, floating in spectral layers above the LZ.

I was in a hurry to get there, to see what had happened, but hesitant to make the turn, afraid of the battle scene that lay just ahead in its eerie, silent shroud. Cold sweat trickled down my sides as we finished our check of the tree line and flew across the bulldozed clearing at top speed.

The outer defense of barbed wire was torn to pieces. As we crossed five feet above the ragged green line my mind could barely comprehend what lay in front of me. I had seen our soldiers killed and our war machines destroyed, but not on such a scale, and never with such force. The four or five acres of LZ Jamie had been churned by mortar and rocket fire into a smoldering stew. Howitzers were reduced to scrap, an insane litter of bent and crumpled men lay frozen in confusion everywhere, enemy beside enemy. Bunkers with their roofs blown off exposed indecently the smoking remains of men trapped in those dark holes. As we sped over the firebase the scene never varied; everything had been blown to pieces. Scattered about were the few men who had survived: disheveled, motionless figures bearing silent witness among the carnage.

We circled back to land by the remains of the TOC. A lieutenant and a sergeant sat on a wooden ammo crate, the sergeant hunched over, staring at the bloody hands he kept wiping on his fatigue pants. Behind them was a row of ten cots, side by side, piled several feet high with soldiers' bodies and body parts. Funnels of blood poured from the bottom of the cots. "Did you see any of them?" the lieutenant asked as he stared right through us. The two soldiers' pale, tired faces were expressionless, their eyes too dark to see into. The sickly-sweet odor of blood was overwhelming.

"None in the tree line . . . What happened?" Crab asked. They did not answer. They could not or did not want to remember.

Several Hueys clattered over the tree line, then flared and landed beside our LOHs. Wolfman and I walked away from the cloud of dust they kicked up. "I've seen it before, been there, but it's always unbelievable," he mumbled as he wandered off toward the smoking remains of a howitzer emplacement. "This is just not worth it."

I couldn't go with him, not past the piles of dead GIs, already puffy in the first rays of morning sun and alive with the buzzing of big blue flies. I walked back out to the perimeter wire where we had seen a bunch of dead NVA soldiers. My AK-47 was out of ammunition, and those gooks were not going to be using theirs. (I carried an AK-47 in my LOH because it had a folding stock and fit in the corner of my armored seat where I could get it, even if I was pinned in the aircraft. It was a good machine gun, heavier but much more dependable than its American counterpart, the M16.)

The young North Vietnamese soldiers lay everywhere, caught in strange contortions, their black eyes now as pale as their bloodless skin. Some of their heads were oddly misshapen with tears in the skin, where flechets from the 105 howitzers had hit them in the face.

I had known this kind of thing was possible—a total NVA victory. From my first week in Scouts, the North Vietnamese Army had won my respect as hardworking, dedicated, and capable of anything. LZ Jamie was satisfactory proof of that, but there was no honoring their effort. What I felt was despair, for the dead and the living on both sides.

I was standing deep in my thoughts, my hands full of ammo clips, when a pistol shot cracked in the air behind me. I hit the dirt, clips flying. "Sorry," a voice called behind me. One of the crewmen from the Hueys, his helmet on and visor down, was standing over a dead North Vietnamese soldier with .45-caliber pistol. He apologized to me again and then shot the dead soldier a few more times. Each time the pistol went off the corpse twitched in the dirt.

A while later Wolfman found me there, wondering what had happened at LZ Jamie. Did we want it to happen? Wasn't it a mistake? Look how many people got killed. Whose fault was it, goddamn it? Why didn't I hate the enemy? A Scout team from the 1st/9th Cav came, and we left the job of looking for the NVA in their hands.

Days like that made me want to quit flying Scouts, maybe get into Cobras or something where we did not have to get right down in it as we did at Jamie. Cobras, our seldom-seen high birds, looked like a nice change from Scouts, circling lazily in the cool blue sky at three thousand feet. They were flying weapons platforms, armed with rockets, miniguns, and 20mm cannons, just waiting for someone to shoot at the bait below them, the LOH bait. We got

Tom "Atom Ant" Smith (with helmet)
and Carl "Ski" Barowski right after a mission.
(*Courtesy Carl Barowski*)

Craig "Flea" Fielding (*sitting*), and Mike "Lurch"
Ward (*right*), take a break. When they weren't sleeping,
eating, or drinking, they flew around "low level" in
their "Charlie Model" Huey, shooting rockets.
(*Courtesy Craig Fielding*)

Mike "Crab" Foster said he would shoot me if I took his picture, but had to rethink his position when I reminded him that I was the only scout pilot left to fly cover for him.

In the middle of November we flew into a helicopter trap. With our engine shot out and the helicopter on fire, we crashed into the only swamp for miles. The slimy bog saved our lives, but the helicopter burned to the water line.

I flew us into trouble, Wolfman shot our way out,
and Little Wolf Buddy (*middle*) put the helicopter
back together when we got home.

The last helicopter I flew in Vietnam. Some landings
were better than others.

Wolfman sights down the barrel of his M-60 machine gun. What he could see, he could hit. Finding the enemy was one thing, getting back with information was another. The accuracy of Wolfman, and later, Cisco, kept us alive.

Wolfman poses for the camera beside our LOH (light observation helicopter)—the hunter part of a scout hunter-killer team. I used the opportunity to show off my new Russian AK-47.

The officers club excluded, this was the nicest building in our company area. The tin-roofed sheds we lived in were built on baked dirt that had been sprayed with oil—particularly pleasant when the temperature climbed above 100 degrees.

Characteristically mellow and showing his lack of respect for privacy, Animal cut a hole in the wall of my hooch so we could "rap."

Carl "Ski" Barowski (*left*), our company clerk, kept the pilots and the RLOs (real live officers) of our aviation platoon from doing any permanent damage to each other. And Ken "Cisco" Gardner (*second from right*) accomplished the impossible: he kept me alive after Wolfman left. (*Courtesy Ken Gardner*)

Atom Ant aka Tom Smith.

A howitzer, the centerpiece of the 1st Calvary's
airmobile operations, dropped into a new fire base
in the jungle (by a Sikorsky CH-54, Sky Crane).
The cannons were the grunts' main defense.

After a long day of hunting the enemy, Wolfman
relaxes with a book in my hooch. We had the luxury
of leaving the jungle at night, but the next day the
advantage was theirs—they got to shoot first.

Although a different perspective always helped,
no matter where I sat, I was still in Vietnam.

a Cobra for cover every now and then, on the odd days when they were not off working with Slicks on troop insertions.

Too bad we did not see more of them; we had a wonderful relationship. They would circle above us, well out of harm's way, waiting for us to get shot at. When we did come under fire they simply had to roll into a dive to get the target in their sights. Halfway down they'd go to work, with bursts of smoke erupting from their weapons' racks, flaming rockets screaming down. We liked to work with the Cobras, because the NVA respected them and were less likely to shoot when they were around.

When we got back to Tay Ninh after Jamie, we quit for the day and got drunk, then went to the "Steam and Cream." Besides getting drunk at the officers' club, going to the Steam and Cream was the only way to unwind after a hard day's work.

The Steam and Cream was conveniently located next to the PX, a square sort of whitewashed adobe place, left by the French colonists, someone said. Right inside the door, behind a little card table, was a mama-san, her teeth stained red with betel nut juice, collecting admission fees in a gray metal box. Fifty cents for a steam bath, a buck-fifty for a massage; anything else had to be negotiated with the girls in the cloth cubicles behind mama-san.

The steam bath was a large, white-tiled room with pipes spitting and drooling hot water into a trough along one wall. On the other side was a stair-stepped tile bench decorated with a dozen or so comatose Americans wrapped in towels. As I sweated and watched the steam curl into the room, dissipating into the gray mist, all I could think about was the men on Jamie. Those poor grunts—terrified and dying in the rocket attack, unable to stop the enemy charges, trapped and killed in their bunkers, while I slept. I wondered if the old lady outside might be letting the VC replace the steam with poisonous gas.

Later as I lay on the vinyl massage table in one of the cubicles, watching the young girl give me a massage, the thought struck me that even she might be VC. Her smile was phony, not as bad as Captain Brisa's, but a fake. Maybe I was unusually paranoid that day, but how could something like Jamie happen if we were as strong, as right, as we had been told? The young girl's smile vanished when she noticed I was looking at her. She stared back, confused. "You want han' job? Two dolla', numba' one."

"No, no hand job." I just wanted to go home. I closed my eyes, put the hopelessly dead out of mind, and thought about my mountain home and friends. But the thoughts would not hold; my mind inevitably went back to the maze of the jungle, where the enemy lived, where I worked.

One exhausting day followed another, so close together that I had written only one letter to Peter and a short note to Uncle Pat and Aunt Kitty since arriving in Vietnam. When I finally got a break after fourteen straight days of Scouts I tried to catch up by writing two letters in a row.

The 21st August 1969

Dear Norm,

The more I get into this war the more fucked up it seems and the more fucked up I get. I would sort of like to describe the last two days for an example.

I don't know what day of the week it is today, but let's say it is Saturday. Thursday night I go to bed at about eight after one CC & water. I am woken up at 5 Friday morning. I go over to the TOC and get our morning missions. I go back to the hooch and shave and plan what kind of explosives I want to carry, i.e., frags, incendiary, percussion, Willy Pete etc. how much ammo for my gunner, how much for my minigun, how much fuel etc. Just as it gets light I take my personal weapon and flight gear and go pre-flight my aircraft. The wing man and I coordinate and by seven we take off. We fly all day only stopping for fuel and two meals. It is really hard flying. It is hot and dirty and you are continually nauseated by the smell of gun smoke and bomb strikes and rockets. Every minute or second something pops up that is trying to kill you. Your own grenades, your buddies' fire, the enemy gooks, trees, aircraft malfunctions, enemy traps, your artillery, more enemy fire, tiredness. You fly around all day in the trees trying to find things, i.e., enemy bunkers, trails the troops use, troops, you try and blow things up, kill people and determine what they are doing. At the end of the day I am so tense even the muscles in my jaw are cramped, and I cannot open my hands all the way. What I have been saying is that it is a real war and work. When you get back that evening you are just a civilian in shitty living conditions. . . .

My roommate woke me up and introduced me to this dude in regular civilian clothes who is a "youth controller." He told me he was going into Tay Ninh to see the Cao Dai temple with him. It is really weird. The rest of today I have spent drinking straight whiskey with my Irish door gunner and making a collage on my wall. Yesterday a company commander of a lift company next to ours took all the ration cards off all the officers under 21 and punched out all the liquor rations. About 5 minutes ago one of my buddies came in and said that a burst of AK-47 fire came through his aircraft about 8 inches above his head at 2300 ft. The AK is the smallest weapon the gooks have. About four days ago I took pictures of about forty dead gooks all blown to pieces for a friend and it was normal. Yesterday some tracers came up between my legs when I was checking out some bunkers and I almost blew lunch. It is really weird.

Tom

And:

The 22nd of August 1969

Dear Norm,

Wow! I am so cool you would not believe it. Took off this morning at 0700 and got about 20 miles out and had a complete tail rotor failure. But the kid was really cool, rolled down the throttle and flew it back. They cleared the active, got out the crash rescue, but through the most deft throttle and torque control brought it in for a beautiful, no damage running landing. I had to do it, my gunner didn't put his seat belt on this morning, and he and I are going to make a fortune populating Vietnam with chickens. I really feel good about it. I just hope I am not using up my luck too fast!

In reference to your letter and the commander in chief. He is full of shit if he thinks they are slacking up. Maybe the killing has decreased, but that is for only one reason and it is temporary. We are not fighting the VC here, they have petered out pretty much. Being a Scout I can definitely tell you the NVA, very hard core dudes, are coming in very much force, very well equipped. NVA don't shoot unless they know they can kill you. An example: I was hovering over what I thought to be old bunkers. There were beau coup of them. All of a sudden I caught some movement and saw signs of gooks. Poncho liners, a covered bike etc. But it was so damn calm that I didn't see how they could be around. If your regular gooks were there one of them would have gotten pissed and taken a shot at me. So I directed some troops into the AO and they got their asses kicked by NVA. When we came back they were only too glad to shoot at us because they knew we were there to call in air strikes. They are moving into this AO in very large force and it will not be long before they try and blow us away. We have already had an LZ run over, and anywhere 10 miles north of here you will get .50 and .51 cal. ground-to-air fire. This is definitely heavy equipment.

In your letter you mentioned food and a bill. I think I have misplaced the bill so please send it again. And for food! I would really appreciate it if you would send off a case of Nutriment. Nutriment has some good energy in it.

Well my aircraft is all screwed up so I am going to take a few days off and try and make it to Saigon for some good "boom-boom."

Love,
Tom

Well, I did not make it to Saigon that time, but my brother did start sending me Nutriment. Within a week I was hooked on the stuff. Those twelve-ounce cans were full of energy, and energy was as important as luck for surviving in Scouts. It was demanding, the physical stress of radical, low-level maneuvers, the intense concentration needed to hunt armed men, and worst of all, the stress of knowing we were going to get shot at, soon, from very close. Energy helped me stay alert and kept my reflexes sharp.

Once I got hooked on the high-energy foods, an exercise regimen naturally followed. Before too long, my morning program included fifteen chin-ups, fifteen pull-ups, fifty sit-ups, and twenty-five push-ups. It felt great.

I was beginning to feel good, both physically and mentally, about flying Scouts, but the reviews were still mixed. Uncle Pat wrote in the beginning of August, "I have always had a profound respect for a guy who can function in a plane, while holes are being banged through his machine. Don't know that I could have done it." That part sounded great, but the next line was, "I sure wouldn't have done it by choice." There was no doubt about it, Scouts was crazy. That is why I was surprised when Gordon, the same fool who went through flight school with Crab and me, volunteered for Scouts at the end of August, as the first and only volunteer since Crab and I had started flying together.

Gordon was just too normal; he was a gung-ho brownnoser maybe, but there wasn't an insane bone in his body. Why would he volunteer for Scouts? The answer came after Crab went up with him for the first time. "Atom, Gordon's an idiot!" Crab complained over a drink at the officers' club. That was it. Only a crazy person or a fool would fly Scouts voluntarily. "You should have seen what he did today. Wolfman doesn't want to fly with him, neither does Slater. They don't even want to train with him," he added.

"Cletus, not Gordon. He wants to be called Cletus," I reminded Crab. No one had any idea what Cletus meant, but that was what Gordon said he wanted for a nickname in Scouts.

"Cletus, my ass, how about Clitoris?" Crab said, but thought about it a second. "No, I like clitorises too much; he'll always be Gordon to me."

Crab was lost in thought about Cletus or clitorises and had completely forgotten what he had been telling me. I prompted him, "You were telling me about what an idiot Gordon was. What did he do?" We all liked to hear stories about others' screwups because we all made them.

"Oh, yeah, it was amazing," Crab went on. "He

was doing tight circles; thought he had some bunkers or something. Wolfman and I were circling around, covering the idiot. I asked him, what's up? He keyed his radio to answer and nosed over into the trees." Crab looked at me in wonder. "He can't fly and talk on the radios at the same time! All I heard on the radio was 'Weaaaaaah *crunch!*'" Crab took a long swig of whiskey. "Flew right into the trees, broke both chin bubbles."

We must have remembered simultaneously that I had smashed the chin bubbles out of my LOH two months earlier, because we both started laughing. "Yeah, but Gordon is an asshole," I pointed out.

"A bigger asshole," Crab corrected me.

The next day I went up on a training flight with Gordon. I tried, but it was hopeless. Instructions went in one ear and out the other. His control touch in low-level flight was spasmodic at best. Worse, he showed no ability or even desire to work as a wing-man, or even with his own door gunner. There was no way he could be trusted to have his door gunner in position to put down cover fire for the other LOH when the shooting started.

To Gordon the fact that he was flying a LOH, a task above and beyond the call of duty, was enough. He honestly believed all he needed was the right attitude, the right *military* attitude. He was a danger-ous man. In the few hours I flew with him I grew to dislike him intensely and voted to keep him out of Scouts. But Crab liked to watch him fly around like a headless chicken and said he would fly with him. At first it turned out to be a blessing in disguise. On the days Gordon flew, I got a day off. However, as soon as Brisa figured that out, he started filling up my time off with Ash and Trash missions, which was almost as bad as Command and Control.

One place he liked to send me was up to Katum, a small town built around an old French border outpost, situated across a low valley from Cambodia and the massed forces of the North Vietnamese Army. There was a special forces camp in the old fort, with a few advisors and some ARVNs stationed there to protect the townspeople. It was a weird place that seemed to generate its own weather.

The first time I went to Katum it was bright and sunny as we flew up the road past LZs Barbara and Christine, but a few miles away from the outpost the air picked up a chill. Before long we were in a haze. By the time we got to Katum the sun was gone; a strange fog hung in the trees and floated over the exposed ground. The whole scene was right out of a French Foreign Legion film: the desolate outpost, with wisps of gray curling over the empty stucco battlements; the hovels of the townspeople nestled in the shadow of the southern wall, hidden from the threat across the valley.

Before the rotor blades had stopped turning, the illusion that Katum was protected by the fort disappeared. The few civilians who had come out to watch me land looked scared; the soldiers walking around looked like the survivors of LZ Jamie. I asked one of the ARVNs for directions to the special forces officers' quarters. Without a word he pointed to a door in one of the thick walls of the fort. In a cramped, musty room I found the officer who had the sealed envelopes for me to take back to the TOC.

"This place is pretty spooky," I told the young lieutenant.

"You're not shittin'," he said as he let out a tired

sigh. "We sit in here while the NVA run their con-voys by. Waiting for the day they get bent out of shape by something we do and decide to blow us away."

"How many troops you got here?" I asked.

"Two hundred ARVNs and eight advisors. Even if the ARVNs decide to fight, the dinks could kick our ass." He was not a happy man.

"Why don't you pack up those civilians and get the hell out of here?" I said. It seemed like a logical idea considering what he had just told me.

The thought seemed to bring some life back into his tired face. "Outstanding idea. And while we're at it, why don't we just keep going, get right the hell out of Vietnam!" The lieutenant looked as if he was enjoying the idea, about to laugh, even, but his eyes had a glazed look that dispelled any notion I might have had that he thought any of it was funny.

The only thing more depressing than visiting Katum was the thought of having to stay there, and I was glad to get back to Tay Ninh. That is, until I opened a letter that had just arrived from Uncle Pat.

8/13/69

Dear Tom,
   I am sure you are thrilled over your draft classifi-cation. What a screwed-up deal!!

Enclosed in the letter was a draft classification from my draft board in the Virgin Islands, the one that had sent me my induction notice. The same one that had caused me to join the Army in Albany, New York, to avoid being inducted in Puerto Rico. The classification stated that I was 1-Y, "unfit for military service." For a minute I could not comprehend what it meant. Then it became painfully clear. I could have stayed home and . . . Before too long I was laughing about it, and crying, as I slugged down Jim Beam after Jim Beam. The governor had called, just a bit too late.

A few days later Slater almost blew himself up with one of his own grenades. We were checking out some bunkers; he told me he wanted to drop a grenade in one of the bigger ones. It was an old complex and there were no signs of activity, so I brought the helicopter back to a hover about twenty feet above the door.

"Far out, no problem, I can get it right in from here," Slater told me over the intercom. He was smiling and flashed me a thumbs-up when he saw me looking at him over the bulkhead. It was not often that we found bunkers we could hover right down on top of.

"Let me know as soon as you drop it. We're really close," I told him. A few seconds later I heard him start to say something and then there was a loud explosion behind us, along with the sounds of pieces of steel from the fragmentation grenade peppering the helicopter.

Fortunately Slater was not seriously hurt. However, he did get enough shrapnel in his legs to be grounded for a while. My first impulse was to give him a hard time, but it seemed there was a stronger force at work—bad luck. Recently there had been a lot of it going around the Flying Circus.

Bad luck is supposed to come in threes, and my suspicion that Slater's accident was part of a string of bad luck was confirmed a few days later when Wolfman got hurt. A bullet hit the skid gear next to his foot and exploded, sending shrapnel into his legs.

No doubt about it, we were in a run of bad luck. The question was, if Wolfman's wounds were the second piece of bad luck, who was going to get it next?

Everyone I knew in Vietnam who lived in a combat zone was superstitious about good and bad luck. Superstition is part of the logic that says the other guy is going to get it. If a combat veteran did not rationalize death that way he would go slowly crazy, with all-consuming paranoia. Of course, there was good reason to fear bad luck. One little piece of it could be lethal.

So we were all pretty happy when the Scouts were grounded for a few days for lack of door gunners. Even Crab could not get any volunteers, with Slater and Wolfman limping around the company area with their legs bandaged. It was just as well; going out in the jungle during an unfinished run of bad luck made it that much easier to get killed. With a day or two off, I decided to take care of a medical problem of my own. A cyst had formed under the skin on my forehead, probably from the irritation of my flight helmet, and it was starting to get in the way.

I could have, and in hindsight should have, gone to the hospital, but instead opted to go to our flight surgeon, Dr. David Brainard. Dr. Dave did a better job of pretending he was not in Vietnam than anyone in Tay Ninh. From all outward appearances the good doctor had never left home. He was neat, clean, and always looked refreshed and alert, but what really set him apart was that Dr. Dave never talked as if he was in Vietnam. He did not have the standard-issue sullen attitude, never used the jargon, never talked about the war or the country. Dr. Dave was a time-space warp, a breath of fresh air.

Unfortunately, what Dr. Dave had in character, he lacked in medical facilities. "I'm really not set up for this kind of stuff here," he said, poking at my cyst. "The 'surgeon' part in *flight surgeon* is actually a misnomer." He poked and pushed on it a little more and finally said, "Well, what the heck, it's only a small cyst."

As if to restore my waning confidence, Dr. Dave made quite a fuss over putting a clean sheet on his examining table and laying out his surgical tools. Then he had me lie down and covered my head with a large cloth, humming confidently as he numbed me up and went to work on the cyst, which protruded through a hole in the cloth. Every so often he had to replace the cloth because it had become soaked with blood. Twenty minutes and many pieces of cloth later, he was still working away. Finally he said, "Well, that's it."

"Did you get it all out, Doc?" I asked. He had explained to me that a cyst had many little roots and he would have to go after those as well as the cyst itself.

"I think so, but you've lost too much blood to keep poking around." He stitched me up and told me not to fly for a couple of days. Dr. Dave even gave me a note that said, "Flight restricted two (2) days." Using that piece of paper as my passport to Saigon, I headed to the airport. In order to avoid any complications with Captains Crane or Brisa I waited until my flight was boarding before calling Corporal Wilson at company operations to tell him I was on medical leave and would be back the next day.

8

Tricks

Late August 1969

A C-130 transport took me as far as Bien Hoa, where I jumped on a helicopter headed to the military heliport in downtown Saigon. We came in low-level over a residential area of the city with wide boulevards and fine homes, and a business section with a maze of winding streets following a stagnant brown river. The city looked like a great place to explore. We circled the heliport, a bright green playing field that seemed out of place in the surrounding canyon of bleached concrete. The buildings, streets, sidewalks, even the telephone poles were concrete in this part of town. The only color contrast in the scene was the bobbing mass of people in the streets and the laundry flying from balconies above.

We landed near the heliport office, a cement pillbox with three-inch walls and a tier of sandbags on the roof, barely enough to stop bullets, much less a B-40 rocket or mortars. In the office, a freshly starched young corporal told me a bus had left minutes ago for the USO downtown but would be back in half an hour. Conveniently, there was a bar in a building only fifty feet away. The seven businesses crammed within seventy feet of the building's frontage were two bars, a restaurant, a camera store, an electronics store, a clothing store, and a bakery.

Middle-aged men sat outside in the shade of the storefronts, squatting around makeshift tables, playing card games and arguing with each other. Older men sat quietly in the corners, staring serenely at nothing in particular. The oldest of the lot were little more than skeletons, their venerable faces tight masks of mottled brown leather worn shiny with time. Punk kids hung out in the alley entrances, trying hard to overcome the handicap of their round baby faces.

Young and middle-aged Vietnamese moved in every direction at a hectic pace in the hot sun, in such numbers that they covered the sidewalks and most of the street. Stuck in the flow of humanity was an intermittent stream of motorbikes, pedicabs, and small black automobiles, moving in concert with the beeping of horns. It dawned on me that most of the men in the crowd were of military age. Why weren't *they* out fighting the communist threat? For some reason I had assumed that we had come all the way around the world to fight a war alongside the South Vietnamese, that all the citizens were already in the war and needed our support. No one had mentioned to me that we were going to Vietnam and the stinking hot jungle to fight a war for them while they stayed in town having a good time.

Seeing those young men walking around, going about their business, made me feel like a sucker. It also lent real credibility to the negative feelings that were circulating among the U.S. soldiers about the South Vietnamese and the support they gave the war effort. Guys who had been around Vietnam for several years estimated that about half the South Vietnamese population was Vietcong and the other half was helping them. There were stories about how ARVN soldiers would do anything to avoid a fight, even help the enemy, and how they would turn and run if they accidentally stumbled into battle. I had heard accounts of ARVN Air Force pilots purposely missing the target to avoid getting ground-to-air fire. There were even tales of the ARVNs shooting their American advisors so that there would be no witnesses to their cowardice.

About the only ARVN troops I had seen by the time I went to Saigon had been a battalion of ARVN Airborne Rangers on their way through Tay Ninh. The U.S. advisors who worked with them had said they were the elite of the South Vietnamese Army, pretty tough dudes. Two weeks after they arrived, they left, heading back to Saigon for repairs. They had run into a bunch of NVA northwest of Tay Ninh and were torn to pieces. It seems the NVA had gone out of their way to wipe out the Rangers, as much for political gain as anything, but they had really put the poor ARVNs in a world of hurt, with more than fifty percent casualties.

I walked into the camera store to check out the prices. Evil Eye had come back with a beautiful Nikon from Saigon but warned me to be careful. There were some good deals, and there were some rip-offs. One scam he fell for was the bogus watch trick. "Don't buy an Omega from the little pricks," he cautioned, sounding a little hurt. "Thought I had a deal, seventy-five bucks for a two-hundred-dollar watch. The kid looked like a choir boy, for Christ's sake. . . . Stopped running two days later."

The camera store doubled as a home. The whole family was there. The father, papa-san, was behind an ornate antique glass cabinet full of cameras. The young boy beside him grabbed his pants leg for security and gave me a worried look as he blew bubbles in the snot dripping off his upper lip. Baby sister was sweeping, and teenage brother was opening boxes in the back room. Behind a stained screen mama-san was cooking a rice lunch on a gas grill. They all stopped what they were doing when I walked in. "You got Nikon camera?" I asked the papa-san.

"Any kine. We got," he reassured me behind a face full of smiles. "If no got in store, can get. How much you pay?" I did not know what to say next— the whole scene was odd, bartering with a guy who looked a lot like the little men who had been shooting at me for the last few months. The teenage son had come out of the back room and was staring at me, the dark eyes hostile in his scowling face. The hell with it, I said to myself and stepped back out into the crowd on the street.

The sun seemed to be coming from everywhere, bouncing off the concrete, blinding me as I made for the bar. I stepped through the door and into another world, dark and blessedly cool; the only sound was the mechanical gurgle of an air conditioner. As my eyes adjusted to the darkness, I felt more relaxed than I had in months. In front of me was a normal civilian bar scene. Well, almost normal, except everyone looked a little foreign, and there were six beautiful young girls and only two sleazy young men with them. But just like most bars, everyone seemed comfortable, hanging out, waiting for something to happen.

As I sat down two of the girls walked over. "Hi you today?" the shorter of the two said as she slid into the booth beside me. "You buy me beer?" She could not have been more than fifteen, but she leaned right up against me with a brazen smile. It was a phony smile, part of the act, but she was trying so hard it would have been rude to say "no." Besides, the young girl's audacious advance had intimidated me.

"Sure. Two beers, Heineken if you've got it. Thanks. OK with you?" I asked the girl beside me. She had not heard me; she was giggling and watching her friend do an exaggerated Mae West-type sashay back to the bar for the beers. A Heineken sounded like a good idea, anyway. My throat was dry and the air was thick with the odor of burning cloves, the distinct odor of the local cigarettes. The only cigarettes the Vietnamese liked to smoke besides their cloves were Salems. Snuffy said he once got laid in Saigon for two packs of Salems. To which Evil Eye had responded, "Two packs is the discount rate for guys with little dicks."

"What you name?" The petite cologned cutie snuggled up against me. She had done everything she could to make herself look older: high heels, tight silk sheath dress, perfume, earrings, but there was no disguising the immaturity of her hipless body and childish reactions.

"Tom." Should I have told her that? I wondered.

"What's your name?" I asked back.

The name she said sounded like "Cow," but when I repeated it she gave me a funny look. The Heinekens arrived, and as her friend put them down on the table, Cow slipped her hand into my crotch. I jumped so high my knees hit the table. That really cracked them up. My new drinking partner took a sip of her beer, smiled a genuine smile, and gave me a little squeeze. "You OK, numba one, you bic?" Cow asked, still tee-heeing now and then. Bic meant "Do you understand?"

"No bic," I told her, and took a gulp of my beer.

It smelled and tasted like the perfume of the girl who had delivered it. When I made a face and almost spit it out the two bar girls went into fits of laughter.

"You dinkydao," Cow's friend said to me as she walked back to the bar.

It was obvious these girls were just playing around with me, having a good time, but Cow had not removed her hand from my crotch and, predictably, emotions started to rise. Feeling this, Cow's attitude changed. Gone was the humor and genuine smiles as she tightened up to start fooling around in earnest. She was very cute, and I knew she had to make a living, but a hand job under the table was out of the question, especially with everyone watching. Under protest she stopped her advances and let me leave, just in time to watch my bus head downtown again.

For an hour and a half I watched shiny Hueys, flown by pilots in starched flight suits, land and take off at the heliport. The bus driver had been on his way to lunch when he left me waving and yelling at him from the bar door. But it was worth the wait. When he came back he took me to a different world, not too far from the USO, but a long way from the mass of poor people around the heliport. It was an older part of the city, with wide streets and beautiful shade trees that cooled off the sidewalks and softened the features of the old colonial buildings.

Caucasians wandered everywhere, dressed in civilian clothes, looking so neat and comfortable. It was obvious by the way they moved that they slept well at night. Their skin was clean, not encrusted with dust and sweat like everyone's back in Tay Ninh. As I stood there in my cloud of rancid body odor, I wanted to be like that again but knew it was not going to happen. Feeling more like a street urchin than a combat veteran of the butt-kicking 1st Cav, I kept my distance from them.

At the USO it took me five minutes of wandering around, reading pamphlets and posters, before I felt comfortable enough to walk up to the round-eyed girl at the information desk. It was my first opportunity to speak to an American girl since my airplane ride over. "Uh, excuse me, but do you know of any place around here where I can spend the night?" It came out more like a proposition than a question; I felt my ears turn red. "You know, a decent hotel."

"Sure, I'll give you the names of some of the middle-priced ones," and she wrote down a few names and addresses. No one was waiting in line behind me, so we talked for a while. She was from California and had started working for the USO after she had been turned down by the Peace Corps. I told her a little bit about Keene Valley and my days out in California before the draft got me. She saw the pilot's wings on my fatigues and asked me what I flew.

"Scouts? What's Scouts?" she asked.

"Aerial reconnaissance," I told her. "We keep track of people on the ground." There was no way to tell her that we hunted people and tried to kill them, without sounding like a weirdo.

"That must be exciting," she said, exhibiting interest in our conversation. But I was hungry and the thought of a couple of drinks and a thick civilian steak got me out of there, checked into the Stars Hills Hotel, showered, and back on the street again in half an hour.

An Air Force lieutenant gave me directions to an old hotel where the steaks were "as good as back home in Texas." It was only a few blocks away, but I hired a three-wheeled pedicab because I liked the

idea of being pedaled around town. In the pedicabs
the passengers sat side by side in a carriagelike seat
suspended between the two front wheels, with an
unimpeded view of the street scene. The drivers, sin-
ewy monkey men, sat behind on a bicycle attached
to the passengers' seat and pedaled their hearts out.

The restaurant was all that anyone who had not
had a decent meal in two months could ask for. On
the top floor, the dining room was open to the stars
and balmy night breeze; with linen and crystal, it
was the perfect setting for a sumptuous meal. The
maître d' did not even bat an eye at my dirty fatigues
and seated me at a table by the railing where there
was a nice view of the city lights. The French influence was apparent everywhere in the decor and service, but the steak was one hundred percent American,
thick and juicy. As my teeth sank into the succulent
piece of beef, my eyes closed and an involuntary
moan escaped. Relaxed in body and soul, with a hint
of fresh tarragon lingering on my palate, I rediscov-
ered the tranquility of eating for pleasure instead of
survival.

Two hours and three cognacs later, a leisurely
stroll seemed like a good idea, so I headed back to
my hotel on foot. The main street was quiet by then,
and the temperature had dropped a few degrees.
People were hanging out in small groups, talking
quietly and relaxing in the cool night air. A breeze
mixed the heavy city smells with the spices of Asia
as singsong music faded in and out of the shadows.

Feeling an empty pack of Lucky Strikes in my
pocket, I stopped to buy more at a newsstand. The
unshaven Arab proprietor wanted more than two
hundred piasters, over two bucks, for Lucky Strikes,
but only a quarter of that for the local brand, so I

bought a pack of the clove cigarettes. The coarse tobacco was bitter and the cloves crackled as they burned, but the cigarettes had some nice side effects: a pleasant aftertaste and a mild buzz, plus a cloud of clove smoke that followed me around, blending me into the Saigon night.

Walking along the darkened street that night, almost invisible, I felt like a civilian again. I was relaxed, walking in a strange place without fear. The stroll and my fantasy ended in the bright lights of the lobby. Looking back at me from the mirrored surface of the bar door was a short, skinny kid dressed in faded fatigues, quite forlorn and pathetically out of place—not at all how he wanted to appear.

The bar in the hotel's lobby, the Key Club, was just as the billboard outside had advertised: COZY ATMOSPHERE, EXCELLENT REFRESHMENTS, LOVELY HOSTESSES, AND HI-FIDELITY MUSIC. The bar itself was beautiful, a big old marble-and-brass affair, clean and cool, with a professional-looking Vietnamese bartender. The cocktail waitresses were indeed lovely and extremely friendly.

Halfway through my second glass of whiskey five Vietnamese kids, dressed like polyester Beatles, took the stage across from the bar and belted out a couple of American and British rock-and-roll hits. They were amazingly good, a little high-pitched, with some funny twists on the lyrics, but really impressive. As the bartender put a third drink down in front of me a beautiful young girl, pale green silk sliding all over her tight body, walked over and sat on the barstool next to me. She gave a little smile in my direction and then stared into the mirror behind the bar, watching me watch her.

It was not the first time she had caught me looking at her. She had been in the bar for an hour, sitting with some guys in civilian clothes at the other side of the room, and I must have spent half an hour stealing peeks at her. She was so beautiful, with her jet black Asian hair falling around her face, a face very different and very attractive. I thought she was most likely Eurasian, judging by her light skin and long torso. Her beautiful young body was enhanced by perfect posture; most of her back, a smooth arch of golden skin, was exposed in a valley of emerald-green silk.

I stared unabashedly when she got up to leave, adjusting the silk of her dress where it rode up in wrinkles across the curves of her buttocks. But she did not leave with her friends—friends or customers—and two drinks later we were on our way to my room. Her name was Tuu and getting her to agree to go with me was surprisingly easy. Maybe it was the originality of my opening line, "Excuse me, do you have a match?"

Tuu looked even better with her clothes off. Her European blood, French she said, had filled out the contours of her congenitally firm Asian body. Her long limbs had stretched tawny skin into graceful smooth flows over her hips and belly. Tuu told me she was eighteen years old, but she wasn't.

A while later, surrounded in a veil of smoke from a local cigarette, I wondered how prostitutes always managed to be somewhere else when they were making love. Or was it just me? As I lay there listening to street sounds, waiting for the sweat to stop running down my chest into my belly button, I told her about the war in Tay Ninh.

Tuu got the gist of it. "Hericopters. You fry hericopters?" I nodded in the affirmative. "You dinky-dao!" she said, getting out of bed, annoyed at the dingy sheet that had stuck to her lovely rear end. She took a small bowl from her enormous pocketbook and walked into the bathroom. The door was open so I watched as she took the bowl, filled it with water, and douched herself.

The next morning came slowly. I was completely hungover and incredibly tired. The unfamiliar commotion of the city street had kept me on the edge of sleep all night. At least it was quiet in Tay Ninh between incoming enemy rounds, I thought, and fatigue from long days of flying made it possible to sleep on the most unbearably hot nights. It would have been nice to stay in bed for the rest of the day, but I had not made the long trip to Saigon just for a hangover; I was also there for a fan. After half an hour in the shower and a wonderful breakfast of fresh fruit, I checked out, climbed in a pedicab, and headed for the main Saigon PX.

"You want see animals in zoo first?" my driver asked as he pedalled us along at a comfortable speed in the busy morning traffic.

"Sure. Why not?" I replied as he made a turn down one of the side streets. It was great riding along in the pedicab at a breezy five miles an hour or so, watching Saigon, the "Paris of the Orient," come to life. Children dressed in blue-and-white uniforms played games on their way to school. Shop owners were working industriously, taking advantage of the relative cool of the morning, as old men slowly took up their positions from which to watch another day.

We did not spend much time at the zoo. Most of the cages were empty, and the animals that remained were horribly neglected, starving in their own filth. "All money go to army," my driver explained. As we continued on to the PX we passed the gilded palace of President Nguyen Van Thieu, which had only recently been completed for some astronomical sum of money. Tanks were parked on the manicured lawn behind a wrought-iron fence, with the cannons pointed into the street. ARVNs were everywhere, armed to the teeth, but otherwise characteristically idle.

The PX was almost as heavily guarded as Thieu's palace. For a good reason; the place was packed with incredible treasures, including shelves *full* of fans. The rest of the day was consumed in fits of shopping and eating, leaving barely enough time to catch the last scheduled flight to Tay Ninh. Looking down on the moonlit jungle from the late-night flight, it was hard to imagine going back to work in such a forbidding place, but I wanted to. Thirty-six hours by myself in Saigon had been time enough to shed a few habits of a Scout pilot, but it had not been enough time to forget the feeling of flying a LOH in combat. Of course, there was no way to rationalize the risk involved, but for me flying Scouts was worth going back to.

I felt so comfortable back in Tay Ninh that even Captain Crane's and Captain Brisa's tirades the next morning did not bother me—it had become part of the way of life. It started, as usual, with Brisa glaring at me during the morning operations briefing. After the meeting Captain Crane asked me to step into his office. Brisa followed us in. "Mr. Smith, you did not have permission to go to Saigon the day before yesterday, did you?" Crane started in.

"Why yes, sir, I did. Got it right here, a note from the flight surgeon," I said innocently.

Brisa was just about to burst; his hands were clenched and his shoulders were hunched in pent-up frustration. "You're joking," he screeched. "You can't get a note from the flight surgeon and leave a combat zone." As he emphasized *flight surgeon* a vein popped out on his neck. "That's desertion. That's what you are Smith, a deserter." Beads of perspiration started to ooze from his forehead and it looked as if he was having trouble breathing.

"But, sir, I had a note from the flight surgeon— grounded for two days," I tried one more time.

"Not a note to go to Saigon, goddamn it!" Crane joined in. "I'll tell you where and when to go. I give the goddamned orders around here." Brisa shot him a hurt look after that statement. "Do you understand me, Smith?" Crane concluded.

"Yes, sir."

"And get a goddamned haircut! And that's an order, mister. You look like a goddamned hippie," the captain said. Crane was starting to lose control and he hated that. "You're supposed to be an officer!" he finished with more composure.

"Yes, sir."

They were really getting down on us about our haircuts. A few days before my trip to Saigon, Crab had received an Army Officer Efficiency Report from Brisa. Under "Appearance" he had a very bad rating with a note about his hair being too long.

A few days later, when I wrote Norm, Saigon had already become a dim memory.

The 29th August 1969

Dear Norm,

I am sorry that I have not answered you sooner, but we have been flying our asses off. We have been averaging nine hours a day. We will have a few days off now because we have no more door gunners. Our last two are laid up for about a week to three weeks. One took a couple .30 cal. rounds in his right leg, and the other took some frags in his leg from one of his own grenades with a quick fuse. For the last five days we have not gone up without taking fire. I almost got blown away the other day just because I dig ruins so much. There is this old busted up temple up by the Black Virgin Mountain. I went down to look it over and the next thing I knew I was in a three way cross fire from the mountain and both sides of the temple. These gooks really are cool. They knew damn well one of these stupid chopper pilots would get curious and come down and take a look, so they just sat there and waited. These NVA are real hard core. The day before that temple job I was out looking for 15–20 gooks who had shot up a recon patrol. I tracked them down a trotter and saw one of the last ones jumping in a bunker. I made four mini gun runs and then went away to let the high bird roll in with his rockets. The whole time I never took return fire. After one pass the high bird called up and said he had lost the target. I was only about a 100 meters away so I came back. They were waiting with a .50 cal., and if I had not been going 120 knots, there is no doubt they would of had us.

There is one sure way to have every gook and his mother after you and that is to blow up his bicycle. Sometimes you catch them by surprise and they have to drop their bikes and run. If you blow their bikes away they will shoot and throw everything they have at you. They really get pissed.

On a little higher note, I have bought some $450 worth of stereo equipment down here, value in states $825, and you would not believe the beautiful music

I have brought to Tay Ninh and probably most of Cambodia.

Boston is one of my favorite towns. You will have to stay there till I get back so I can come play with some of the BU [Boston University] students. Where are you going to school?

Actually I might not be back for another 17 months. There is this new deal down here. If you extend for 8 months you get out of the Army. This would give me a 14 month early out. I am still thinking about it.

Love,
Tom

With my new fan and a Sansui stereo the quality of my life in Tay Ninh had come a long way. Not far enough to justify extending my tour of duty, but I thought about it. The first time was in the midst of a drunken tirade in the officers' club. It was one of those nights after seeing too many young men fight hard for their lives and lose—fighting for a cause that had little value to anyone except a few American and Vietnamese politicians and some generals—dying for the people of two countries who really wanted nothing to do with them. I needed a reason to be in Vietnam, a reason that made sense to me. With the help of a little bourbon, I found one in a late-night brainstorm.

"Look, the only thing we can do to straighten out this fucked-up war is win it," I stated emphatically. Animal was the only one left at the table, and he appeared too interested in the bubbles rising in his glass of beer to respond to my statement. "We've got to extend," I said—that got his attention. "If we all stay till the war is over we would end up kicking their ass. Once and for all so we can all go home—

a victorious army—to parades and young women who are completely in love with us! Think about it."

He did, for about two seconds. Just long enough to screw his face up in a look of disgust. "Real good, Tom. That's a great idea. You do it."

"No, listen, everyone who's here stays, and everyone who gets sent over stays. Before long we got this enormous army and we kick the shit out of them," I said, trying to sound as logical as I could.

"I got a better idea. Let's move the war back to California or someplace a little nicer than this armpit. Then maybe I'll think about extending," Animal muttered, on the verge of falling asleep.

I don't think I was seriously considering extending my tour. Even writing my brother Norm about extending for an early out was as much to get a reaction as anything. It was like back in North Creek in 1968, when I told the girl at the White Water Derby that I was thinking about joining the Army to fly helicopters.

My primary reason for extending was to take advantage of the "14 month early out" I had mentioned in my letter to Norm. By volunteering for eight more months of duty in Vietnam I could reduce my overall commitment to the Army by fourteen months. This would get me out of the Army as soon as I had finished serving my extended tour of duty. Military life was getting to me even more than the rigors of combat. I was especially tired of the Mickey Mouse games Brisa played. Anything that could reduce my exposure to the bullshit of military life was worth considering—even extending.

It was odd, but most of the guys I knew who extended were combat veterans—the small percentage of soldiers in Vietnam who actually went out to do the killing. Their reasons were similar to mine; they wanted out at any expense. Mostly because they wanted to get away from the rear-echelon troops, and out of reach of the apathetic bureaucracy that had gotten them into the mess they were in. Some of these men preferred to keep their self-esteem and extend their tour for an early out rather than go back to the trivial games of regular army life.

A letter from Evil Eye, who was back home, reinforced the idea that the best thing I could do was get out of the Army as soon as possible.

1 Sept 69

Peace Perrius,

Well, I arrived here in California the 28th of August even though my DEROS was the 25th. Once again the Army fucked me.

I was home 24 hours when my wife told me she was too young to be married. It figures. She will be begging back in a month, but I won't be there. Oh well I'm getting off cheap, all I have to do is give her my TR-4A.

I just bought a cherry '65 Corvette Roadster that I paid around $600 too much for, but I don't really care as I want the car and it is ultra-cherry. From now on I'm living the way I want.

Evil Eye's homecoming did not sound as happy as I hoped mine would be, but his problems did not really surprise me. Evil Eye was naturally disposed to find fault and administer punishment, regardless of the price. But the last line of his letter, "From now on I'm living the way I want," echoed my sentiments exactly: master of my own fate. Extending would get me out fourteen months early and let me resume control of my life.

Actually, as much as men can be in a combat zone, we were the masters of our own fate. Control was what kept us alive; get in and get out without getting shot; control the situation. We could not even consider following direct orders. Almost everything was improvised or reflex; making plans only limited our options. Change course constantly, never hesitate, and don't focus on any one thing too long. The maneuvers we did use repeatedly were designed for a specific job and we believed they could not be improved upon. One example was our highspeed turn, a modified crop-duster's turn, which allowed us to keep the target in sight.

If we were buzzing over the treetops at a hundred knots and my door gunner saw some NVA below us, we could not use a standard banking turn, or he would lose the target. Any flight path other than straight up would take us past them, putting the jungle between us. By the time we could find them again they would be well hidden, or set up and waiting for us, or even worse, both.

The highspeed turn was basically a short hammerhead stall with a pedal turn. First I would pull the machine back into a fairly radical nose-high climb with a little right pedal kicked in. The pedal twisted the LOH to the right so that my door gunner could keep his M60 trained on the target behind and below us. Carefully reducing the power after initiating the climb helped decrease airspeed and rate of climb. As the airspeed dropped to about fifty knots, at a hundred feet above the trees or less, I would roll the helicopter on its right side, giving it lots of forward cyclic while kicking in more right pedal. The LOH would pivot and we would be looking straight down into the trees. In the few seconds it would take to dive back to the treetops again we would be going eighty, the target a little off our right nose, still exposed to my door gunner and under my minigun, making them easy targets.

When we came upon them like that, at top speed and low in the trees, they would not even hear us coming. It helped if the wind was blowing in the right direction for us, but the whole maneuver took less than fifteen seconds, not enough time for them to get organized. We got some easy kills with that turn. The downside to the maneuver was popping up above the cover of the trees, only to discover the easy pickings below us were part of a larger force that had us surrounded. For this reason I usually spent the interminable seconds at the top of the turn looking for holes in the jungle canopy large enough to accommodate a stricken helicopter.

Most of our maneuvers were developed to attack the enemy, others to escape from him, and some just for the fun of it, but they all had to be coordinated. A maneuver was coordinated if all the sequential moves joined in an uninterrupted flow. Flying the helicopter that way not only maximized its performance, it felt good. Not everyone liked to fly that way. Take, for instance, the time Gordon decided to climb up and call in some marking rounds for the troops we were working with.

He started his cyclic climb at about a hundred and ten knots. A cyclic climb is designed to get the aircraft to maximum altitude as quickly as possible; it is executed by pulling the cyclic back until the nose of the aircraft is pointing straight up in the air, trading airspeed for altitude. At the top of the climb the pilot can either level the ship, with at least fifteen knots airspeed so it will still streamline and fly, or he can take the airspeed all the way down to zero and then try to roll it over into a dive to get a little airspeed back. Gordon showed us another alternative. He held the nose straight up until he hit zero airspeed and then leveled it. As we watched horrified from below, his helicopter hung above us for a second, perfectly flat and unmoving, and then started to spin to the right, faster and faster. Slater came over the intercom: "Wow! Did you see the stuff flying out the back?" Sure enough, he was spinning so fast his door gunner's grenades and ammo belts were flying out of the open door.

Gordon regained control of the ship by at least having the sense to dive out of the spin. I promptly called him on the radio and asked him if he was having a good time.

"Roger that, two-four, getting arty [artillery] now." He acted as if nothing unusual had happened, but his voice was trembling.

All of our new maneuvers came through experimentation. Once in early September, Crab was trying to lose me on our way back to Tay Ninh. I was on his tail, a little above him in good dogfighting position, chasing him across the rice paddies. Crab was right down in the rice stalks, going flat out for a hole in the tree line off his nose. From quite a distance I could tell the hole was not wide enough to accommodate his rotor blades, so I started to climb early, sacrificing my airspeed for the altitude necessary to get over the trees. Crab started to pull farther ahead, but I knew I would catch him when he would have to climb over the trees. To my utter amazement he never even slowed down and never went over the trees. He simply turned the machine on its side and slipped through the hole!

I reflexively flinched as he went through the hole, sure he was going to crash. It was an incredible stunt; helicopters do not fly on their side without losing altitude. When I mentioned this to Crab back in Tay Ninh he told me how he had done it. "I came at the tree line at an angle. Just before the break I rolled it almost on its side, not quite, and pulled it into a climb against the angle. It's the climb that kept me from falling. . . . I guess it works." He was as happy with my incredulous reaction as he was with the feat. Both of us ended up using modified versions of this maneuver to escape hostile fire.

Some maneuvers we discovered out of desperation, like my "Frisbee" climb. Late in another stifling day I was trying to get some sleep in the back of my LOH. "You the pilot for this bird?" came a question as a rude hand started shaking my foot, which stuck out of the door hole. Nobody called a helicopter a "bird" except idiots. I looked up—sure enough there was a brand-new, squeaky clean second lieutenant. "I've got orders for you to take me to Firebase Ike ASAP," he told me.

I didn't feel like going anywhere, much less as soon as possible. "There's a Huey leaving Stingray Pad right now for Ike. Why don't you jump on that?" I said, and rolled on my side to go back to sleep. I wasn't trying to be rude, just practical. Animal was leaving Stingray Pad and it was part of our job to save fuel and blade time. The lieutenant, however, flipped out.

"I've got my orders, mister. Now get your sorry ass out of there and take me to that firebase!" He was screaming at me and it sent flashes of pain through my head.

"Fuck it," I said, and sat up.

"What was that, Mr. Smith?" he said, making a point of knowing my name.

"I said, 'Fuck it,' let's go."

The lieutenant strapped himself in the helicopter but was so angry he would not look at me. That struck me as funny and I made sure he could see me chuckling every time I looked at him, which was often. About halfway there, as we were hugging the grass of a big clearing, he said, "It's attitudes like yours that make this war unwinnable."

I'm afraid I overreacted to his antagonistic remark. He began to realize something was not quite right when he looked at me and noticed I was not laughing at him, but staring straight ahead at the approaching tree line. After one look he could not take his eyes off it either. We were approaching at over a hundred knots, only two feet off the ground, and the time to make a normal climb over the trees had passed quite a way back. What I was doing was approaching suicide, but what mattered to me was that he had shut up. Finally, like waking from a dream, I realized we were in big trouble.

I yanked the cyclic back to its stop so we started to climb straight up the two-hundred-foot trees. About forty feet from the tops it became obvious we were not going to make it. We had plenty of airspeed for the climb, but the arc of our climb was going to carry us into the trees about twenty feet from the top. In a desperate move I started a right turn with cyclic and pedal to try to get back down to the field. At the same time I pulled in power, even bleeding off rotor rpm, to keep us out of the trees. We never completely turned around because to my complete surprise the helicopter seemed to catch the air like a Frisbee: we actually pulled away from the trees.

When we got to the top I turned it back to our original course with pedal, nosed it over, and got my airspeed back. The lieutenant was slumped back in the armored seat, his face chalk white, and the crotch of his pants soaking wet. He did not say another word for the rest of the flight. It was not the brightest way to develop a new maneuver, but it sure was fun.

As our knowledge and skills grew so did our confidence, a necessary ingredient in Scouts, but overconfidence was dangerous and hard to detect. Crab and I first noticed it when it almost got us killed.

We were on our way from LZ Ike to LZ Jamie when Crab decided to check out one of our favorite trails. It was a major NVA supply route, which followed a north-south stream for a few miles and then disappeared into some dense undergrowth. There were a few narrow fields along the stream where we could get down and inspect the trail. Crab dropped down into one of them and called back, "Two-four, two-one. We got fresh bike and foot traffic heading south. I mean real fresh."

"Roger that, Crab, better get your ass up here," I called back.

"Yeah, comin' up, but I bet they kept walking to where they take their lunch breaks." Once before, Crab had found some garbage about half a mile away in a clearing where the trail crossed the stream. Ever since then he had called it their "lunch break" spot. "It's noon. I'll bet they're eatin' fish heads and rice right now."

I didn't think we would catch them sitting down for lunch, but if we could it was worth the try. Catching them by surprise in the open made for some easy shots at low risk. "Two-one, two-four, OK, let's do it, but how about coming in low and fast. Think you can find them if we come in over the trees?" I asked.

"No problem." Crab sounded really pleased with the idea. "Follow me." We swung off to the east a mile or so, the downwind side, and flew parallel to the clearing. "Two-four, two-one. This is it," and Crab rolled his LOH into a right turn back toward the stream. He went over the tree line doing a hundred knots; no way they could have heard him, but instead of the excited call of "Gooks in the open!" from Crab, he started yelling, "Taking fire! Taking fire!" as he practically disappeared in a cloud of tracers. In my zeal to be in on the turkey shoot I had fallen right in behind Crab, so close I had to fly right through the same wall of tracers. It was a rough ride; we took over twelve hits between us, but no one got hurt.

Crab was right, they were having lunch at their favorite spot. Someone back up the trail must have radioed ahead that we might be joining them.

9

Hard Core

Mid-September 1969

On the nineteenth Gordon screwed up and was shot down. The Scouts had been called in when a recon patrol from Bravo Company heard people chopping wood on the trail ahead of them. Bravo Company was staking out a major NVA resupply route west of LZ Jamie and coming into contact with NVA troops everywhere they turned. Crab and Gordon had taken off in their LOHs with a Cobra gunship from Phuoc Vinh flying cover. Slater was with Crab, and riding behind Gordon was a guy named Mason who was in his second—and last—day as a door gunner.

"It was unbelievable, the little dinks were setting up housekeeping right on the side of the trail—bicycles parked everywhere," Crab said, laughing as he told an attentive group of pilots the story of what happened. "It looked like a friggin' convention." Usually it was a bit nerve-racking when we caught up with the enemy; we had no idea what was going to happen. However, when we found things like bicycles and other personal gear lying around, it meant we had caught them unaware, that the advantage was ours.

Crab explained how he started to set up a circling flight path around the area. "But Gordon, the douche bag, blew it," he said. "As usual, he got all excited.

You know, his voice climbed a couple octaves and he started to lose it. I thought the asshole was going to crash into the trees again—he could barely talk. He didn't even know I was there. I was spending more time watching him than I was the trail."

Crab took his time opening another beer, giving the impression that his story wasn't important, and obviously loving the undivided attention he was getting. "The trees thinned out and I could see movement—people running around—so I kept my speed up and said to Gordon, 'Hey, we got movement and bunkers off to the right.' I kept going and swung left to circle. He cut hard right and started sayin', 'Yeah, we got bunkers. Yeah, we got gooks in the open!' He flew right over them, did a sharp turn, and came to a hover—unbelievable. They all started shooting at him at once. By the time I turned around he was spinning. Crashed right on top of a bunker. The Cobra rolled in, pumping rockets while I directed the grunts to the wreck. I knew Gordon had made it 'cause I saw Mason drag him out."

Gordon's door gunner, Mason, was quite the hero that day. They had indeed crashed in the middle of a large bunker complex, right on top of one full of angry NVA. Mason had no sooner gotten Gordon (who had been hit several times by AK-47 fire) out of the wreck than the NVA rushed them. Mason pulled out his .45 automatic and started shooting. When his gun was empty he calmly asked Gordon if he could borrow his .38 revolver and continued firing. He killed six NVA and was later awarded the Silver Star for bravery.

Everyone thought Mason was pretty cool—except Wolfman. "Mason was just tryin' to save his own hide," he maintained. "What kinda choice did he have?

It was shoot or get shot, what else could he do? Hero, my ass." Wolfman sounded angry as he continued, "He came back to Tay Ninh to get out of fighting in the field. He was a cook's assistant till his buddy Short Round told him how cool he would be if he flew Scouts."

Even though we didn't particularly like Gordon, Crab and I stayed around the 45th Surgical Hospital to make sure he was being taken care of. Our front-line hospitals were famous for parking guys and forgetting about them. It was not that they didn't care about each soldier; they were usually overbooked.

When we found Gordon in the Quonset hut they called the hospital, a nurse was putting a patch on the bullet hole in his arm and two doctors were working on his left leg. A bullet had gone through his thigh, broken the bone, and exited down by his knee. As we watched, doctors were putting traction on his broken limb. This must have hurt quite a bit; despite the fact that Gordon had a lot of drugs in him, he was still screaming. Just as the doctors were finishing up, Gordon slipped on the cot, so they had to start all over again.

Crab and I sat to the side cracking jokes, trying to make the best of an unattractive situation. Actually we were in pretty good spirits, happy that Gordon had not killed one of our door gunners on his way out of Scouts, and extremely happy that it was not one of us stretched out in that Quonset hut, bleeding all over the floor. In fact, Gordon had not stopped bleeding since they brought him into the 45th Surgical Hospital. A half hour had passed, and there was still a steady stream of blood flowing from the bottom of the canvas cot they had parked him on. When a doctor walked by I pointed the puddle out to him.

"Runoff," he said, and kept on walking.

Twenty minutes later Gordon was still there in the hall, still bleeding. This time Crab and I badgered a doctor until he looked him over. After a brief examination the doctor grunted and told the nurse beside him to get some instruments—there was a bullet stuck in Gordon's ass, which they had missed. By the time they finished working on him, I had gone back to the company area and picked up my camera. We spent the rest of the afternoon getting Gordon to pose for us.

It was not until later that day when we looked at the wreckage of Gordon's helicopter that we realized the extent of the damage done by his crash. He had landed on his minigun and crushed the cowling, the last one we had. There were more miniguns, but without the cowling to eject the spent rounds and belt links, they were worthless. Crab and I had no choice but to ground the Scout operations until we had a new cowling. Neither of us would fly without the minigun for protection.

My respect for the minigun had grown considerably; I had shot at least a dozen NVA with it in the last two months. I knew it was a good offensive weapon, and one day at the end of September, I found out firsthand what a good defensive weapon it was. We had been sent out into the jungle to find a mailbag that had blown out the open door of a Huey, which we found without incident in some light bamboo near a river.

I was the first to find a landing spot, a little shelf of the riverbank just large enough for my LOH, so I told Crab I would go after the mailbag while he covered me. While I crept nervously through the bamboo, Crab, unbeknownst to me, decided to work on some potential ambush spots with his minigun. Even had I been warned, I would not have been prepared for the shock of four thousand bullets a minute being fired a hundred feet above my head. I was paralyzed by what sounded like the end of the world. Barely audible above the deafening roar of the minigun was the spattering of hundreds of bullets shredding bamboo trees.

We got our weapons man to call around and find us another cowling. It was not easy, but the next day he had found a whole warehouse full of them. "The good news is that I've found more than you can shake a stick at," he said. "The bad news is they are in a warehouse and can't be delivered for a week or two. The other good news is that that warehouse is in Vung Tau."

Vung Tau was the rest-and-recreation center of Vietnam. It was rumored that the beautiful, white-sand beaches were littered with voluptuous, half-naked, round-eyed women. We discussed our options.

"If we tell Crane that we have to go to Vung Tau to pick up a minigun cowling, he is going to say 'fat chance,' " Crab said.

"So let's not tell him," I replied.

"That's going AWOL," Crab said, feigning horror.

We had to decide on how to get there and back. "If we do the military transport trip it will take us four days, man. Let's split with a LOH. They won't miss it and we'll be back tomorrow," Slater put in, joining the conspiracy. We all agreed it was the only way we could get the Scouts back in the air.

Crab told Operations that we were going on a maintenance run and the three of us jumped in a LOH. As we were running it up in the revetment,

Little Buddy left the Huey he was working on to come over. "Where you goin'?" he asked. When we told him he smiled from ear to ear, jumped in the back, and said, "Let's didi [go]."

The trip to Vung Tau was great. Like a bunch of high school kids in their dad's borrowed car, we were excited about breaking the rules. Two and a half hours later we arrived at Vung Tau. We circled the town a few times and then flew low-level down the coastline. Sure enough, the place was a sea of scantily clad bodies. We landed at the airport and headed for the beach.

It was even better than we had anticipated. We found a spot centrally located in a bevy of beauties, and within minutes were light-years away from Tay Ninh and combat. It was hotter on the beach than it was in the jungle, but in Vung Tau that wasn't a problem. We had barely broken a sweat when a little girl of ten or so came along with a basket full of ripe, already sliced pineapples. Right behind her came a little boy selling beer and, of course, the "Saigon special" watches.

"We don't want any of your rip-off watches," Little Buddy told him. "You got anything we can smoke? You know, pot, dinkydao."

"I get," he said as he ran off. Minutes later he returned with something that would have made the freaks in Haight-Ashbury stand up and applaud. It was a marijuana cigarette about six inches long, shaped like an ice cream cone. We bought several of them. By the time Little Buddy and I had finished one, we had a name for them: "Bombers"—total destruction. Four hours later the sun was going down and we still could not move, which was all right with us because we did not know where we were.

If it were not for Crab and his insatiable desire to win the hearts and minds of the people, and maybe meet a few young girls, we probably would have smoked another one and spent the night right there. But he finally got us moving; before long we found ourselves in a little shack on the outskirts of town eating rice with four generations of an extended family who all lived in one room. It was more like a tribe than a family, and I could not help but be a little paranoid as they talked about us in a language I didn't understand. The main entertainment for these people that night was watching Crab share their dinner with them—fish heads.

We were having a good time with the family, but I knew if we stayed there too long Crab would fall in love with one of their teenage daughters, and we would never get out of there. So after we finished our rice and beer we dragged Crab off to a whorehouse where we shared a room, three nice young girls, and a lot of laughs. Unlike in Saigon, the girls in Vung Tau actually seemed to enjoy our company.

The next morning we found the minigun cowlings and loaded them in our helicopter. We thought so much of ourselves for getting the job done that we unanimously voted to extend our vacation in Vung Tau for another day. Little Buddy came up with a few more Bombers and we went back to the beach, but within an hour our guilty consciences had us back in the LOH heading to Tay Ninh.

When we checked in with Operations Crane hit the roof. "I've had it with your arrogance and complete disregard for the goddamned military system!" he screamed. "It's out of my hands; this time you're up for desertion. Crab, you've really let me down."

"Captain Crane, we needed that minigun cowling,

sir. We would have been grounded without it," I interjected.

"Who gives the orders around here, goddamn it, Smith? I'll let you know when it's time to get a goddamned cowling. I've cut you a lot of slack, but the colonel knows about this." He glared at me for a while and then said, "You're dismissed."

Captain Brisa was waiting outside Crane's office. "You're in a world of shit, Smith!" he sneered. "And you had better get a haircut before you see the colonel, mister."

As it turned out the colonel was not as upset as Captain Brisa and it was several weeks, and a few more atrocities, before I got to see him.

Most of the officers around Tay Ninh deserved more respect than Brisa. For instance, there was Captain Mink of the U.S. Air Force, a FAC pilot stationed in Tay Ninh. We worked with him a lot marking and BDAing air strikes, and we spent a lot of time with him after work in the officers' club. One night he asked me if I would like to take a ride in his OV-10 Bronco, a beautiful twin-turboprop aircraft reminiscent of the old P-38s used in World War II, in exchange for a ride in my LOH.

The next day he strapped me in behind him and we took off in his airplane for the jungle. We were looking for some of the areas we had worked together, but had trouble getting down low because most of our area of operations was covered in a thick morning mist that hung in the treetops. It was interesting seeing the war from where he sat, more like Command and Control than Scouts, but interesting.

Just as the flight was starting to get boring, Mink climbed up to five thousand feet, above the layer of clouds covering the jungle. Without a word he

pushed the machine over into a power dive, straight
at the jungle below us. By the time we got down to
a few hundred feet above the layer of clouds, we
were going over two hundred knots. At what seemed
like the last minute, Mink pulled back on his control
stick until the aircraft started to shudder from the
strain.

Pulling out of the dive put a strain on us as well
as the aircraft. At somewhere around seven times
the force of gravity I lost consciousness. It was like
watching a movie slow to a halt. Everything was normal, then the film started to flutter, each scene going
by slower and slower, and finally the last frame
froze—I passed out.

When I came back around, it was the most amazing sensation: I was hanging upside down, weight-
less, in my seat belt and shoulder harness, looking
at the jungle from a completely new perspective.
After Mink had knocked me out he rolled the agile
Bronco on its back. As we skimmed along the tops
of the flat mist layer at a hundred and fifty knots,
upside down with trees just barely visible through
the mist, Captain Mink asked me, "Can you dig it?"

Not long after that Mink told me it was my turn
to show him a good time—he wanted to fly as my
door gunner. The young Air Force captain wanted to
do a BDA with us to see what one of his air strikes
looked like from a slow-moving helicopter.

The next day I strapped Mink into the backseat of
the LOH and took him out for a little practice with
the M60. I didn't tell the captain this, but if he could
not shoot the machine gun I was not going to take
him anywhere near a bunch of NVA soldiers. But he
did pretty well, so Crab and I set up an air strike for
a bunker complex we had been working around. The

complex had shown signs of activity, but we had been unable to catch anyone at home. This time we arranged the air strike so that we would come in at high speed on our first pass, and mark the target at the same time the jets were rolling in from an altitude where they were undetectable by the enemy.

It worked perfectly. As we dropped the Willy Pete grenades we saw NVA running all over the place. The bombs exploded seconds behind us. It was one of the best air strikes we ever orchestrated. We caught them so unaware that when we came back in for the BDA hardly anyone had it together enough to shoot at us.

Mink kept asking, "How many gooks did we get?" It was hard for him to see the twenty or so dead enemy that were scattered in the bomb craters and opened-up bunkers. People blown into pieces do not look like people at all. Finally I said, "Look for things that look like sides of beef." The rib cages are easy to recognize once you know what they look like; for some reason they stay intact. When I looked back to see if he had recognized any of the NVA below us, he was throwing up.

Flying Scouts was different, and took some getting used to, but then almost every day in Vietnam took getting used to. Even days off had their moments. On one such day I was listening to my stereo in my hooch, trying to relax, when Animal almost broke the hinges off the door in his haste to get in. He looked at me wild-eyed and asked, "Atom, where's your AK-47?"

He was a mess, out of breath. His jungle fatigue shirt was ripped, and blood was trickling down his forehead. "What the . . .?" was all I could get out.

"Where the hell is it? Got to have a Russian machine gun to shoot up nine-four-four," Animal raged. "Crane is heading out there right now. He'll bust my ass!"

Earlier that morning Animal had stopped by my hooch to tell me he was taking out one of the LOHs to do a little fun flying. Every now and then Animal would take a LOH out under the pretense that he was thinking of getting into Scouts. He had gone out to LZ Grant and was screwing around doing some ground-level tight turns when his engine quit. Being so low and slow, he did not have time to set up for an autorotation and ended up smacking into a pile of stumps and totaling the machine. This in itself was not a punishable offense, but crashing it because he had let it run out of gas was.

"I've got to shoot up the fuel cells so the pricks can't prove I ran out of gas. That geek Brisa will probably dig the slugs out, so they had better be from an AK."

I gave him my AK-47 and an extra clip of ammo, and he was off at a run to get back out there before Crane and Brisa. Animal pulled it off, shot it up and got away with it. Brisa knew what Animal had done but could not prove it.

Life at home, Tay Ninh, was getting pretty unbearable with the widening schism between the officers and pilots who sat around doing nothing and the other pilots who were actually fighting a war. We couldn't help but resent it. Actually our resentment encompassed more than a couple of men in Tay Ninh—it included everyone who was responsible for us being there.

There was even a believable rumor that Lyndon Baines Johnson was directly involved in our not being able to get replacement parts for our LOHs. Evidently he was using his influence to get the Army to replace the Hughes OH-6A, our LOHs, with the Bell OH-58, a helicopter made by a company in which he reputedly was a major stockholder. We were upset because the OH-58 could not maneuver like the OH-6A and was therefore more vulnerable to enemy fire.

We probably would have been more upset with our situation if we had more time, but the NVA had a way of keeping us busy. They were bringing in more troops, and it was getting hard to keep tabs on them. We were constantly bumping into whole companies of NVA with so much firepower that we did not stand a chance if we ended up in the middle of them. One group of NVA we called Charlie Company had taken over five square miles of bombed-out jungle right in the center of the firebases we were supporting, and set up helicopter traps, three .51-caliber machine guns arranged in gun pits to form a triangle. They would hold their fire until we flew right into the middle of the triangle, where all three guns would have us in their sights.

They kept changing their tactics, using different trails and setting up decoys for us. They even came up with green tracers, which were perfectly visible to them against the blue or gray sky, but were invisible to us against the green jungle. They could see when they were hitting or missing us; we could not tell where the fire was coming from.

The combined effect of the pressures in Scouts and the bullshit in Tay Ninh was giving me a bad attitude, which I took with increasing regularity to the officers' club, where I got it drunk. Every day my bitterness toward the Army and my fear of dying grew. Climbing back into that cockpit, trying to be a hero in a war where heroes were suckers, was becoming more of a chore with each passing day.

Something else that was bothering me was the letters coming from home. Besides the ones from my family, most of the letters seemed to fall into two groups. The first group consisted of relatives and friends writing to tell me that they respected me, and then they'd go on to explain why their sons could not be in Vietnam. The second were from girls; girls I did not know, girls from ten to thirty—it was great. They were really sweet, thought the war was horrible, and told me I was a wonderful guy for trying to make the best of a bad situation. The letters full of excuses and lies disappointed and angered me, whereas the letters from the girls made me homesick.

Late in September, after a company party in the maintenance tent, the dam broke. Crab and I had put down the better part of a bottle of Canadian Club whiskey before we went over to the party where a Vietnamese band was playing Beatles hits. We grabbed a couple of cold Budweisers from the makeshift bar set up on the engine overhaul counter and found some empty seats near the back of the tent. It was a typical Army party with a hundred or so tired men sitting in neat little rows of folding metal chairs. Ten minutes later we were bored stiff.

"What a joke," Crab said.

"Let's go back and finish off that Canadian Club," I suggested.

The band was so bad that even the colonel had walked out. Before we could get up and leave, Skinner, whom I had grown to dislike because he loved to tell war stories yet did everything possible to stay out of a fight, walked up onto the stage. "I know you guys are all having fun," he started in among boos and hisses, "but I just want to take a minute of your time to thank this great band." He started clapping his hands and beaming back and forth from the band to bored soldiers below him.

"Sit down, Skinner, you asshole," I yelled.

"We all have a lot to be thankful for here," he continued, waving his hands around like an evangelical preacher. "Our Vietnamese allies here . . ."

It was more than I could stand. The next thing I knew, my full beer can was flying at Skinner's head. It missed by a foot, but hit the drummer sitting behind him. "You worthless hunk of garbage!" I screamed at him as Crab dragged me out of the tent.

Outside I broke Crab's grip and fell face first into the "cleagy pit" (Crab's name for the fetid drainage ditch full of green scum, waste oil, and assorted vermin). After several attempts I pulled myself up the slimy bank and threw up on his boots. It wasn't the cleagy pit itself that made me nauseous, but the surprisingly vivid memory of a drunk soldier relieving himself in the ditch as we had walked by on our way to the party.

After rinsing out my mouth and innards with the rest of the bottle of Canadian Club, Crab and I got down to some serious talk about the war and our comrades in arms. "I can't take it anymore, Crab. I can't live with these shithead hypocrites and this bullshit war."

"Come on, Atom, it's not all that bad. Crane told me the other day that he wanted you to take Skinner's job as the colonel's pilot, and he wants you to move into his hooch with him," Crab ribbed me.

Crab was really enjoying getting my goat. He had always been an instigator, and that night he knew he had some good material to work with. Unfortunately he had no idea how much rage had built up in me. We started talking about Wolfman and Little Buddy, and the next thing I knew I was throwing a CS (choking gas) grenade into the Wolf Den. My intentions had been amiable enough—I wanted to get Wolfman and Little Buddy up to drink with us—but in my inebriated, crazed condition I had gone way too far.

Wolfman came out coughing and swearing. As soon as he could breathe and see again, he realized that Little Buddy had not come out of the hooch. He ran back in to drag the unconscious mechanic out. Without a second's hesitation Wolfman bent over his friend and began mouth-to-mouth. It seemed to take forever, but after a couple of breaths Little Buddy coughed and regained consciousness.

Later that night, after hours of apologizing to my irate friends, Wolfman finally forgave me with, "The whole thing wouldn't have pissed me off so much, Atom, if Little Buddy hadn't barfed in my mouth when he came around."

Usually that kind of loss of control would have taken the edge off my aggravated, belligerent nature, but the situation I was in would not let me escape the frustration and fear that had pushed me so far. Two days later my hostility manifested itself again, but this time it was against an NVA soldier.

I had gone in to do a BDA on an arc-light while Crab covered me. The B-52s had been right on target and the bunker complex they dropped their tons of high explosives on was pulverized. Our initial pass brought no hostile fire, so I slowed down to take a closer look. One of the bomb craters had exposed part of a large bunker. As we flew by I thought I saw someone moving around in the shadows of what was left of it.

"What's up, Atom?" Wolfman asked as I brought the airspeed down and turned toward the opening in the bunker. He could not see what I was looking at because the helicopter was pointing straight at the bunker.

"Atom! What are you doing?" Crab called over the UHF radio. "Jesus Christ, are you nuts?"

"Got some movement in this bunker," I told them both.

"There were people moving all over here a minute ago. Get your ass out of there," Crab barked.

Right about then an NVA soldier crawled out of the bunker. We were about twenty feet from him, and it seemed he was not even aware we were there. I could see blood coming out both of his ears. "Hey, you guys, he's got a rose behind each of his ears," I told Crab and Wolfman over the radios, referring to the blood. "Don't worry, he's too screwed up to hurt anyone."

"What about his buddies in the trees, Atom? Get the hell out of there." Crab sounded stressed but was trying to keep his temper. I should have gotten out of there, but for some reason the wounded man in front of me was all I was interested in.

"Hey, wait a second, he's got a gun," I told Wolfman as the bleeding solider dragged an AK-47 out of the dirt. He valiantly struggled with the bolt of his machine gun, trying to put a round in the chamber as I hovered there watching. He was having a hard time, his bloody hand kept slipping off the operating lever, but no matter how much trouble he was having, it was obvious that he would eventually get it loaded and take a shot at us.

"Goddamn it, Atom, let me get him!" Wolfman yelled at me over the intercom. It was one of the few times he raised his voice while we were flying. Just as Wolfman finished, the bloody soldier tried to raise his rifle, and I squeezed the trigger of my minigun.

When we got back to Tay Ninh, Wolfman followed me to my hooch. "Look, Atom," he started, "I really like flying with you, but that was really stupid out there today. You could have gotten us both blown away—coming to a hover like that and not letting me have a shot at him. You can't trust that minigun for pickin' off gooks. What the hell is wrong with you, anyway?"

"Yeah, you're right, Wolfman. That was pretty weird; I just sort of got hung up on him," I tried to explain.

"Crab would never have done anything as crazy as that," he said, not wanting to drop the subject.

That comment hurt, because sane, safe Crab was getting into kicks that I thought were crazy. He had always been jealous of the high bird's capabilities to shoot rockets. As our LOHs had no weapon system designed for rockets, Crab made his own. He took a minigun mount and modified it to hold a rocket pod. It worked pretty well, considering, but in order to shoot the rockets he had to get the helicopter up out of the trees, a hundred feet or so. If he punched off the rockets low-level, the shrapnel from the blast peppered his LOH. The trouble with getting up to a hundred feet to shoot his rockets was that the enemy got a good clean shot at him. He admitted it could get him killed but added that did not make it any less fun.

"Maybe you should just fly with Crab, then!" I snapped back, losing my temper completely.

"Don't get pissed, little Ant buddy. I really like flying with you—you and I have a lot in common, but when it comes to keepin' your cool, forget it.

Crab is safe, Atom, he stays in control. But I have a better time with you. Remember that time I saw the gooks playing basketball?" he asked, trying to take the edge off the situation.

Wolfman and I had been clipping along at a hundred knots when he yelled over the intercom, "Atom, come around, I got some gooks playing basketball back there." We were right in the middle of thick jungle, and I knew he had not seen anyone playing basketball, but I came around anyway just to try to find out what he had seen.

"Yeah, I remember," I told him.

"Crab would have just laughed at me and kept flying, but you went back. I really appreciated that, but get real, Atom; blowin' 'em away is my job. The minigun just isn't as good as my M60—*dig it!*"

"Yeah, you're right," I had to admit, but Wolfman was a fine one to be telling me I wasn't rational. It was the last week in September, Wolfman had two weeks of leave coming to him, and his tour of duty was up the middle of October. He could have stopped flying that day and never gotten shot at again, but he just kept on going up.

"I have fun with you too, Wolfman, and I would not be able to let it hang out like that if I didn't think you could get us out," I said, dreading the day he would go home.

It seemed like the very next day that I got a message to report to the brigade commander's office. He came right to the point. "Mr. Smith, Captain Crane and Captain Brisa have brought some very serious charges against you," he said, sliding a sheet of paper across his desk for me to read. I had gotten used to Crane and Brisa chewing me out, but the colonel was a new experience, and a little scary.

"I have reviewed their statements, and before you there is a copy of the letter of reprimand that will remain in your personnel file until you leave Vietnam," he continued solemnly. The letter read:

Department of the Army
Headquarters, 1st Brigade, 1st Cavalry Div.
2 October 1969

WO-1 Thomas L. Smith
HHC, 1st Brigade
1st Cavalry Division (Airmobile)
APO San Francisco

1. It has been brought to my attention that during the Aviation Platoon party on 27 September 1969 you threw a CS grenade into an EM billet.

2. It has also been reported that earlier in the evening you threw a full can of beer at WO Skinner, missing him and striking a member of the band. Incidents such as these are inexcusable and are harmful to U.S. and third-country relations.

3. On 16 September 1969 you were picked up by Military Police in downtown Tay Ninh for being off post without authorization. Your name appeared on the Military Police blotter for this violation.

4. During the first week in September you absented yourself from the 1st Brigade area without authorization and went to Saigon for two days.

5. You have failed to meet the required standards of personal appearance, specifically regarding haircuts.

6. Acts of this nature are immature and dangerous in addition to being entirely devoid of humor.

7. The duty position that you hold in this brigade is one requiring the utmost in responsibility and maturity in addition to your demonstrated skill as an aviator. Irresponsible acts and conduct such as these bring discredit upon yourself and your organization.

8. It is my intention to place this letter in your

personnel file here for the remainder of your tour in the 1st Brigade. Providing your conduct and behavior are flawless during the remainder of your tour, this letter will be destroyed. You will indicate receipt of this communication by endorsement hereon.

Richard B. Lansing
Colonel, Infantry
Commanding

Later I learned Captain Brisa had written the original statements against me, and that they had been in the form of court-martial charges, including desertion in a combat zone, a crime punishable by death. The colonel was a practical man, however, and needed Scout pilots more than he needed retribution for his junior officers.

Crab read it and broke out laughing. "Sergeant Schultz [his name for Captain Crane] and Brisa can't even win a battle in base camp."

When I showed the letter to Animal he said, "Big deal, what are they going to do, send you to Vietnam and make you fly Scouts?"

10

Mayhem and Medals

Early October 1969

A change in the weather provided me with a little time to work on better behavior around the company area. The monsoon season struck with full force, and we had more days off, since we could not fly our LOHs in the rain. The tail rotors were made of plastic, and they turned so fast (thousands of rpm) that they disintegrated after just minutes of flying in heavy rain. The rains also slowed the enemy's activities, leaving us with no one to chase. So for a few weeks everyone got a break.

The days off and time away from the jungle gave me a chance to forget about combat and concentrate on my relationship with Captain Crane. Helping me, and everyone else in the company, to get along with Captain Crane and Captain Brisa was the new company clerk who replaced Wilson. His name was Carl Borowski, and he was quite a character. Ski, as he soon became known, had a way of slipping in between our company commanders and the pilots, defusing a lot of potentially volatile situations. Somehow he managed to take the petty manipulations that they called orders and turn them around into comical scenarios we could deal with. Crane and Brisa liked him, and we loved him.

On the days we did fly there were so many clouds

it was hard to find our way around our area of operations, and the humidity from the saturated jungle made the hot days unbearable. Before long we realized that hot, humid, cloudy days were better spent having fun than chasing the enemy. Crab and I would climb up to ten thousand feet, where the air was about twenty degrees cooler. Flying around the great snowy white clouds with cool air blowing in the open doors was truly a blast. Eventually we came up with a new form of recreation using some of the smaller clouds—our own game of chicken.

We would pick a cloud about three thousand feet from base to top, with less turbulence than the taller ones, and center ourselves over the top as we rolled the throttle off, putting us in an autorotation right down through the middle of it. It was cold, dark, and spooky inside as we were dropping, powerless, two thousand feet a minute through the moist gray marshmallow insides. Time dragged in the gray void; our senses were deprived of reference. The chicken part was determined by when we rolled the throttle back on to stop the descent of the helicopter.

The bottom of the clouds usually stopped about five hundred feet above the tops of the trees, so if we waited until we dropped out of the bottom to roll the throttle back on, it wasn't always possible to stop the descent before hitting the trees. If we rolled the throttle on inside the cloud we were "chicken."

Another consequence of the heavy rains was my getting a rating as a tank driver. Heavy rains were covering Tay Ninh, making landing there impossible. I turned around and was heading back to LZ

Barbara to wait out the storm when I noticed a tank company stopped in the middle of the road just outside of town. It looked secure enough, so I landed next to the lead tank, got out, and asked the driver how long he was going to be sitting around there.

"Don't know. Got a broken-down half-track, could be hours before we get going again," he told me.

"Great!" I said. "I can't get into Tay Ninh until that storm passes, and I don't really feel like sitting out here by myself with a bunch of NVA."

"Well, if you got nothin' to do, how about giving me a ride in that whirlybird of yours?" the driver suggested.

"No problem, if you'll let me drive your tank," I responded.

Sure enough, after I took him and his whole crew for a ride, he let me drive the old Patton tank around the rice paddies for a while. Actually, it was not as much fun as I had imagined it would be. The diesel fumes were overpowering; it was like an oven inside, and it drove—not surprisingly, I guess—"like a tank."

Like all good things the heavy rains passed in a few weeks; the NVA started moving around again, and the war was back on. Besides a nice break during those first few weeks in October, we also got another Scout pilot to replace Gordon. His name was Don McNeil, a big, round-faced, jovial guy who was named Spud by someone the first day. He was easy-going, a good addition to the brigade Scouts. Spud also was in touch with a friend of his from flight school and said his buddy was going to transfer to fly Scouts with him.

On one of my days off, while Crab was training Spud, I wrote a long letter to my brother Norm.

The 11th of October 1969

Dear Norm,

I would like to write you more often, but I keep losing my head and get involved in this war. Half the day you go out and kill and get killed. The other half you sit around and wait for your year to be up, feeling quite shitty because you have to be down here and you may not go home. I don't know which half of the day is worse. The second part of the day is definitely not constructive and basically makes you a pretty lousy person. It is a waste of time in a lousy place. The first part of the day to some is constructive and eventful, but some of the after affects such as death or loss of limb are definitely not desirable. The second part of the day could be all right, considering war is hell, if you could find motivation or justification for being here, but no one likes to fight for a lost cause especially if it is not your own. The first part of the day is easy to find motivation in that it is interesting to see if you can find them and then hit them with your bullets before they hit you with theirs. Sort of like a really hard treasure hunt with a very tense race at the end involving skill and technical know how. Your basic justification is you are doing it to help others know where the enemy is so they can go get killed. When they make contact on the ground then you try to save them. It is a very good way to fight a war in the jungle. We find them, and the troops with air support kill them. Having a pretty solid knowledge of how to beat them (I swear to God it is not hard). I get so pissed that every eligible male is not down here fighting. The enemy is elusive, but he can be found and easily killed. He is not equipped for heavy and prolonged contact. He relies on mobility and stand off attacks to even keep the war going. We unfortunately do not have enough

men to corner him and stay with him. Also we are
only allowed a certain amount of casualties a month.
We go far enough to get a few of ours killed and
then break off and move to a new bunch of gooks.
At times it seems we want his type of war to keep
us fighting. Coordination is really outstanding until
the part where we move in to finish a job. Then
someone screws up and all we did was make him
move again which is his bag anyhow. I can say we
win in combat, but in combat we are understaffed.
Vietnam is a pretty big place for 75,000 combat people. It is rewarding to know you do good work and
get a job done even at the risk of forty or more years
of life, but it is easily outweighed by the fact that we
will not win, unless it is by a few people who will
have to pay too much, and that you are only required
to die for a year and not a cause. Basically what I
am trying to say is as far as wars go this one sucks.

One problem now is that I have a bad case of
nerves. Unlike most aviation jobs, in Scouts the more
time you get the more likely you are to be shot down.
No matter how good you are you get shot at every
time you can, actually the better you are the more
you get shot at. In a jungle the only way you can
find them is to make them shoot at you. Oh well, on
December 24th I am going to quit and fly Command
and Control ships.

Well today was tomorrow and I got your letter last
night and I would like to thank you very much. All
except for the part about fall in the Adirondacks. My
memory torments me enough without reference to
the world I once knew.

Four days after I wrote Norm, Wolfman finished
his tour of duty and left Tay Ninh. He flew right up
to the last day, removing any doubt that what he
had always said was true: "I just like to fly." For
four months Wolfman had been responsible for keep-

ing Crab and me alive. A few weeks before he left he even saved the lives of several of our enemy.

Crab and I had been keeping an eye on a new NVA resupply trail that seemed to be getting quite a bit of use. The trail ran through heavy jungle and the only way to check it out was to hover down two hundred feet through a hole in the forest canopy that was just big enough to accommodate a helicopter.

Wolfman and I were down in the hole with Crab and Slater circling above us. The trail had signs of recent use, bike-tire tracks and lots of Ho Chi Minh sandal tracks all over it. Wolfman keyed his intercom switch and in his usual calm, controlled way he said, "Atom, get the hell out of here fast—real fast!"

Looking up from the trail below us and back over my shoulder at him I saw what the problem was. Wolfman was staring off into the jungle on our right side and was bringing his M60 up to firing position. I followed his stare, and no more than fifty feet from us, next to a big tree on the edge of the clearing, was a man in black pants and a T-shirt—frozen in position, looking straight ahead. Leaning against the tree next to him was one of the biggest rockets I had seen. It was at least five feet tall.

I pulled in all the power the machine would give me, and we started very slowly to climb up out of the hole. I knew we could never get out of there before someone shot us down, and I shrank down and waited for the sound of AK-47s. But there was no sound of machine gun fire, none at all, not even of Wolfman's M60. I yelled over the intercom, "Shoot him, Wolfman, goddamn it, shoot him!" but still not a shot was fired. After what seemed like forever we broke out of the jungle canopy and I rolled the nose over, putting our tail to the enemy.

"Wolfman, what the hell is wrong with you? That guy could have blown us away, and you were just sitting back there like a dufus turd. Jesus Christ, you trying to get us killed?" I shouted at him, on the verge of hysteria.

"Atom, he had a wolf shirt on. I couldn't shoot anyone wearing a wolf shirt" was all he would say.

True enough, he had a T-shirt on that looked a lot like Wolfman's favorite T-shirt, but he could have easily killed us. For the next few minutes I was so mad at Wolfman I couldn't think straight. Then it dawned on me that if he had shot at that guy and hit the rocket beside him—a very likely possibility—we would all have been blown to pieces.

Perhaps I wrote my brother Norm that I had decided to get out of Scouts on Christmas Eve because with Wolfman leaving I was afraid. I didn't think anyone else could keep me from getting myself killed. Slater and a big guy named Ben were the only regular door gunners left. All too often I was ending up with part-timers in my backseat. Guys like Short Round, whose gun kept jamming, and someone called Lenny, who had been shot down once and was almost incapacitated with his premonitions that it would happen again. Every time we wanted Lenny to fly we had to convince him that it was his paintbrush, not his bad luck, that had gotten him shot down and almost killed.

Several months earlier Lenny and Wolfman had decided to make a statement supporting the peace movement back home. Lenny painted a big white peace sign on the bottom of one of the Scout ships; the first time he went up in it they got shot down. There were almost twenty holes in and around the peace sign and only four holes in the rest of the LOH's fuselage.

There was no doubt about it; by the third week in October I was feeling pretty lonely and insecure. Wolfman was gone and Crab was in Vung Tau, of all the places, for two weeks of LOH Instructor Pilot School. Spud wanted me to train his buddy Loftin, who had finally transferred to our company, so Loftin could fly with him instead of me. Crane and Brisa hated me, and every time I went flying the NVA tried to kill me. All my good buddies with their non-military negative attitudes, like Evil Eye and Snuffy, had finished their tours of duty and gone home, and all the new guys who were joining the company had not yet realized what a lousy war it was—they were too new and too gung-ho to talk to. I was bummed. The only friend I had left was Animal, until "Cisco" showed up. Sharp introduced us with, "Got some new meat for you, Smith. He actually asked to be a Scout door gunner."

His name was Ken Gardiner, formerly an infantryman with the 2d of the 5th, 1st Cavalry. He was friendly and polite, but a little hard to understand because of his strong New Jersey accent. "Why do you want to fly Scouts, Cisco?" I asked.

"Jeez, you know, walkin' around, being a grunt an' all, I'd watch youse guys up there, flyin' around, having a good time. And when I was out on point and youse guys would fly over to help us I'd just want to cheer. Saved my ass a bunch of times," he said. Then he looked at me with an inquisitive look, smiled a shy sincere smile, and added, "I always wanted to get together and party with youse guys, sir, and I figured this was a good way."

Sir! Usually when someone called me "sir" it

sounded more like a swear word than a title, but he actually said it with respect—and he wanted to party. I liked him right away.

"And it's got prestige," he continued on without encouragement. "You know, everyone respects the Scouts. And you get to come home and sleep above ground—I can dig it."

Cisco had plenty of combat experience and lots of experience with the M60 and M79, which helped in trying out for door gunner, and the next statement he made confirmed that he was crazy enough for the job. "Yeah, I had to extend my tour to fly Scouts," he said. "No kiddin', when I told my company commander I wanted to extend to fly Scouts he sent me to the chaplain."

Our newest door gunner moved his gear in with Loomis, a door gunner for the colonel's helicopter, and the next day we went up for a tryout. He was a good shot, and I felt he was going to be a great door gunner once he got used to shooting out of a helicopter. He wasn't as cool and calm as Wolfman, but he was not afraid of getting shot at, loved the flying, didn't get sick in tight turns, and he could shoot as well as anyone I had flown with. The only problem I had with Cisco was getting him to stop calling me "sir."

The first couple of times he called me "sir" I let it pass because it was good for my ego, but up in the air, at the end of every sentence over the intercom, it was getting to be too much. Not only was it wearing on my nerves, but our LOH was no place for the typical officer-enlisted man relationship. I didn't want him relying on me to make decisions. On our way back to Tay Ninh from our training flight I tactfully tried to explain this to him.

"Cisco, you know in Scouts the door gunners don't have to call the pilots sir," I told him over the intercom.

"OK, sir," he said.

"Actually, Cisco, I'd rather you call me Atom, or Tom, or anything," I tried again.

"Yes, sir," he replied as if he had not heard a word I had said.

"Don't call me, sir," I yelled over the intercom.

"OK, sir," he came back meekly.

I didn't know whether to laugh or cry, but he was not getting my message. "If you *ever* call me sir again I will land wherever we are and leave you there," I told him, in as menacing a tone as I could muster.

Shortly after Cisco started flying Scouts full-time Little Buddy finished his tour of duty and went home. I hated it when my friends reached their DEROS. For those of us left behind it was almost as bad as losing our friends to enemy fire—he was gone and that was that. It was a personal loss that left me feeling empty and ever more alone.

Cisco made it easier to take. Not only was he becoming a great door gunner, he also had a sense of humor. If he was not talking about "chicks," he was trying out one quip after another. Cisco liked Scouts so much he brought in a friend of his, Ogre, who started flying door gunner with us. Ogre was able to move into Cisco's hooch the third week he was in the company because Loomis got an early out. Loomis had been standing right beside the colonel's Huey, shut down on LZ Christine, when an NVA mortar came in and landed right at his feet. The Huey didn't even get a scratch and no one else was injured, but the shrapnel from the mortar tore Loomis to pieces.

That third week in October I had my hands full; Spud and I were the only Scout pilots. We flew every day, getting shot at every time we went up. When I was not flying missions I was trying out new door gunners or training our new Scout pilot, Spud's buddy, Loftin. Crab was still down in Vung Tau, the lucky SOB, and I really missed him. I had always looked to Crab for advice and support, not only because he had a few more weeks of experience than I did, but because he knew what he was doing.

Loftin—he wanted to be called "Lofty"—had potential, I thought, but he had a major ego problem. A good-looking guy, he was completely absorbed in himself and the role of being a cool Army pilot. He dressed neatly, not the usual military starch, but aviator cool, and even walked with a swagger. His mustache was neatly twisted up at the ends, and I am sure he would have worn an ascot if it had not been so damned hot. He could fly a helicopter well enough, but underneath all the show was a high-strung young man who too often lost control.

After Cisco had flown with Lofty I asked him what he thought about our newest pilot. "He's a trip, isn't he, Atom? How the hell does he keep his hair combed so neat after eight hours in a LOH?" he asked. Cisco thought about it for a minute and then said, "And I think he's flyin' Scouts more to be with his buddy Spud than because he digs it."

No sooner had I gotten Lofty trained and flying with Spud than we got another volunteer Scout pilot, a guy named Duck. He was a lot like Crab, had good control, and compared to the skittishness of Lofty, he was a pleasure to fly with. However, it really didn't matter whom I was flying with on training missions;

I was glad when they were over and I could devote my attention to regular missions again.

On 20 October, southwest of LZ Ike, once again I broke the golden rule I had been preaching during the weeks of training missions just completed—don't get low and slow. A company of infantry, making their way through the torn-up jungle left behind by an arc-light, requested a Scout team. When Spud and I arrived the company was strung out in the first hundred yards of the arc-light clearing and were pinned down by sniper fire from the front and both sides. We checked out the trail they had come in on and then advised the company commander that there were no enemy behind him and that his best bet would be to pull out the way he had come in.

"No can do," he said over the FM radio. "Got two boys badly wounded up at point. Can't get back by themselves. How many gooks we got up there?"

We made a few quick passes, and from the amount of fire we took we guessed that at least fifty or more very hostile NVA had them pinned down. There was no way they could move up, get the wounded, and pull back without suffering more casualties. After a few calls we got the Air Force to send us two jets loaded with napalm, which was good for dropping on the enemy when they are close to friendly troops.

After the Air Force dropped their ordinance, we flew down the smoking tree line to see if things had calmed down. From the amazing amount of fire we took again, it seemed that there were more NVA there than before the air strikes. Spud and I were running out of ideas and we had only enough fuel to stay on station for fifteen minutes. The chances of getting the wounded men out were looking slimmer all the time. Something had to be done; besides that

I was famished and the mess hall was going to be closed within the hour.

Without really thinking I radioed the company commander, "I'm goin' in for the wounded."

All that came back over the radio was an incredulous "What?"

I can't remember who my door gunner was that day, but I do remember him coming over the intercom as we headed down into the tangle of downed trees of the arc-light: "This isn't funny, you know we could . . ."

He was cut short as we started taking fire from both sides of the clearing. He returned fire with his M60, and I let off a few bursts with the minigun. As we came to a hover over the wounded soldiers, the hostile fire was blocked from the sides by some large trees piled against each other. Some dirt-and-sweat-soaked grunts threw one of the wounded up front with me as we started taking fire from straight ahead of us. The soldiers around me opened up, I leveled the minigun, and together we hosed down the trees about two hundred feet off my nose. An NVA soldier fell out of one of the trees, and the shooting slowed down while my door gunner helped load the other wounded soldier in the back with him.

After a quick cross-check of my engine instruments I looked up at the tree line off our nose, started to pull in power and plan my climb back out, but my plans fell apart as my eyes focused on a projectile coming straight at us, very fast. At first I had no idea what it was. It looked dark and pretty big, and it wavered a little as it closed on us. What gave it away was the propellant and exhaust spreading out behind it as it homed in on my head. It was a B-40 rocket, the first one I had seen shot directly at me.

In a desperate attempt to get out of the rocket's path I pulled in all available power, knowing that the aircraft would barely have time to move a foot in the few seconds it took the B-40 to cross the clearing to us. As I watched in amazement the projectile snaked toward us and right on by, less than a yard from my door.

I have no idea what happened to the B-40 after it missed us. Nothing made sense for a few seconds because I was still waiting for the rocket to hit us. The great god of lunch must have been watching over us that day because we got out of there with only a few new bullet holes in the tail boom and were back at Tay Ninh before the mess hall closed.

Usually the trip home after an incident like that would have been spent in an endless cycle of euphoria and self-incrimination, but that day I was kept too busy by the wounded soldier in the seat beside me. He had been thrown in without being buckled into his seat belt and shoulder harness, and he kept flopping over onto my left arm. Every time he fell on my arm his weight pushed the collective down and forced us dangerously low to the tops of the trees. I was pushing him up for the hundredth time, it seemed, when his weight seemed to quadruple and the cockpit filled with the smell of excrement—he was dead. It was amazing how heavy he became and how hard it was to get him up off the collective. I ended up yanking on the dead man's hair, cursing him for trying to kill us, as I fought to pull him off the collective—it was perverse.

For the rest of the day I sat in the officers' club trying to find something in my job or myself that could get me to go fly Scouts again.

Just as I thought I was not going to make it, Crab

got back. Somewhere he had found a little white stray puppy, and the two of them came strolling in the door together.

"Atom, meet Frederick Bauser," he said. Crab and his mangy puppy were a welcome change. I took a few days off and relaxed.

With Crab back we had two Scout teams, our workload was reduced, and for a few weeks life seemed to go by uneventfully. When Captain Crane sent Ski for me, I was surprised, not having been in trouble for weeks. Reasonably expecting the worst, I was pleasantly surprised when I walked into his office and found him all smiles. "Here's a little something for your efforts, Smith," he said, handing me a piece of paper.

Award of the Distinguished Flying Cross

For heroism while participating in aerial flight evidenced by voluntary action on 20 October 1969, while serving as aircraft commander of an observation helicopter during a reconnaissance mission in Tay Ninh Province, Republic of Vietnam. When a friendly company made contact with an unknown size of enemy force in bunkers and trees they requested and received the support of an aerial Scout team to assist in their maneuver. During the active exchange of fire, Warrant Officer Smith, flying at treetop level, relayed key information to the ground commander. He spotted and marked enemy locations for tactical fighter air strikes, and even though his reconnaissance mission was completed, he voluntarily offered his assistance to the ground commander in order to evacuate two seriously wounded soldiers. With great skill, Warrant Officer Smith maneuvered his aircraft to a location where the wounded could be lifted onto the aircraft. Before the second man

could be placed on the ship, they began receiving
fire from snipers. Without regard for his own safety
Warrant Officer Smith remained at a low hover while
his gunner and ground troops placed suppressive fire
into the trees so that the second soldier could be
loaded onto the ship. His outstanding flying ability
and devotion to duty is in keeping with the highest
traditions of the military service, and reflects great
credit upon himself, his unit and the United States
Army.

The award hit hard. I had no idea I had been put
in for a medal. It was almost embarrassing, and
at the same time one of the proudest moments of
my life.

A copy of my citation made it to *Stars and Stripes;*
and they ran the following article a few weeks
later:

> November 26, 1969
>
> *Tay Ninh*—It's not often that you find one aircraft
> performing low-level reconnaissance, MEDEVAC and
> ammo resupply all within a matter of thirty minutes.
> Particularly not a LOH.
>
> Unusual though it may be, all three missions were
> performed by a 1st Air Cavalry Scout helicopter pi-
> loted by Warrant Officer Thomas Smith . . . a pint-
> sized 22-year-old Scout pilot for the 1st Brigade's
> Aviation Platoon. . . . The action possibly saved the
> lives of two Skytroopers and illustrated what flexi-
> bility and imagination can produce in airmobile oper-
> ations.

Better than the medal was meeting the captain of
the company I had helped in that arc-light. His company had gotten a stand-down (a week's break in

Tay Ninh from life in the field) and he caught up with me in the officers' club where I was sitting at the bar by myself, pondering the medicinal qualities of the amber glass of Jim Beam in front of me.

He sat down beside me and just stared at me for a while. The captain's bars on his collar and his level gaze made me a little nervous, but I figured at worst it would only be another lecture on military discipline. "I can tell by the tag on your fatigues that your name is Smith, but are you Warrant Officer Tom Smith?" he asked politely.

"Uh . . . Yes, sir," I replied as noncommittally as possible, trying to figure out what this guy could possibly want from me.

"I guess that jade bear paw where your rank insignia should be threw me off." He laughed.

Someone had sent me a tiepin made of jade and set in silver; it looked like a bear paw to me too. I decided it was a good luck piece and started wearing it on my collar where my warrant officer's bar should have been.

"Brings me luck," I told him.

He laughed again and said, "Well, it brought you and me both good luck back in October when you saved the lives of—I don't know how many of my men. I was commanding Delta Company 2d of the 5th, pinned down in an arc-light, and if I'm not mistaken, you're the guy who pulled our fat out of the fire." He gave me one of the nicest smiles I have ever seen. Without another word he put out his hand and we shook. "Thanks!" he said. God, it made me feel good.

Maybe it was the recognition for my efforts or perhaps it was coincidence, but the next day I wrote my

brother Norm, thanking him for his help while I had
been in Vietnam.

                              The 7th of November 1969
Dear Norm,
    Thank you very much for the letter and let me
apologize for not writing more often. Actually around
this point I have pretty much given up on writing
letters. All I have to think about is Vietnam and war,
and I really don't care too much about either. This
tends to limit creative or worthwhile letters. I really
want to thank you for the Nutriment. With school
and home and all it shows a lot of thought and effort
on your part, and I thank you.
    I really appreciate your letters and what you
have to say. In your letters and for at least the last
three years the things you have done and said
make me feel pretty good. They didn't always, but
as of late they have held, letters and memories, a
little more meaning for me and what is happening.
It appears to be a thought pattern, which down
here usually distinguishes between a man who
will get you and himself killed. It is not really a
matter of trying hard or being good down here. It
is more important to be current all the time. To do
it takes a lot of effort, especially on my part it
seems. It is work, mostly mental, and the only
thing that keeps me at it is a deep concern for the
life span of Tom Smith. You seem to work the same
way with most things. I can do it when it concerns
my life, but not livelihood. Are you sure you never
went to a war? Maybe it was all those good past-
war movies.
    Before I forget something that is quite important
to me. I was wondering if you had ever seen Sally
Daniels. If you have, send me a description, physical
and mental. She has been writing to me for a few
months, and you might say I am curious. This is
strictly confidential of course. . . .

Actually I had not told Norm the truth about not writing. Duck was flying full-time and leaving me more time to write letters. Consequently I started getting letters back. To quote a few of the letters I received from family and friends:

"How are you? Tonight President Nixon gave a speech on how he plans to end the war. I hope he hurries it up cause I really miss you so much."

"Remember, discretion is the better part of valor! You have to keep your ass out of the sling so that you can pick me up a shot gun and some lenses in Hong Kong."

"I hope you are able to keep some peace within yourself, even though you may be forced to do some ugly things. Peace."

"What about you dear Tommy, have you been able to feel the goodness of giving, maybe when you save a life?"

"Keep the Reds off our back lawn."

"I have your jacket—security Tom, really—and I listened to Led Zeppelin earlier, closed my eyes and just thought of you, your camp on the brook. . . ."

"You can do me a favor if you will. I have seen some small ceramic elephants, about 6 or 7 inches tall, made in RVN. I'd like to have a pair."

"Come home, I'll scratch your back, it's quiet here."

"I know you won't die because if you did it would kill part of me, and that's not possible because I won't let it happen."

"You write very good letters when you're stoned."

"Is that your home that you are standing in front of? If so, I hope that you aren't paying much rent."

"Peace and love for your mind."

Some were deeper than others:

"Tommy I learned something from your last letter. . . . In spite of all the protesting I've been doing and all the draft counseling I'm involved in . . . that you, Tom Smith, who has already been through more pain and suffering than one person should have to bear, can go out and time after time risk your life above and beyond what is necessary, just because you feel the panic of the wounded or the starving of the ammunitionless. God, Tom, you are beautiful and I think it is time the protesters stopped to look at the love and brotherhood that takes place among the troops and stop denying heroes their heroism, stop making them martyrs and killers when they return home. It's so different now, in my mind, it's all so different. Kind of a loving and peaceful feeling."

Some were weird:

"Wow, about that dream. It took place in the church at Keene Valley. . . . It was some sort of tribute to you and the whole service was unique because you were headless. . . ."

One brushed on a point that wore heavily on the minds of most combat soldiers in Vietnam:

> "We just received your letter on flying Scouts and I am glad to hear that they are not boring you to death over there. I have to say that besides being a little drunk, I am quite jealous of your exploits. If I could come over for a few days. . . ."

The key phrase in that letter was *come over for a few days*. Most able-bodied men, with an ego, would not mind proving themselves in combat for a few days. A lot of my peers who didn't go to Vietnam even thought a year's tour of duty wouldn't be all that tough because it was only for one year. No one, not even the designers of the one-year tour of duty for each soldier, had any idea what the mental effects of a limited tour of duty would be.

In previous wars a soldier usually could not go home until his side won or lost. This gave him incentive to win, to do his job and continue to do it well because the sooner his army won, the sooner he could go home, along with everyone else. No one in Vietnam thought the war would end in the one year they were going to be there. Also, it was hard to justify getting killed in a war we knew we could not win.

In Vietnam, as in any war, the new soldier did not know what he was doing and was even dangerous. In a few months he developed the skills necessary to be productive, reliable, and to get himself home. But in Vietnam, as a soldier got closer to his DEROS, he became increasingly aware that he didn't have to use his skills in order to get home, he just had to stay alive X number of days. For the last few months of their tour, most of the men in combat zones were paranoid wrecks from the knowledge that all they had to do was just stay alive for a few more days and they would be home. A lot of men started worrying about making it to their last "wake-up" from the first day they arrived in Vietnam; they suffered.

Instead of soldiers feeling relieved that they only had to stay alive one year, most felt that every day was a death sentence until the year was over. On top of the mental stress of the one-year tour, they had to suffer the ever-increasing weight of those fears by themselves. Everyone had a different DEROS depending on when they arrived in country. Each man was in his own boat, alone.

I was still too far away from my last wake-up to be involved in the DEROS-paranoia syndrome, but I had developed a few mental disorders of my own. One was a kind of schizophrenia; one minute I would be calm, going about my job in a rational way, and the next would find me trying to kill the enemy with a lust that defied reason. An example was the time Cisco and I were on our way out to LZ Jamie to check out some enemy contact they'd had.

We were skimming the tops of the trees at a hundred-plus knots when we came upon a wide field stretching across our flight path. As we dropped down into the clearing and started across, just a few feet above the ground, Cisco suddenly yelled over the intercom, "Gook in the open, one o'clock," and started blasting away with his M60.

The lone NVA soldier was a hundred yards in front of us, running for the tree line on the other side of the field. When Cisco's rounds started hitting around him he dove into a clump of bushes a couple of hundred feet short of his objective. As we flew by his cover Cisco filled the bushes with M60 slugs. We checked out the tree line to make sure he was alone and then flew back over to see if we could find the body. As we went over, still doing a hundred knots, the fearless guy opened up on us. I dodged his fire while Cisco shot back. We made two more passes and each time it was the same.

Finally Cisco said, "Atom, he's got to have a bunker in there. No way that brush cover could stop me from hitting him. Let's drop a few grenades on him." A little risky, I thought, but we had to get him. It should have been an easy kill and he had come really close to hitting us on each of our passes; I could feel my anger rising.

We flew right over him and Cisco dropped a grenade in the bushes. He was shooting at us as we flew over, then there was the dull thud of the grenade detonating, followed by the popping sound of his AK-47 shooting at us as we flew away.

"That little prick is unreal," I told Cisco.

I was so mad, there was no way we were going to leave there until he stopped shooting at us. On the next pass Cisco's grenade landed close enough to do some damage. He came reeling out of the bushes, blood running down the side of his head, arms flailing about—he was obviously out of his mind. I laid the LOH over on its side and dove down right behind him, hugging the ground. When I closed to within twenty feet of the frantic, fleeing figure, I squeezed the trigger and hit him in the back with a burst of four thousand rounds a minute from the minigun. The impact drove him to the ground, leaving behind a haze of blood and flesh, which splattered the Plexiglas front of the helicopter as we sped over his mutilated body.

11

What Luck

Late November 1969

Spud and I were on our way back to Tay Ninh for more fuel when we got a radio call that a company of ARVNs was being beaten up by the NVA not far from where we were. Operations told us to go over and see if we could help them out.

We found them and established radio contact with the American advisor on the ground with the ARVNs. "We're pinned down," he said. "If you can find a hole in their line we might be able to get back into the jungle and outmaneuver them." The ARVNs were strung out in the trees along the side of a field and the NVA held the jungle in front of them.

Our aircraft were getting low on fuel but had plenty of minigun ammo left, so Spud suggested we strafe a section of the jungle in front of the ARVNs, try to blast a hole for them, and then head home. He called the American advisor, told him our plan, and asked him where he would like us to strafe. "I'll pop smoke, hit them real hard on a zero-one-zero-degree heading from the smoke, might be able to get through," he came back.

On the second pass he told us that it was working, a lot of the NVA were pulling back from the area we were strafing, but there was still a pocket of NVA off on the right. Spud and I each had enough ammo for one more pass; Spud went first. After he was done I called the advisor to see if he wanted me to make my strafing run in the same spot. Instead of the American advisor on the radio, a South Vietnamese soldier came on. It went something like this:

"Two-four, you want me to strafe the same spot or move it over some?"

"You keep shooting, please?" he said in pidgin English.

"Two-four, who's this? Where is the advisor I was talking to?" I asked.

"He hurt bad, very bad. You shoot over there please, on right, OK?" was all I could get out of the ARVN soldier on the ground.

"Which right? Right of the last run or right of the smoke?" I asked, not wanting to waste my last rounds.

"Yes right, OK?" was all the ARVN said.

By this time I was getting dangerously low on fuel and Spud was telling me he was running on fumes. Once again I lost my head, but this time it was more of an attempt to kill myself than the enemy.

"Show me where, where you want fire put down," I yelled at the ARVN on the radio. I was flying so low and slow that I could plainly see the man with the radio on his back, speaking into a handheld microphone.

"Point," I tried again, as we moved slowly over him. He looked up at us, smiled, and waved. "Jesus Christ," I said to myself, and to him I radioed, "Point where, show where!"

Up until then we had not been shot at when we were over the ARVN positions, so I was not too worried about keeping my airspeed up. Exasperated, I brought my LOH to a hover twenty feet above the

ARVN's head, got his attention, let go of the controls for a second with my right hand, and demonstrated how to point. As I finished my demonstration and grabbed for the cyclic, I looked off toward where we had been strafing, just in time to see an NVA soldier stand up from behind a fallen tree.

As I watched, he brought an old SKS bolt-action rifle to his shoulder and then lurched backward. In the same instant that it dawned on me that he had shot at us, my right foot flew off the tail rotor pedal. Several weeks later the incident was reported in the *Stars and Stripes*.

December 3, 1969

Tay Ninh—"I'm hit, man, I'm hit." This frantic reply came from Warrant Officer Smith, 1st Brigade Scout pilot, in answer to his wingman.

Warrant Officer McNeil, piloting the other light observation helicopter of the Scout team, was justifiably concerned when he saw Smith's aircraft dive sharply to the left, headed for the scrub jungle below.

"I knew I was in trouble when my right foot was suddenly knocked up in front of my face, instead of being on the pedal where it should have been," said Mr. Smith.

Smith and McNeil were flying reconnaissance in support of fierce contact involving the 114th Company, 11th ARVN Airborne Battalion, about 20 miles north of Tay Ninh.

"For a minute I thought the aircraft was out of control, and I would have to put it down in one of the open areas," said Mr. Smith.

Tightening up on the throttle, Smith and his team headed instead for Tay Ninh's 45th Surgical Hospital for treatment of his wound.

"I could feel a sort of dull ache in my heel, not very painful, just numb," said Mr. Smith.

With the 20-minute flight from the jungles to the

hospital completed, Smith was in the treatment room pulling off his right boot.

"Not a scratch," said the doctor to the unbelieving pilot. An X-ray confirmed the diagnosis.

Further investigation revealed a bullet hole in the radio compartment of the LOH, just under the pilot's seat, and a slightly bent protective metal plate in the heel of Smith's jungle boot.

The first part of the flight to the 45th Surgical Hospital I had kept thinking, "He shot me. That son of a bitch shot me, and I just watched him do it." Not once did I consider going back after him. The second part of the flight I forgot all about it when I considered the positive aspects of getting shot in the foot.

A bullet in the foot was the helicopter pilot's million-dollar wound. A hit in the foot, a relatively minor part of the body, meant that you would not be able to fly for months and would be sent home. I had visions of myself, rocked back in the seat of a Boeing 707 with cocktail in hand, grinning back at Saigon as we took off for San Francisco. There were stories of pilots flying around with their foot hanging out the door, hoping for just such a wound.

When the doctor at the 45th told me there was no bullet wound in my foot, I asked him, "Are you sure the wound isn't self-sealing? Maybe there's no blood because the skin closed over the bullet hole. Take another look, will you?" He looked at me as if I were nuts, but was nice enough to take an X ray.

It was frustrating getting shot, actually seeing the guy shoot me, and not having anything to show for it except the bent slug I found on the helicopter floor. I wasn't even helping our own troops. I didn't dislike the ARVNs, but it was hard enough fighting for our troops, much less the disorganized troops of the corrupt, puppet government of Nguyen Van Thieu.

Maybe someone knew I didn't like working with the South Vietnamese because a week or so later we were called into the TOC where a short, fat major told us that the Scouts were going to start pulling random ID checks of civilians in the agricultural areas around Tay Ninh. The purpose of these missions was to catch NVA or VC trying to sneak into Tay Ninh in disguise. I could not help thinking, "Disguised as what? Vietnamese?"

On our way out to the flight line Cisco said, "Hey, this ID check-in, could be a good way to meet chicks, y'know."

The first people we decided to investigate were two groups of men walking along a rice paddy dike. Duck, who was flying the other LOH that day, said he would take the first group. Cisco and I circled the second group and came to a hover almost on top of them, kicking up dirt and small rocks as the thirty-mile-an-hour winds from the helicopter's rotor wash whipped around them.

The saucer-shaped straw hat of the man nearest me flew off his head and cartwheeled away in the wind, revealing the terrified face of an eighty-year-old man. The wind flattened his black cotton clothes over his emaciated old body and whipped dirt into his face. As I watched in horror the old man fell to his knees and put his gnarled old hands up to protect his eyes; he was so weak and scared. "Fuck this!" I said to Cisco and took off. It was bad enough killing the enemy in combat—I could not terrorize old men at work. The same old men who long months ago I thought I was defending.

Things were changing so fast around Tay Ninh

that it should not have surprised me when I got a letter from Aunt Kitty in the second week of November saying she, Uncle Pat, and two sisters-in-law were planning to visit me in Vietnam.

> Dear Tom,
>   I am going to Bangkok the end of February, and have been wondering what the chances are of seeing you. . . . I believe we get to Bangkok on the 30th and attend the International Council of Women's meeting from January 31st through February 12th. . . . I found out yesterday that we can even come to Saigon, but I'll have to wait until I hear from you.

Aunt Kitty was serving as the Vice President and United Nations representative of the National Council of Women, an organization that represented various women's organizations throughout the country. Every three years the National Council of Women met with their counterparts from some ninety countries around the world. This year they were meeting in Bangkok. I wrote her back and said I would love to see them in Saigon; assuming I was still around.

It was unbelievable that Aunt Kitty and Uncle Pat could come visit me while I was in the war, but I was getting used to hearing things from back home that were impossible to believe. For instance it was impossible to believe what Nixon was telling the people back home about the war in Vietnam. The *Stars and Stripes* had the witless audacity to quote him as saying we were winning the war; and even more preposterous, that we were winning the hearts and minds of the people.

One day while walking around the grizzly aftermath of an LZ overrun by the NVA I picked up one of the leaflets the NVA had left behind.

Officers and Men in the 1st Air Cav. Div.

Why does Nixon always mouth peace and the withdrawal of US troops home yet the Air Cav. Div. is still stretched out along a line of more than 200km in these dense, rough and dangerous jungles?

Why do you, day to day allow yourselves to be helilifted to remote strange and dangerous areas and never got back all safe?

Sure Nixon doesn't live up to his words!

Don't let the war-like ruling clique continues to deceive you and misuse your blood and sweat any more.

Be resolute and take action promtly:

—Refuse any operation orders!

—Demand withdrawal of cavalrymen an all US troops home

—Let the Vietnamese people settle their own affairs themselves!

Don't be the last man to die a worthless death in the last battle in Vietnam!

No denying they had a point. With the student demonstrations raising many fundamental questions about the values of the Vietnam War, only the most fanatical military mentalities in our midst thought the war was worth dying for. I knew I did not want to die a "worthless death" in Vietnam; however, days later I came as close as you can get. In fact Slater and I came real close several times within a few long minutes.

First we made the mistake of flying right through the middle of a helicopter trap. Three heavy machine guns opened up on us from three sides as we flew across the jungle trees—we didn't stand a chance. They hit us so quickly, I didn't even see a tracer round before I felt the impact of the large-caliber slugs. There is no telling how many times they hit us. Usually when we took hits, it would be a bullet here and a bullet there, each one making its own thunk as it hit the helicopter. This time it sounded like a hailstorm of copper slugs ripping away our thin fuselage.

Some of the first rounds went through the compressor section of the engine. The sound of the steel compressor blades, rotating at thousands of rpm's and broken loose by the slugs, was unmistakable as they ripped through the engine and engine compartment.

My training was to check my engine instruments to confirm that our engine had been hit, but I never got a chance to. There was an explosion behind me and the aircraft gave a violent shudder. Almost simultaneously, an orange ball of fire rolled over the bulkhead and across the cockpit from the left. I had just enough time to close my eyes before the fireball rolled over my face, burned off my mustache, and left me with the distinct impression that my mouth was full of light, spongy, angel-food cake. The sensation of angel-food cake was in fact the fire burning the oxygen out of my open, probably screaming, mouth.

An incendiary round had penetrated the fuel input tube, igniting the trapped fumes. The ensuing explosion blew the right side of the aircraft (just behind Slater) apart, releasing the small fireball that swept through the passenger compartment.

The fire disappeared as quickly as it came, but the heat of the flash fire had melted the synthetic nape strap of my helmet into the back of my neck. The pain of the plastic burning on my skin was so intense that I let go of the controls, ripped my helmet off, and threw it out the open door beside me. It almost hit Slater, who had left his burning backseat and climbed outside onto the skid and up to my door.

He was holding on to the door frame beside me, staring at me with one of the most wide-eyed, confused expressions I have ever seen. Slater's glasses were gone and his eyes seemed to bug out more than usual as he stared at me, speechless. When he saw that I'd thrown my helmet out the door he reacted instantly, ripping his helmet off with one hand and throwing it away too. He must have thought it was what everyone did when they caught on fire.

Slater's simple action, irrational as it might have been, broke him out of his momentary shock, and he started yelling in my ear, "It's burning, the whole goddamned ship is burning. Atom, we're on fire!"

I knew we were on fire, but what Slater didn't know was that our engine was out and we were losing lift. If we crashed in the trees on fire we were done for. Fortunately we had been flying into the setting sun when we were hit, and I caught the glint of sunlight on water through the trees off our nose. Instead of putting down the collective to save the remaining rotor rpm for an autorotation into the trees, as we had been conditioned to do since flight school, I held the collective up, gambling that we would make it over the tree line and to the water before our decreasing rotor rpm let us fall from the sky.

I took this gamble, risking our ability to do a successful autorotation through the trees, because I knew that a burning helicopter often blew up at the end of an autorotation, as Pokey's had done. As long as the burning aircraft was flying, the wind would keep the flames back behind the helicopter and our chances of exploding were reduced. If we could just get to the water and do a run-on landing we might make it, I thought.

We broke over the tree line with the blades turning slowly enough to see them individually, but it didn't matter because, as hoped, there was a nice, soft, watery bog stretched out in front of us. I nosed the burning helicopter over, dove to the water, and just before we hit, leveled it for a running landing. As the skids dipped in the water I turned to Slater and yelled, *"Jump!"* which he did without hesitation.

The belly of the aircraft hit the water, bounced, and slid along for another hundred feet before the drag of the minigun rolled the helicopter over onto its left side, bringing it to a stop. As it rolled over, the rotor blades hit the water and the machine thrashed violently about as they bounced and broke up on the water's surface.

I could hear my instructor back in flight school warning us: *You only have seconds before you drown.* I grabbed the right door frame and started to pull myself up and out the open door. That is when I should have paused to remember the rest of my flight instructor's ditching-at-sea instructions: *but whatever you do, wait until the blades stop turning before you try getting out.*

The broken rotor blades were still whipping around, sometimes only a foot above my door, as I tried to climb out of the sinking helicopter. Fortunately, halfway out, the cyclic, still thrashing about between my legs, hooked me and pulled me back into the cockpit. I would have certainly been killed. Stunned by the events of the last few minutes, I simply sat there in my seat, crumpled and dazed, not hearing or feeling anything.

I didn't want to move, but the helicopter was settling and within seconds water was swirling around my left foot and over the radio console beside my left elbow. Grabbing the door frame once again, I pulled myself out of the sinking machine and into the glare of the setting sun. The helicopter was lying on its left side, almost underwater, as I climbed out and stood on the door frame. In my dazed state, knowing only that I did not want to get burned again, all I could think to do was a simple sailor's dive, headfirst into the water a foot below my feet— straight to the bottom of the swamp.

I wasn't even aware that my steel chest protector had dragged me to the bottom, but my arms and legs knew because they flailed about in a reflexive effort to swim back to the surface. Unfortunately the weight of my chicken plate held me like a magnet on the murky bottom. As my oxygen supply dwindled my swimming efforts began to atrophy and a welcome calmness began to settle out of the panic and confusion. I suppose that is when my life should have flashed before me, but instead only one thought popped into my mind: So this is it?

Then I stood up. I have no recollection of thinking about it, I just stood up in water that was only four feet deep. The first thing I saw was Crab and his door gunner hovering about twenty feet away, laughing at me. As I stood there trying to figure out what they were laughing at, Slater swam up beside me I understood. We looked like very startled, half-drowned rats.

Crab hovered over and we crawled up the skids into his ship and rode to the 45th Surgical Hospital where they put patches on the little shrapnel holes in my legs and shoulder, some ointment on my

burned neck, and shaved off the charred stubble of
my mustache. Slater had a few burns and a couple
of shrapnel holes also. Crab had not taken one hit
because he had been flying far enough behind me to
swing around the helicopter trap after the shooting
started.

A contributing factor to our getting shot down was
the Army's plan to deforest the jungle with Agent
Orange. The idea was that defoliating the triple-
canopy jungle would expose the enemy; unfortunately the opposite was true. As planned, the chemical killed all the vegetation right down to the ground,
but within a month or so the first layer of growth
returned, leaving the enemy all the cover they
needed and a forest of dead trees above them. The
barren trees, over two hundred feet tall, kept us exposed to their guns, with no place to take cover.

It was bad enough having everyone in the jungle
trying to kill us without the Army helping them, but
with the bad comes the good. The good was that the
burns on my neck got me grounded for a couple
of weeks—letting me have some desperately needed
time off.

For days I had trouble focusing on anything. Getting shot in the foot had been much less of an ordeal
than going down on fire. The bullet hit me almost
without warning and then it was over, whereas getting shot down on fire took forever and exposed me
to fears I had only imagined. Bad dreams plagued
me at night and during the day almost everything—
smells, sounds, and the pain of my burned neck—
brought back vivid recollections of the fusillade of
bullets hitting the ship, the engine coming apart, the
fire, crashing, and worst of all, almost letting myself drown.

It was not until Spud was shot down, five days after our crash, that I broke away from my preoccupation with our near-death experience. Spud was checking out a bunker that wasn't as deserted as he thought—an instant later he and his door gunner Ben were on the ground, burning. His good friend Lofty was flying cover for him and watched the whole horrifying crash.

"The entire ship just burst into flames, smoke pouring out the doors. God, it just blew up and went out of control," Lofty said, his voice trembling even though he had finished off the best part of a bottle of Scotch. "It burned forever. . . . Then Ben crawled out of the flames. I thought Spud was dead for sure. His LOH just kept burning . . . but then Ben must have seen him. He ran back into the fire and pulled him out." Lofty took another pull on the Scotch bottle. "The bastards kept shooting at us the whole time."

It was a bad crash. Later we found out that Ben had been hit in the shoulder and leg with small-arms fire and filled full of shrapnel. The shrapnel came from one of the grenades in the box beside him that got hit by NVA fire. The explosion filled Ben and the fuel cell below him full of holes. Spud was also hit and the helicopter went down on fire, exploding on impact.

At the 45th Surgical Hospital they went to work on Spud, but there was not much they could do for his severe burns, and they sent him to the larger 24th Evacuation Hospital in Long Binh. When they took a look at Ben, who was standing around after having helped Spud into the hospital, they found two bullet holes and some forty shrapnel wounds from the grenade.

We found out later that Spud had not died from his wounds, but we never found out what happened to Ben. Ben was the quietest person I had known in Vietnam, strong and silent—the most dependable kind of hero.

12

Time Out

Early December 1969

Spud and Ben's horrible crash made my mind up for me—no more Scouts. Losing two LOHs in five days, both shot down on fire (one with me in it) was too much. I was not alone in my reluctance to get back into Scouts.

Lofty would not go near a LOH. For a couple of days he seemed to be all right, a little depressed maybe, but slowly he started to deteriorate. He became irritable, erratic in his speech and mannerisms, and started drinking excessively. Before long he was really out of it, flitting about the compound with a false gaiety that was scary. At one point he did try to go back up flying cover for Crab, but the next day announced he was switching to Command and Control.

I would have been flying Command and Control right along with him if it were not for being grounded for my burned neck, a wound that not only got me out of combat, but set me up for a trip to the Philippines. Occasionally the company received slots for various schools, like the LOH school in Vung Tau that Crab had attended. The schools were designed to round out an officer's knowledge and skills but were usually viewed more as a paid vacation. Our company had an opening for jungle survival school in the Philippines. As I couldn't fly, they decided to send me.

My orders were cut, and on 26 November I got a ride down to Tan Son Nhut, catching the first flight to Manila. The first two days I spent in the officers' club at Clark Air Force Base, drinking and playing cards with a bunch of jet pilots who had flown in Vietnam. They kept buying my drinks as long as I would tell them stories of the destruction their bombs left on the ground.

The third day a group of us, officers from all around the Pacific, boarded a bus and went to Subic Point, a naval base where the survival school was held. Once again evening found me seated in the officers' club, having even more fun than I'd had back at Clark. The bar wasn't much, concrete and linoleum, but set out in the middle of the floor was the cockpit of a jet mounted on small railroad tracks. At one end of the tracks was an enormous spring, which catapulted the cockpit down the rails to the other end of the bar and into a pool of water.

The occupant of the cockpit had one very small chance to stop himself by dropping a hook and catching a partially exposed brake wire before he hit the water. The whole point of this contraption was to let the fighter pilots show off the skills they had acquired in aircraft carrier landings, but it seemed to me like a pointless exercise. The only pilot who caught the cable while I was there got a short round of applause, and then was thrown in the pool by his rowdy friends.

Bright and early the next morning our survival training commenced. They gave each of us ten students a small rubberized poncho, a poncho liner, and an eight-inch knife. That was it except for the clothes on our backs, and a Negrito pygmy as a guide. Then we were told that we would be spending the next two days and nights out in the jungle, guests of the short guy.

For the next forty-eight hours we dined on exotic foods harvested from the trees, found hiding under rocks in streams, and dug from the ground. Our wild rice was steamed in a pressure cooker made from a cleverly fashioned length of bamboo. After our meals we would wash up with a root that, once it had been debarked and beaten with a rock, looked like a luffa sponge, complete with a lather of white suds. Amidst the cackles, calls, and cries of the jungle night, we slept well in our poncho hammocks. Our four-foot-tall teacher removed any doubts about our being able to survive—that is, if we knew our jungle, its flora and fauna, and did not have to get anywhere else in a hurry.

At one point when our pygmy guide was explaining the medicinal properties of some roots and vines in his hands, I had to wonder if his concoctions were for real. A few hours later an Army lieutenant from California sliced his hand open between the thumb and index finger. Our host bound the incision, which was easily half an inch deep, with his local medicines. Thirty hours later when the bandage was removed back at Subic, the cut appeared completely healed.

The entire survival experience was fascinating, and while in Manila I took care of all my Christmas shopping—and fell in love with a teenage prostitute. The only unpleasant part of the trip was getting on the plane back to Tay Ninh. A sign in the Vietnamese arrival terminal greeted me: WELCOME TO VIÊTNAM

AND ITS CHARMING TRADITIONS. The only tradition I could think of was their four hundred years of war.

When I got back to the 1st Brigade my mailbox was full. One of the letters was from my brother Peter.

> Dear Tom:
>   I have been trying to think of what to send you since I can't send Wild Turkey thru the mail. Everyone says people in Vietnam like food so I am sending you a hundred pounds of rice. . . .
>   I was listed in the newspaper *St. Croix Avis* as being a delinquent draftee so I thought it was about time I went to a physical. . . . I went over and took the physical, and when it came to the time where I talked to the doctor I told him about my knee and he fooled around with it and told me to go to the hearing test. I thought I was halfway to drinking rice wine with you in Vietnam, but at the end of the physical I was given a slip that said I had flunked. . . . When I got to thinking about it I felt that maybe it wouldn't be such a bad life from your description, but I think I will go meet Macy in Aspen. I must say it is a burden having to uphold the fuck-off image without your help so get back here and give me a hand.

Peter was on his way to getting his doctorate in nuclear engineering. He loved his sciences, spending the greater part of every day buried in technical books, but when he was not studying he knew how to have a good time. On this level we had a lot in common and were brothers and good friends. Peter, however, was not much for writing letters or doing anything for me while I was in Vietnam.

He was totally unlike my oldest brother, Norm, who had been more of an antagonist than a friend over the last twenty years. Now Norm was taking care of my business affairs, sending me Nutriment, writing four or five times a month with news from home, and giving me support. It must have been a pain in the butt for him to haul a case of Nutriment down to the post office every other week.

While I was in the Philippines, the Republic of Vietnam awarded me their Vietnamese Cross of Gallantry for the time I got shot in the foot trying to help them out. My feelings toward the ARVN soldiers had changed considerably over the months. This wasn't owing to any new insights concerning their courage or abilities in combat, but because of something a major had told me in the officers' club one night.

"I was in Korea for that stinkin' war. The Koreans couldn't fight worth a damn. Just like our ARVN pals here," he said. "But you know what? I worked with the Koreans just a few months ago, over by the Triangle, and they were some ass-kickin' little dudes." It made sense that given the proper incentive, training, and time the ARVNs would evolve into a respectable fighting force, just as the Koreans had.

Korea, Australia, and a few other countries had sent token forces to Vietnam in support of the American effort. The Koreans were by far the toughest fighters of the lot, but as far as I was concerned no one topped the Australians for trying the hardest.

We got to work with some Australian pilots one afternoon when we took a little fire from a bunker complex we had been exploring. When we called for an air strike we got some Aussies flying two Canberras instead of the usual U.S. Air Force jets.

"White Scouts, Canberra four with you. What've you got down there for a target today?" they called after they had arrived on station.

"Canberra four, White two-four, a bunker complex,

with recent signs of activity. Took a little fire in there," I informed him, looking up at the Canberra's profile. They looked like some of the jet bombers the Germans built toward the end of World War II.

"Bunkers? Good, these old girls like those stationary targets. Not very sophisticated machines," he said lightly. "Takes longer lining things up, but we'll hit 'em."

They did not have a forward air controller, so we marked the target for them while they circled at four thousand feet. After locating the target they moved off to the south and started their bomb run. They came lumbering along in their big old twin-engine bombers at what appeared to be less than a hundred miles an hour. Then, to our amazement, they descended to two thousand feet, flying straight and level at the target well within small-arms range. As they came over the target and dropped a pair of bombs the jungle erupted in light machine gun fire. Through the whole ordeal their course never wavered.

"Canberra four, two-four, be advised you guys are taking boo koo [slang for beaucoup] small-arms fire," I said, wondering if they were still alive up there.

"Roger that, mate, not much choice, old bombsight, takes time," the Aussie pilot came back, without a hint of fear in his voice.

"Canberra four, two-four, how about picking up the altitude," I tried, unable to believe he was so serious about a couple of bunkers.

"Negative on that, two-four, bombsight again," he called back, actually laughing about it. "Not that accurate for small targets. Got to get down low to hit anything at all."

They made the same pattern, got the same amount

of small-arms fire, and the whole thing started over again. I could not stand it; these guys were doing everything they could to let the NVA shoot them down. The bunker complex was just not that important.

"Canberra four, White two-four, if you guys don't climb up to five thousand I'm calling this mission off," I tried once more, doing my best impersonation of a commanding officer. They still had enough bombs for three more runs, and we didn't want to have to pick them up out of a burning wreck.

The pilot didn't even bother to answer me. They just kept flying that ridiculous pattern and dropping their bombs two at a time.

Life had not changed much in Tay Ninh during my trip to the Philippines. Crab and Duck were the only pilots flying Scouts, and they did not give me too hard a time when I told them I would not be getting back in a LOH for a while. In fact I did not get back into an aircraft for an entire week after my return, but finally, on 10 December, I started flying again in a Command and Control Huey.

It was amazing what a little vacation time and a change in missions did for my nerves. I actually looked forward to flying the Hueys, learning the capabilities of the big machines, and I had no desire at all to strap myself into a LOH. Because of my low time in Hueys I had to fly copilot. It wasn't too bad, however, as Animal was an aircraft commander and our good buddy Ski had no trouble scheduling me as Animal's copilot.

Flying with Animal was a trip; no one was smoother. He would show me a maneuver, and then I would try in vain to duplicate his finesse and economy of movement. When we had the Huey with no passengers aboard we would take the long way home along routes that took us up over Nui Ba Den and down along meandering rivers, flying low level whenever possible. I loved low-level flight through the rice paddies, as the Huey's stable bulk skimmed the tops of the rice stalks while the heavy two-blade rotor system beat out a deep, resonant *whoop-whoop-whoop.*

When Animal and I had night missions we would detour by LZ Barbara and watch the fifteen-inch cannons blast flame into the night sky. Frequently we would have the opportunity to watch the LZs repel a night attack. The jungle lit up in flashes around the 105 and 155mm cannons as shots were fired into the surrounding tree line, while tracer rounds from the machine guns streaked across the open spaces and ricocheted up into the night sky below us. Jets sent great sheets of rippling orange flame rolling through the silhouettes of the tall jungle trees. Voices on the radio and the glow of the jets' afterburners, shooting the planes back into the sky, were the only connection between them and the carnage below.

In Command and Control I was able to see a lot more of Vietnam. Scouts had been limited to the LZs within a thirty-mile radius of Tay Ninh, where we spent all our time just above the jungle trees searching the ground for the enemy. Flying Command and Control we traveled hundreds of miles up to Loc Ninh and the old French rubber plantations around An Loc, and over to Phuoc Vinh and occasionally down to Saigon. To the north the topography changed radically, with rolling hills, deep ravines, and large open fields. Down south there were villages and whole towns going about life as if there were no war.

It was all a nice change from the ravaged jungles of Tay Ninh.

As if life was not easy enough then, a few weeks before Christmas we got to trade our old tin-and-plywood sheds at Stingray Pad for the plush company area formerly occupied by a Philippine Cavalry unit, a construction-and-supply company of Filipinos. The Phil Cav had built most of Tay Ninh base camp, so it was not surprising that they had the nicest hooches in town.

When we heard about the impending move Crab and I went over and checked out the different hooches to find the one we wanted. We took Bauser, Crab's dog, along with us to play with the Phil Cav mutts. We had a hard time making up our minds, since there were so many nice big hooches, but finally we settled on a homey two-bedroom place with a large living room. Inside there was wood paneling and even an indoor shower; however, the deciding feature was the four feet of sandbags around the walls and on the roof. Bauser took care of the formalities by marking the front door.

The day of the move Crab and I flew over in a LOH, landed right by our hooch, and claimed it officially. In fact, we had already set up our lawn chairs and were relaxing in the shade when the rest of the company arrived in jeeps and trucks. We were still sitting there, discussing our good fortune, when Bauser showed up with one of his pals, or a part of his pal, in his mouth—tails and paws were all that was left of his pals. It turned out that the Filipinos' dogs had been raised specifically for their farewell feast.

I would have had nightmares about boiling puppies if it had not been for the cockroaches. As I lay sprawled on my cot, sweating from every pore, the first wave hit. One of them, obviously suicidal, dropped from the ceiling onto my face, did a quick dance, and split. Within minutes another one ran up my crotch and stomach, scrambled across my chest, and did a banked turn in my armpit as he headed for the security of my wadded-up, sweaty sheets. Wide awake and fearing the worst, I reached for a cigarette and was surprised to find no less than three of them, each an inch and a half long, munching on my Lucky Strikes. That did it. I grabbed a can of DDT and sprayed the room down. "Let that be a lesson," I lectured the dozen shiny brown forms scurrying around the floor, and lay back on my cot to catch up on some badly needed sleep.

Minutes later I heard scraping and scratching sounds all around my cot. When I turned the light back on I was shocked to see hundreds of roaches in various stages of their death throes covering the floor, walls, and ceiling. I turned the light back off, put toilet paper in my ears, and tried to forget the macabre vermin war I had started. They, however, would not let me, as they kept crawling onto my cot and dropping on me from the ceiling, twitching and scratching as the poison slowly killed them. Cockroach hell went on all night—as one wave died off another would come staggering out of the DDT-contaminated sandbag walls.

The roaches did not seem to bother Crab, but the foot-long rats that had nightly run of the hooch did. One night when he blasted one of them with his .38 revolver just outside my door he almost gave me a heart attack. When I ran out of my room, pistol in hand, he was already back asleep.

It was bad enough having to share our hooch with

the roaches and rats, but the next day it got worse when Lofty moved into our living room. No one else wanted to live with him because he was getting weirder by the day, flitting around talking gibberish. Crab started calling him Lori because he kept trying to give him a hug or a kiss on the cheek.

Not long after Lori moved in, Crane went home, leaving Brisa in charge. Up to that point Brisa had been tolerable because all his attempts to run our lives were processed through Crane. Unless something was really important the good captain would usually say "I'll look into it," and would then forget about it. Most of the pilots knew there was going to be trouble when Brisa took over, and we did not have to wait long to see what it was.

The first crusade Brisa pursued as our commanding officer was to try to get rid of the drug problem in the aviation platoon. He got chewed out by a colonel who thought he smelled pot when he was getting on one of the Command and Control helicopters. The colonel told Brisa to bust anyone who was smoking pot on the Flying Circus flight line. The next day our CO got right on it and started sneaking around the helicopters and revetments.

Brisa may have looked ridiculous, but his efforts almost paid off when he saw Little Buddy standing behind a LOH puffing on a pipe full of pot. Like a shadow, our captain slipped from behind a Huey, over to the jeep and along the LOH revetment, while Little Buddy waited for him. Little Buddy had seen the captain sneaking around and had stashed the pipe down the exhaust cone of the LOH he was working on. Brisa's frustration was quite evident as he frisked the stoned mechanic and searched all around the helicopter, with Little Buddy asking, "What's the problem, sir?"

Brisa also wanted to bust Animal. It was not an easy undertaking because Animal kept incense burning all the time, effectively covering up the smell of the pot. Brisa knew that he would have to catch Animal red-handed in order to get a bust. He would burst through the door of Animal's one-room hooch several times a night, with only the lamest excuses for the rude intrusions. The nightly raids bothered Animal, so he took a big reflector, hung it from the ceiling a few feet inside the door about head height, and put a high-intensity bulb in front of the reflector. Every time Brisa pulled the door open, a piece of string turned on the light and blinded the frustrated captain.

Brisa started picking on me also, to no one's surprise. One evening a sergeant from the TOC caught me on my way to the officers' club after a long day of Command and Control.

"Sir, Circus Operations said you'd take me out to the ARVNs out by LZ Rose," he said.

"At this time of night?" I inquired.

"Captain's orders," the sergeant responded. When he said captain, it occurred to me that this was a mission from my friend Captain Brisa.

We were supposed to fly some radio frequency changes out to some ARVNs in the field—a pointless and dangerous job. Pointless because the ARVNs did not use the frequencies to which the changes applied, and dangerous because it was already starting to get dark. Trying to find a bunch of ARVNs was hard enough in the daytime, since they usually had no idea where they were, but trying to find them in the dark would be nearly impossible. The thought of getting shot down in the jungle at night made my skin crawl.

Nevertheless I did what I could. We went out to the flight line, buckled ourselves into a LOH, got the machine running, and picked it up to a hover. Then I put it back on the ground and shut it down. "What's up, sir?" the sergeant asked.

"As the aircraft commander of this LOH, I have, while in flight, determined that this mission cannot be accomplished without unnecessary risk to the aircraft and the lives of its crew," I stated, trying to recall some military regulation about an aircraft, while in flight, being the sole responsibility of the aircraft commander. Supposedly even the commander in chief could not order an aircraft commander to continue a mission if the AC determined it would get everyone killed.

"But the captain waited all day to give you this mission," the sergeant said, smiling from ear to ear. It was obvious he did not want to go on the ridiculous escapade any more than I did. As we parted company I suggested that he tell the officer who had assigned the mission (Brisa's name had not been mentioned) that it was an asinine and irresponsible order.

Then next morning I was in front of Brisa's desk, his beady eyes flashing at me as I tried not to smile. "Mr. Smith, did you tell Sergeant Hasting that my order was asinine?" he demanded.

"No, sir; I said whoever assigned me that mission was irresponsible, sir," I told him. "Sir, that mission was way too dangerous to be done at night and I just thought whoever had assigned it—I didn't know it was you—should know that it was not a good idea." Brisa was as frustrated as I had ever seen him.

Two days later I was back in front of his desk with Crab and it was payback time—he had the goods on us. The day before I had been assigned an Ash and Trash mission to take a couple of special forces soldiers to their camp on the edge of Tay Ninh city. Crab came along for the ride because one of them was a friend of his. Crab's friend took us to a camp that was actually a bar they had commandeered for their headquarters. Even though they had taken the place over, they had been considerate enough not to displace the bar's former occupants, a bevy of prostitutes.

One thing led to another, and before long Crab and I realized that we were overdue back at the base. Unfortunately, by that time we were both in love with two of the working girls. It was probably the girls' mama-san who came up with the plan that now had us standing in front of Brisa.

"You take girls and me home with you. Maybe invie frens, have big party," she suggested, realizing an economic opportunity when she saw one.

What a great idea: we could drink, fool around, and not have to worry about driving home. The mama-san saw such potential for profit that she demanded we take two more of her best-looking girls. That made five of them and two of us—definitely an overload for the four-seat LOH, but Crab and I were accustomed to difficult missions.

Everything went pretty well except takeoff. Crab was flying, so his girlfriend got to ride between us up front—on top of the radio console. As we started to lift off she became so excited that she threw her arms around his neck and tried to climb into his lap, wedging her knee against the cyclic in the process. That put us into a dive, and we bounced off the ground twice before Crab could get her back up on the radio console. The rest of the flight to our hooch went without incident. As per our deal, we brought some of our friends over and the party started in earnest, the girls turning in a stellar performance for their young mama-san.

Many hours later, as Crab was leaving my room, where we had been entertaining our dates, he froze in the doorway and exclaimed, "We're in deep shit, Atom!"

Looking over his naked shoulder I saw what he was referring to—a major was standing in the front doorway surveying the debauchery before him. We would have run, but he was blocking the only way out. We knew the major, he worked at the TOC, and he had always impressed us as a real straight arrow. He noticed us, and a big smile lit up his face. "Is this party for junior-grade officers and enlisted men only?" he politely inquired, catching us completely by surprise.

"No, sir." Crab sighed with relief. "Why don't you come on into Atom's room here?" We were so relieved that he was not there to bust us that we gave him our mama-san, the best-looking of the lot, and told her if she charged him a piaster (the Vietnamese equivalent of a penny), there would be dire consequences.

We thought we had gotten away with it, but the next morning there we were in front of the grinning Brisa. He looked so satisfied and secure; obviously the major must have turned us in.

"Where are the girls?" Brisa asked, switching quickly to a look of contempt.

"We took them to the gate this morning, sir," Crab explained calmly. "Told the MPs they were hooch-maid trainees." (We had actually taken a Huey and flown them back to the special forces camp, but if we had told Brisa that it would have just upset him more.)

"I had breakfast with Major Owens. He told me to thank you for inviting him to your party last night," our new CO said as he tapped a pencil on his desk, obviously making an effort to control his anger. "You've gotten away with it this time, but if this ever happens again, major or no major, you guys are going to the stockade, *understood?*"

"Yes, sir. It will never happen again, sir," Crab and I assured him, edging toward the door of his office.

"Just a goddamned minute, you two," he yelled, and turned toward me. "I expect this kind of crap from you, Smith, but you"—he turned to Crab—"I expect more of you." Then he turned his back on both of us and said, "Dismissed." It was everything we could do to contain our glee over the major's support.

That night I went over to Brisa's hooch to apologize. It seemed obvious in his office that he hated me, and I thought it might help if we talked it over—which we did for about three hours. We discussed the war, the military, ourselves, and our motives. It amazed me—we actually seemed to understand each other, and even parted as friends that night. Maybe it was his Christmas spirit, or possibly he thought it wise to have a truce while he took care of other problems, such as Rod, who had just been busted by the doctors for tampering with our malaria specimens.

We had been ordered to take our malaria prevention pills every day, but most guys blew it off because the pills made them sick. When the medical brass heard that the men were throwing their malaria pills in the trash they ordered us to piss in a cup every morning. The samples were collected and analyzed to see if the men were actually disregarding their order to take the pills.

Rod, a sergeant nicknamed after Rod Steiger in the movie *The Sergeant*, was assigned to pick up the cups every morning. Rod spent most of the night riding around in his jeep, clad only in his underwear, checking for enemy infiltrators. For that reason, and a few others, we liked him and he liked us, so one day, when he heard us complaining about the piss test, he offered to help us out.

"No problem," he said. "I take the pills, so I'll just fill your cups for you." Rod was the man for the job. He usually drank a quart of gin on his nightly missions in his jeep, and he never ran out of urine.

That Christmas season in Tay Ninh was like no other, starting with the day before Christmas. I got a letter from Wolfman, who was now living in Seattle, Washington, trying to get a job playing professional baseball.

> Atom,
>   Well Atom what's been going on over there in that world of due? I hope the hell you, Crab and McSpud are flying in the big Hueys now and not in those little stinger eggs, LOH 6-A.
>   Hey Atom did Ben go back to his old Unit? Little Buddy told me old Crane was giving the gunners a hard time so Ben told him to get fucked and went back. Let me know will you. . . .

It wasn't much fun writing him back to tell him that Spud and Ben had been shot down, that they had crashed and burned, and that Ben might be dead for all I knew. We still had not found out where they had taken him after he left Tay Ninh. All we had to go on was what the doctor who treated him in the 45th Surgical Hospital told us—that Ben had a lot of internal injuries and was in bad shape.

Animal wanted to put up the Christmas lights his mom had sent from home, but our COs wouldn't let him because the enemy might use the lights for targets. When it was suggested we might have a company Christmas party, Brisa told us that Christmas would be a good time for an enemy attack, and we should all be on alert.

The only Christmas spirit I saw in Tay Ninh came from the cooks in the mess halls. They worked all Christmas Eve preparing a hundred turkeys with stuffing, hams, sweet potatoes, even cranberry sauce, and apple pie for dessert. Christmas morning we loaded up all the Hueys and flew the feasts out to the LZs. The only thing that made me feel better that Christmas came in a letter from my brother Norm.

> Am sure that I don't have to tell you that everyone is proud of your performance etc. and there were nothing but words of praise for T.L. this Christmas. . . . Take good care of yourself and get back soon.

As I read it my eyes filled with tears.

The new year, 1970, started with Slater leaving for the world. Saying goodbye to my good friend was difficult, not only because we had been through a lot together, but because his vocabulary had finally dwindled to a repetitious giggle.

Just before Slater left we got a new pilot who was

an Army celebrity—the youngest helicopter pilot to go to Vietnam, who arrived on his eighteenth birthday. His nickname was Batman; he was a nice guy who could not wait to fly Scouts. Within a week he and a new Command and Control pilot, Coyote, were up with Crab, who was happy to train them. He and Duck had been doing all the scouting for the brigade since I had been shot down at the end of November.

Shortly after Coyote and Batman were trained, Crab and I were talking about them in the officers' club and about how they were making a team the way we had when we joined the 1st Brigade. "Jesus, I'm feeling old," Crab whined. "What was it, six months ago? We were just like them, getting into it, having a good time. Now you've lost your nerve—"

"Up yours, buddy," I interrupted.

"And I don't get the thrill I used to," he continued with a chuckle. "I feel like a father, a grandfather, for Christ's sake, and those guys are nuts. Batman flies around with a tape deck, listening to rock-and-roll, but I guess that's how we were, nuts when we got into it."

"You still *are* nuts to be flyin' Scouts," I pointed out.

Crab would not admit that flying Scouts was dangerous. He wouldn't even admit that the war was not worth dying for, but he started taking more days off, and even flying Command and Control once in a while. He was also drinking more and getting into trouble. One night he attacked a new guy whom we called J. Edgar, after J. Edgar Hoover, because he had been a narcotics agent before joining the Army.

The incident occurred just after a USO show. J. Edgar had gotten a little drunk, jumped up on the stage, and started dancing with the girls in the show, breaking Crab's unspoken rule that new guys should be seen and not heard. On the way back to the Phil Cav compound, Crab jumped him and threw him in a cleagy pit. Poor J. Edgar almost drowned in the slime, with no idea why Crab had attacked him.

On January nineteenth I wrote my brother about getting out of Scouts and into Command and Control.

Dear Norm,
Well you saved my life. That case of Nutriment got there just in time. Now I am a healthy, well conditioned 98 lb. Hulk. You see I have turned into a physical freak. I do all these physical exercises and soon I am even going to start walking to meals and the helicopter. I am doing these physical things to create a balance between mental and physical exhaustion. I beat my body at night and my mind all day while flying. Working hard and sleeping are the only ways to make it through this thing. I never feel better than when I step out of the aircraft after a good ten hour day. All I want to do is be still and at peace. It is really neat. It will also be neat to get out of the habit, back in the world. I have entered a whole new field in flying Command and Control helicopters. It is no more cut and dry, do it or die—wow—as it was in Scouts. . . . We fly the field commanders around. They love and know how to fight wars, but they do not know how to handle the flying part. Seeing as we are an airmobile division, their lack of knowledge is quite a threat. I think it is because they do not realize the importance of timing in mass or single aircraft maneuvers. Also they think that as long as they are in the air they are safe. They

fail to see that is where it all begins. But anyway it is not as boring as I thought it would be. You can actually miss the tension involved in killing or being killed. . . .

Actually the end of my Scout career was pretty colorful. I got shot down and blew up and caught fire in the air. I got some shrapnel and second degree burns so they gave me a purple heart and a bladder bag so I would not make a mess whenever anyone lit a match. I finished up by killing a whole bunch of people and then one night and next day and next night I was afraid so I quit. If you do a job like Scouts when you are afraid or wanted to quit you die. It is honestly that simple and true. . . .

The week after I sent my letter to my brother, I flew Command and Control every day, and then, impulsively, I was back in Scouts. I didn't go back into it the way I had before. This time it was more for the fun of zooming around in the treetops than for trying to locate and kill the enemy. Besides, Coyote, Batman, Duck, and Crab were taking care of the nitty-gritty stuff, so on the few days a month I went up with Crab I had little trouble convincing him, and myself, that we should take it easy. I really had missed the excitement of tracking the enemy, but certainly not the terror of getting shot up. To avoid taking hits I tried to keep my airspeed up, but sometimes even that was not enough.

Cisco and I had flown over an old abandoned bunker complex just in time to see a couple of NVA jump into the door of a big bunker. We spent a few minutes at high speed checking the place out for any more enemy, but couldn't find any. We felt pretty safe because the complex area had been hit by an arc-light, and there weren't too many places for them to hide. We flew back over the bunker, strafed it with the minigun, and dropped some grenades on it, but it was obvious that we were not getting to them. So we called up the Air Force, and got some jets en route that were only fifteen minutes out.

The jets contacted us when they arrived on station: "White two-four, Dragon one-one, we have a couple five-hundred pounders for you, but no FAC to mark the target. Our FAC will not be here for another one-five minutes. You want to mark the target for us?"

"Dragon one-one, White two-four, no problem. We'll drop a Willy Pete on the bunker. Be advised that we have only one bunker for you; put it in the door," I radioed back.

"Dragon one-one, Roger that."

We flew over and Cisco dropped the white phosphorus grenade right on top of the bunker. Then we moved a safe half mile away to wait for the air strike. The jets rolled in, but a few seconds later they called, "Two-four, we lost the target. How about another Willy Pete?"

"Roger that, Dragon one-one. Be there in zero-two minutes," I replied, not very happy about having to go back in. Returning to an area when the enemy knew that they were about to get blown up with bombs was pretty dangerous. They had nothing to lose by shooting at us, so I nosed the LOH over to its maximum speed of a hundred and ten miles per hour and headed back to the bunker. Skimming across the tops of the trees at such speed, we missed the target by fifty yards. To keep my airspeed up we did a wide turn and came back around on target—

right into the sights of an NVA .51-caliber machine gun.

The NVA had slid the gun out the door of the bunker, so it was just resting on the dirt. I heard the heavy pounding of the large-caliber weapon before I saw that they were shooting at us. As I rolled the LOH over on its left side I felt the helicopter shudder when the large slugs hit somewhere behind my head. Cisco's M60 went silent and I yelled over the intercom, "You hit?"

"Naw," Cisco came back, "but there's a couple new holes above my head back here." We headed straight to the nearest LZ, as .51-caliber slugs can do a lot of damage to the structural integrity of the aircraft.

I called the jets, "Dragon one-one, two-four we are full of holes and departing the area. Sorry, don't know how badly we're hit."

"Good luck, two-four, want us to keep an eye on you?" the jet pilot kindly offered.

My instruments were all in the green, indicating that the helicopter was operating normally, and the LZ was only a few miles away so I radioed the jet pilot, "No thanks, buddy, but we'll be on your freak [frequency] for the next zero-five minutes, in case something goes wrong. When your FAC shows up, the bunker is on the south edge, repeat, south edge of the arc-light with a .51-cal. sticking out the door."

We landed at LZ Rose to check out the damage to the aircraft. There were three big holes less than a foot above Cisco's head that went all the way through the helicopter. The little buggers had missed the main transmission and controls by inches.

Cisco looked up at the holes, and said in a most

reverent tone, "Hollywood," an expression he often used to show his respect for something spectacular.

"Bullshit," I said. "Too close," and vowed never to fly Scouts again.

13

Friends and Foes

Early February 1970

Whatever it was that a Scout pilot needed to survive Vietnam, Crab had it. His aircraft had been shot up a few times, but in more than eight months of flying he had never crashed or been hurt, which was a record of sorts. Crab's first mishap was not until February, when he did suffer some minor injuries, but not in combat.

As the LOH instructor pilot for our company, Crab had been showing a new guy how to do standard approaches to a dirt air strip on the outskirts of Tay Ninh. This was probably the least dangerous mission he had been on. Crab and the trainee were flying four hundred feet above the strip, with the new guy on the controls, when without warning the LOH spun around to the right. As they rotated through one hundred and eighty degrees, they saw their tail boom—which had separated from the rest of the aircraft—hanging in the air in front of them. The entire tail boom, from the engine compartment to the position light, was hanging there, with the tail rotor still spinning. The new guy, being quite pragmatic about the situation, said to Crab, "You've got it," and relinquished control of the aircraft.

Crab leveled the aircraft as best he could and bottomed the collective. Seconds before they hit the air strip he pulled up on the collective, using the remaining rotor rpm's to cushion their landing. Crab and his trainee walked away from the crash. The helicopter was totaled and Crab's back ached, but as we were prone to say in Tay Ninh, "Any landing you walk away from is a good one."

What Crab did sounds fairly simple—one or two control moves and they were on the ground—but there were lots of other moves he could have made that would have resulted in a fatal crash. I had always felt that I could do anything that Crab could in a LOH, but in the same situation, with the whole tail boom missing, I am not sure I could have done nearly as well.

Crab could make a LOH do just about anything, like backward autorotations. The day Crab decided to show me this game we were cruising low-level above a dirt road near Nui Ba Den. He was flying. "Atom, I got to show you a new trick," he said, chuckling the way he always did when he was about to do something crazy, and glancing at me to see if I was getting angry. "See that big stump up there on the left side of the road?" he asked. I didn't say anything, hoping he would forget whatever he was planning if I ignored him. But he continued, "When we reach the stump I'm entering autorotation, low-level, and then I'm going to land right back at the stump, without doing a three-hundred-and-sixty-degree turn."

My immediate reaction was, "Don't be a jerk, Crab." I didn't have a lot of time to think about it, but the stunt he proposed seemed impossible.

As we passed the stump, Crab rolled off the throttle and yanked back on the cyclic. The little LOH's nose came up and as I watched in horror, Crab started pulling up on the collective. He was trading our remaining rotor rpm for lift from the rotor blades. Because we were climbing almost vertically the lift from the blades was pulling the helicopter back toward the stump.

As we neared the top of the cyclic climb, maybe three hundred feet above the stump, just about to fall out of the sky, Crab nosed it over, did a little turn with a radical flare, and landed about ten feet from the stump. He then turned to me and said with a big grin, "I've been practicing."

I should have strangled Crab for taking me through a maneuver like that, but I was too busy assessing the damage a flying clipboard had done to my lip. When Crab nosed the ship over at the top of the cyclic climb, it was so radical we got into negative gravity—everything loose in the cockpit went flying.

Most of the first weeks of February I spent in a LOH, providing me all the opportunity I needed to practice backward autorotations, but I never got as proficient as Crab.

I wasn't flying a LOH in Scouts those weeks; I hadn't been back in Scouts since the day Cisco and I got shot up by the .51-caliber machine gun. The LOH I was flying was on Ash and Trash missions. On most of the missions I was alone, but occasionally I carried a passenger, like the sergeant who was hitching a lift from LZ Barbara to LZ Outlaw.

Halfway up the road between the two firebases, the sergeant noticed a dead NVA soldier on the side of the road. He came over the intercom: "Excuse me, sir, how about we go down and check out that dead gook? Maybe I can get his skull."

It was an unusual request, but collecting trophies—

anything from taking pictures of dead enemy soldiers
to cutting their ears off—was a pretty common practice. We swung around to check the area out, and
then came to a hover beside the body. The corpse
had been there for quite a while, almost reduced to
a skeleton, so it should have been fairly simple for
the sergeant to detach the head.

"Hurry it up," I told him. "It would be pretty embarrassing getting blown away doing this kind of
crap."

While the LOH hovered, the sergeant climbed out
on the skid to reach down and wrench the head off
the body. Then he started making some loud, weird
sounds that I could not understand. He wasn't talking over the intercom, just yelling to himself, so I
looked over to see what was happening. The sergeant
was still out on the skid, holding on to the door
frame with one hand while he waved the other hand
wildly about, shaking a grisly skull that clung to
his fingers.

It looked as if the dead man's head was biting him
and would not let go. The sergeant kept screaming
and shaking the skull until finally it flew off and
rolled away. Apparently when wrenching the skull
free, he had jammed his thumb into what muscle was
left on the jaw. When the smell of the rotting flesh
hit him, he tried to throw the skull away, but his
thumb had stuck in the sinuous tissue.

That night I had a horrible nightmare about the
headless man. In the dream I was flying along, and
when I turned to look in the back at my door gunner,
I saw instead the dead soldier staring back at me.

That was not the only nightmare I had. The one I
disliked the most had been with me since I was shot
in the foot. At least once a week in my dreams I

would be flying along in a Huey when, from out of nowhere, a bullet would hit me in the lower right side of my jaw and exit the left top of my skull. I disliked that nightmare in particular because it always played in slow motion; I got to see the whole show in vivid detail.

Around then Craig, my best friend from flight school, finally made it up from Cu Chi for a visit while I was out flying. He couldn't stay, but he left a note.

Tom:
  3 P.M. Leaving AO—STOP—Fucked up—STOP—Trying to leave for hour now—STOP—But kept forgetting where I left my (your) San Miguel Beer—STOP—Consequently I remember I can't leave until I have drank it—STOP—Call me on Victor if you can come down within the week.

Even though Craig was stationed only forty miles away we had not had a chance to get together. He was flying Charlie Model gunships with the Stingers, flying almost every day. We never seemed to be able to get the same day off, but we stayed in touch on Victor, our prearranged frequency on the VHF radio. The day after I got his note I gave him a call. "Flea [Craig's nickname], this is Atom Ant. Do you copy?"

"Atom! Flea. Come to Cu Chi ASAP. I've two days off starting tomorrow. You've got to make it. Can't talk," was all he said. I tried to raise him the rest of the day, but he never came back up on that frequency.

As good fortune would have it, I too had a day off, so early the next morning I hitched a ride on a Huey to Cu Chi. By noon I was in Craig's hooch, asking him why he had insisted I come down as soon as possible, while I played with his cat, Moon Kitty, a weird, mangy little beast with no tail.

"First, the bar," he said, a little overdramatically, as we watched Moon Kitty walk across the plywood floor, leaping straight up in the air every other step or two.

"Yes, let's get a drink," I agreed.

On the way to the bar I noticed that Craig's company area was a little more civilized than ours, starting with the olympic-size swimming pool. And their air-conditioned bar, even though it was only used by company pilots, was twice the size of ours. When Craig and I arrived, the place was empty except for four pilots playing cards. As we sat down at the bar Craig greeted the other pilots and informed me they also flew gunships. I would have guessed that by the way they greeted each other, like Scout pilots, with respect and wariness.

In three hours I had to catch a ride back to Tay Ninh, and Craig still hadn't told me why he wanted me in Cu Chi. When I mentioned this he grinned from ear to ear and asked, "Are you ready? Follow me."

We walked out of the gates of base camp and into the shanty town that thrived off the enlisted men's monthly paychecks. There were plywood-and-tin sheds full of cameras, food, liquor, tobacco, magazines, and anything a soldier would buy. Not far from the gate Craig stopped in front of one of the larger plywood structures. "Here it is," he exclaimed with a mischievous grin and a wave at the decrepit structure. "Inside is a woman who will help you find your sexual peak."

"No way. I'm not going in there, Craig," I told him. "I'll get bit by a rat."

Craig grabbed my arm and shoved me inside, where a mama-san greeted us with, "You pay now!"

Craig, still grinning like an idiot, paid the hag and came in. She showed us to two of the curtained cubicles behind her. Left on my own I sat down on the only furniture, a plywood bench, tested it for strength, then lay on my back. The cubicle was four by eight feet, with plywood walls that almost reached the tin roof. As I lay there fantasizing about the lithe young beauty who would supposedly take me to new heights of pleasure, I heard the scuffing sound of slippered feet stop outside my cubicle.

The curtain slid aside and in hobbled an eighty-year-old woman. At first I thought she was there to clean up, but then she smiled; the way she smiled I knew she was there for me. With a curse I started to sit up, ready to find Craig and choke him for his practical joke, but he was one step ahead of me. His eyes peeked over the wall and he said, "Try it, you'll like it," and then disappeared again. By that time the old lady was pushing me back down on the bench, still smiling a lovely smile, which revealed a perfectly toothless mouth. As I had noted once before, Craig was weird, but he was almost always right.

It was a comfort to see that the months of combat had not changed the bonds we shared. Being with Craig was like finding the calm in the eye of a hurricane. He had his war stories, and had metamorphosed as we all had, but there was a part of his mind that had not been touched by Vietnam. Not too many people, myself included, still had such a place.

Back in Craig's hooch we drank beer and talked. At one point we discussed the pros and cons of extending. I told him that I had thought about it and couldn't make up my mind, but that a recent letter from Evil Eye almost had me convinced I should go ahead and do it. Evil Eye's letter had read:

Atom,
    You will recall that I never gave you bad advice. It seems I've always been the immortal philosopher in that I can solve anyone else's problems but my own.
    Well, I'm going to give you some advice that I wish you would take to heart because I am giving it earnestly. Instead of coming back here to spend almost two years in the stateside army, extend for six months and get out early. After being over there, society is too much to cope with and be in the Army at the same time.

"Heard the same thing," Craig said when I gave him the gist of Evil Eye's letter. "Been thinking about extending for the early out too."

"The only trouble is, I'm tired of getting my ass shot off in Scouts, and Command and Control is a drag," I said, voicing my primary reason for not extending.

"How about extending and flyin' guns with me in Cu Chi?" Craig asked.

"That's a thought," I stated cautiously, thinking to myself that flying guns was almost as dangerous as Scouts.

The Charlie Model gunship's job description was the same as the Cobra's (aerial rocket artillery), and that was a job I coveted. However, the Cobra was designed for the job, and the Charlie Model was just an early version of the Hueys we flew in Command and Control, which was modified for the job.

Cobras were designed for shooting rockets at the ground while rolling in from altitude where they had good visibility and were out of light-weapons range. They had a small silhouette when attacking, tandem seats, rotating gun turrets, stub wings designed for several different weapon systems, and an engine with enough power to get all that off the ground.

The Charlie Models could not roll into a dive for very long; they were too heavy and slow. Consequently they had to fly a couple of hundred feet above the ground—where they had fair to poor visibility and were well within small-arms range. They had an enormous silhouette from any angle, and weapon systems that were more suitable to a tractor than a helicopter; and the crews were always overloading the old machines with rockets and ammo.

The first thing I did back in Tay Ninh was to ask Ski to get me the paperwork for an extension. Flying guns with Craig sounded like a great idea.

A few days later I was hitching another ride out of Tay Ninh. This time it was to Saigon for lunch with Uncle Pat, Aunt Kitty, and Judy, my brother Norm's wife, who were all flying in from Bangkok.

The helicopter that took me down to Saigon had seven other passengers, two of whom were lying on the floor at my feet in body bags; no one talked the entire flight. Two hours after leaving Tay Ninh I was sitting in the Saigon Airport bar, having a drink with family, after nine months of war.

"How are you, Tom?" someone asked.

"I'm fine," I said, knowing that when they left I would feel more alone than ever.

"Are we really doing any good here?" Aunt Kitty wanted to know.

"Sure, I guess so," I replied lamely.

Most of the conversation went that way, questions with answers far from the truth. There was no way I could tell Uncle Pat, Aunt Kitty, and Judy how I really felt about Vietnam. They had been considerate enough to make the effort to see me and were only going to be there for eight hours. I was not about to spoil the day by trying to explain all the terrible things we did every day, some of which I was even proud of, some of which I did not understand. So we spent the day driving around Saigon, eating and enjoying each other's company in spite of the war.

During our day together I thought I was the only one who felt the disparity between our lives. Days later a letter arrived from Judy showing a reaction like mine.

Dear Tom,
   It was so great to see you. When I think about being in Saigon it seems like a warm little island in time. It still seems incredible that the day before, and just a few days after we saw you, you were in such totally removed circumstances, hovering over villages and rice fields, fully armed and armored. It's like the wives in carriages observing the battle of Bull Run. I suppose all wars have strange things going on during them, but the incongruities in this war seem more pronounced than any I can imagine or have heard of.
   I bought Norm a belated birthday present in Tokyo. . . .

Back in Tay Ninh the big news was a rumor that Lofty was having an affair with one of the mechanics. As it was only a rumor, that afternoon in our hooch I asked, "Lori, is it true love or just a wartime romance?" Lofty reached down beside his cot and pulled out a loaded AK-47, drew back the bolt and let it go, putting a round in the chamber. Then he pointed the weapon at my stomach and started yelling incoherently. The gist of his raving was that he was going to kill me if I ever talked to him, or maybe even looked at him, again. Backing into the safety of my room, I assured him his wishes would be granted.

Several days later Lofty pulled a .38-caliber pistol on Crab under similar circumstances. Crab, who was getting tired of Lofty's shenanigans, called the military police. Lofty had not left Crab alone since Spud was shot down. If he wasn't flirting with Crab, he was threatening to shoot him. After the MPs questioned him, Lofty seemed to calm down, and the next day apologized to all of us, saying it was a just joke and would not happen again.

Even though it was tough on Lofty, the whole thing was pretty entertaining, something the rest of us appreciated—life around Tay Ninh was getting pretty boring. If I had not made aircraft commander in Hueys, I'm not sure I could have stuck it out in Command and Control as long as I had.

My promotion to aircraft commander was an honor considering that, on the average, it took six months in Hueys to make AC, and I had logged only fifty-three days in them. Undoubtedly my time in Scouts had helped, but Sharp, who made AC the same day as I, had been flying Hueys for eight months.

I was pretty proud of myself, climbing into the great big Huey as aircraft commander. I had no idea there was such a difference between being a copilot, even with a friend like Animal, and being an AC in a Huey. As copilot I felt like an overgrown child on an amusement ride, with few responsibilities. As an aircraft commander, with a crew of three and up to eight passengers, my priorities shifted from just flying to thinking about the job. It was too big a machine, and there were too many people involved, to fly by instinct as I had in my LOH. I had to plan ahead and my flying became more conservative—excluding the day Operations sent me after a dropped sling load.

A Chinook, a great big double-rotor helicopter (five times the size of the Huey), lovingly called a "shit hook," was carrying a three-quarter-ton pickup truck full of high-tech weapons on a sling line when the cable broke. The truck fell four thousand feet to the ground. Even though the vehicle and everything in it was obviously a total loss, the guys in the TOC wanted it recovered. No Scout ships were available, so they dispatched my Huey to secure the area until a Scout ship could get there.

We had a very accurate fix on exactly where the Chinook had lost the truck, but when we got to the spot, a nice clear field next to a town, there was no evidence of anything having fallen from the sky. Had it not been for the suspicious nature of some of the town's residents fleeing the northeast corner of the field, we never would have found it.

We dropped down from three hundred feet to twenty feet and searched the field. Before long we found a suspicious-looking hole next to a fresh pile of dirt. In the half hour it had taken us to get to the area, the townspeople had located the truck and buried it in the crater it had made upon impact. As we turned to make a second pass someone shot at us from the tree line a hundred yards away.

I saw where the shots were fired from and my reflexes took over. I whipped the cyclic over to the right, hoping to put the left door gunner in position to shoot back, but the big aircraft just rolled like a whale into a long slow turn. By the time the Huey came around the door gunner (who was no Wolfman or Cisco) had no idea where the shots had come from and wouldn't fire for fear of hitting a noncombatant. We circled around to the edge of the tree line and flew down it to the spot where I thought the shots had been fired from. He was there all right and shot at us again as we flew over.

Once more I tried a Scout maneuver to get a door gunner on him, but the Huey just wouldn't do it. Meanwhile havoc reigned on the intercom system with both door gunners yelling, "Where is he? Turn left. Turn right," while my copilot kept saying, "Let's get out of here." I finally realized that the only way we were going to get that little SOB was to keep flying around until he shot us down—then maybe we could crash on him. Frustrated, I climbed back up to three thousand feet and waited for the Scouts.

It was the smart thing to do. Flying Scouts was dangerous enough in a LOH with a competent door gunner, but suicidal in a Huey, and suicide was out of the question so late in my tour. I had only three months left, and besides going home, I had my R&R to look forward to. R&R, rest and relaxation, was a two-week vacation everyone got toward the end of their tour. When I had visited Craig in Cu Chi we made plans to go on R&R in April, to Australia—we were allowed to go almost anywhere except home.

Toward the end of February I started getting letters from friends who had not heard I was planning on extending my tour and were anticipating my return home.

25th of Feb

T.L.,

How is the war? Isn't it about time you quit playing that game and came home to play the life game?
That isn't quite honest of me since I am still avoiding
that life game. I finally finished at North Carolina
and am now heading for Europe. I fly to Rome in a
few days. Will probably be in Europe for five or six
months. After Rome I head for Greece, Ouzo etc.
Maybe after Europe I can grow up and play the business dog, exec, stocks and bonds, buying and selling
merry-go-round.

Life has been tres boring. Spent two days in New
York with Dave and Erica, lots of Ballantine ale, gig-
gles, pass-outs. I haven't been to the valley since November. Talked to Carol last night. Her mother took
her out of Denver and now has her seeing a shrink
three times a week. She didn't sound too zippy. Apparently Fred is in jail, tried to break into a liquor
store somewhere in Vermont.

I haven't talked to Peter since Christmas. I guess
he is at Vail or Aspen with Pia, irresponsible lout,
jealousy.

When I am in Europe I will try to get to Paris and
swing my weight at the Paris Peace conference. This
joke has gone on long enough. Besides, too many of
the hard core booze rock artists are getting out of
shape sitting in Vietnam swamps, picking their noses
and forgetting how to go-a-million etc. When may
we expect you back in the valley?

Rock on,

Robin

I also started getting letters from friends who knew
that I was extending for six more months in Vietnam:

"Damn it Tom, I'm not even gone a month and
you are talking about extending. Well I hope they
turn it down. Tom, you don't know what you're

missing. Nobody is dying or getting hurt here except the ones that want to or have a real good reason to. It is such a gas I couldn't even begin to tell you about it. So just cool it on that extending bit."

And:

"Where is your head at?"

And:

"Don't extend no matter what. It's foolish and no matter how bad it is here in the Army, it is worse over there."

February slid by uneventfully, with my nerves healing during long days of Command and Control. The only day I flew Scouts the entire month was the day "Boss FAC" got killed. Boss FAC had replaced Captain Mink as our local Air Force Forward Air Controller. Since he was a major and outranked Captain Mink, we called him Boss FAC.

The Scouts were tied up with a company in heavy contact when Operations was notified that Boss FAC was overdue from a mission. Knowing it could take hours for the Air Force to get someone up to Tay Ninh to look for him, I jumped in one of the extra LOHs with a mechanic for a door gunner and flew to the area where he had been last reported. As I took off Captain Brisa came on the radio and started yelling at me for going on a mission that he had not assigned to me. I turned the radio off and marveled at the fact that he had managed to get his wings as a pilot and had no concern for the plight of another pilot.

It was not too hard to find the spot where he had

gone in. Boss FAC must have been going full speed when he hit the trees, in almost level flight, because he cut trees in half for more than a hundred yards. There was not a piece left of his OV-10 (twin-engine spotter plane) bigger than a lunch pail, and the only part of Boss FAC I found was his flight helmet.

14

Getting Shorter

Mid-March 1970

Captain Brisa was on my case again. Our delicate truce was considerably weakened when I took the LOH and went looking for Boss FAC. It completely fell apart with the introduction of a recreational diversion we called "soap bullet wars."

Soap bullet wars involved taking the shells out of our .38-caliber revolvers, pulling the heads off them, and dumping out the powder. Then we crammed the shells into a bar of soap to fill the empty casing. The shells were loaded back into the revolver, and when the trigger was pulled the soap wads were shot out by the small percussion cap in the end of the shell casing. The average soap wad could travel one hundred and fifty feet and hurt like hell. Our revolvers loaded with soap bullets, we stalked each other around the company area—every man for himself.

One of the first days we played soap wars I was in the operations office, crouched down behind Ski's desk taking careful aim at Animal's back through the louvered window. I was just about to pull the trigger—it was a simple shot, maybe fifty feet—when Brisa walked in the door. I looked up just in time to see his jaw drop to his chest as he took in my cocked pistol aimed at Animal's back. He made an attempt to speak but absolutely no sound came out.

It never occurred to me that he thought I was really going to shoot Animal, with a real bullet, that is, so Brisa's next move came as a surprise. He crossed the room in two enormous steps, ripped the pistol out of my hand, opened the cylinder, and started shaking bullets on the floor. He was out of control, but he was at last beginning to make some sounds, a few squeaks and gurgles, so I tried to communicate. I explained that we were playing a game, but instead of calming down, he grabbed my shirt and started shaking me.

A couple of nights later Brisa got even. One of the LZs was attacked just after dark. Before long they were in danger of being overrun, and started calling for help on the radio. Brisa had been listening, and when he heard the radio man at the LZ say that their sandbagged fortifications were not holding up he decided that our company could help by bringing out more sandbags, *empty* sandbags. It was absurd to think that soldiers in the middle of a close contact firefight would have the time to sit around and fill sandbags, but Brisa told Ski to get me for the mission.

There is no way that I can actually prove that he was trying to kill me, but it was obvious that he had singled me out for reasons other than my ability to get a Huey in and out of a night firefight. In the ten months I had been in Vietnam, I had only five hours of night flying time, and all of that was as a copilot. When I showed up at Operations to get a briefing on the mission, Brisa asked me, "Are you ready, Smith?"

"Other than the fact that I have absolutely no night time as an aircraft commander, and that this is a ridiculous mission, I'm ready," I told him, hoping he would get mad and take me off the mission.

"Pick up the sandbags over on the runway, next to the tower, and take them out to LZ Kramer. Your copilot will be Rawlins," Brisa replied, displaying his reptilelike smile.

Rawlins? I had not even heard of a pilot named Rawlins in our company. Company policy was that the AC of an emergency night mission like this got to pick his own copilot, someone who was good at night flying. Brisa had assigned me a guy who was so new in country that I had not even heard of him. When I confronted Brisa with this policy he snapped, "Don't talk back to me, Smith; that's an order."

We picked up our sling load of sandbags, a large (four-by-four-by-eight-foot) box on the end of a twenty-foot cable. As soon as we were airborne the box started spinning and swinging back and forth on the cable, making the helicopter rock and lurch from the strain. The machine was barely flyable. We should have had a drag chute on the box, but every time I thought about returning to Tay Ninh and Brisa, I decided to keep flying.

It was a ridiculous mission from the start, but as we neared LZ Kramer, what little ground reference I had from the moon started to disappear in the smoke from the battle ahead of us. Two minutes into the smoke, and still five minutes from the LZ, I started to get vertigo. I tried to switch from visual reference to my artificial horizon, but went right back to visual. My instruments for night flight were useless, jumping all over the place every time the box swung around on the end of the cable.

A pilot can have vertigo in various stages. When it is minor, it is like a bad dizzy spell. When it is severe, it creates such an intense reaction that it can cause nausea and complete disorientation. With a severe case of vertigo it is absolutely impossible to control an aircraft. After trying to switch to instruments my vertigo started to leave the light stage. I told my copilot, "You're going to have to take it. I'm getting too dizzy to fly."

"Forget it," Rawlins said. "I've had vertigo since we left Tay Ninh. I don't know which way is up."

Just as I was about to jettison the sandbags to stabilize the aircraft, the flashes from the heavy firefight ahead of us created a horizon, and my vertigo dissipated. I radioed the LZ that I was coming in. "Kramer, Stingray four-seven, where the hell do you want these goddamned sandbags?"

"Sandbags, you've got to be shittin' me!" someone came back, ignoring radio protocol. "Where the hell is the medevac? We've got to get these wounded outta here!" Then someone else came over the radio: "Four-seven, Kramer, be advised there's no place to land here. The whole LZ is torn up."

With that bit of information I came to a hover between the antenna farm and a flaming howitzer emplacement. I told my door gunners to clear me below and started down with the load, but the cannon and mortar smoke curled up into my rotor wash, intensifying my vertigo. "This is bullshit," I said to my copilot, and punched off the load from fifty feet.

On the way back to Tay Ninh I considered my options. I could go back to the operations office and shoot Brisa; I could continue to fly Command and Control and let him slowly drive me nuts; or I could get back into Scouts. The next day I rejoined Crab, Cisco, and the boys. The last week in March and the first two weeks in April I flew a LOH almost every day. It did not take me long to remember why I had left Scouts—we got shot at four out of the first five days.

I had not forgotten what the stress of getting shot at did to my nerves; hunting and shooting people wasn't fun anymore. It made me nervous, but flying Command and Control would have meant sacrificing my pride for a few weeks of safety. Anyway, I didn't get a lot of time to think about it; the hard work involved in Scouts put everything else in the background.

For the last time I slipped back into being a member of a hunter/killer team. A letter to my brother and his wife reflected the change in my attitude.

April 2nd, 1970

Dear Norm and Judy,

I appreciate the Nutriment very much and hope it gets here soon. The war has really picked up here again. It is getting really scary now that I am getting short (two and a half months until my first tour is over). Four days ago they overran LZ Jay. The place got really blown away. The morning it stopped I went out there in my LOH and it was just a pile of dirt with a dog looking very confused standing on the green line. All the grunts had split into the jungle to get away from the rockets etc. The next night, night before last, LZ Hillingsworth got hit. They just drove up in trucks, let the troops off, and blew the place away. When I got there in the morning there was no problem finding the grunts. They were scattered all over the LZ. I have never seen so many messed up people since I have been here, and most of them were ours. The gooks really won. They had the place completely, but they left instead of going in and killing all these blown up guys. Every piece of metal on the place was full of holes.

This particular battalion on Hillingsworth has been almost wiped out three times since they have been in our AO. There is this one gook battalion, 95 C, which really hate them. Every time they come around they get beaten up. Anyway the Nutriment will help me keep my strength up to get through this new offensive. The last two nights we have had gooks get through the wire into the base camp here at Tay Ninh, so we nail the doors shut at night and get drunk. I always said the best defense is a good offense.

My extension has not been approved yet, but I think it will be. If it is approved, three of us are going to England on June 5th to go to the Isle of Man motorcycle races. We are going to buy some bikes in London and drive down to the races. I think I might go to Stuttgart, Germany and see if Dr. Porsche will sell me a car.

I will probably get back to the US about the 20th of June and stay around Keene Valley until the 10th of July and then come back here.

Even though I had picked a lousy time to get back into Scouts, with a big NVA offensive going on, I made the best of it. I kept my airspeed up and my curiosity down—until I saw the panda bears.

Cisco and I were sticking to the edge of a clearing, following a small stream and a trail that followed it. We were talking over the intercom, having a pretty good time, cruising along at ninety miles an hour. As we passed an island of trees in the clearing, I looked out my door and there in the middle of the clump were two panda bears sitting on a log. "Cisco, did you see something that looked like panda bears in the middle of that clump of trees back there?" I asked over the intercom.

"Pandas? I don't know, Atom, do they even live around here?" he asked.

It did not surprise me. I had seen wild boar, tigers,

elephants, in Vietnam, so why not pandas? "I swear, they were pandas," I said. "Let's go back and take a closer look." We came around and flew over the clump of trees, but the only thing we got to see were tracers from AK-47s flying around us.

I had to assume that Cisco was right, pandas did not live around there. From then on my curiosity and my imagination both were put on a short leash. In my last months, I became so conservative in my desire not to get killed that I even started questioning the motives of others, like Crab.

One night in the officers' club, after having listened to one of my lectures on the futility of getting killed in Vietnam, Crab said, "Atom, you're just getting short, or shorter." After he chuckled at his own joke for a while, he continued, "Two months left and you can see the light at the end of the tunnel. There's no difference between your first day and your last. Get a grip." Then he laughed and continued in a lighter tone, "Look, what is it, for Christ's sake—next week?—that you're going on R&R to Australia? Take it easy; when you get back, call in sick for the rest of the month. You'll make it."

Crab was probably right about the first day being the same as the last, and he was definitely right about my needing to get a grip. Every time I tried to rationalize my situation, an overwhelming desire to be away from it all, almost a panic, pushed all rational thoughts aside. The pressure was inside me, unlike the external pressures of combat, a feeling that I had made a terrible mistake and was going to have to pay for it. I was beginning to regret extending.

On the fourteenth, Craig and I met in Bien Hoa and flew to Australia for our rest and relaxation leave. Sydney was exactly what a stressed-out helicopter pilot needed. Lots to do with the friendliest people I had ever met. We slept late, went sailing, took in *Easy Rider* at a theater up by Kings Cross, spent hours strolling around the beautiful city parks and botanical garden, and then went back to the pubs. When the time came to get back on the plane to Vietnam, I did it almost willingly. Five more weeks and my tour of duty would be over, I thought to myself; I can make it.

My first day back on the job in Tay Ninh, after two weeks of debauchery, Brisa had me out flying before daylight, assigning me one flight after another until after dark. I logged twelve hours of flight time, and half again that time sitting in the cockpit between flights. The next morning Brisa had me up before daybreak again, and told me to take my LOH out to where the Rome plows were working west of LZ Kramer.

Rome plows were enormous bulldozers, clearing a road through the jungle in preparation for Nixon's invasion of Cambodia. When I asked Brisa who was going to fly cover for me, he said, "It's a single-ship operation, Smith."

"You're sending me out on a single-ship Scout mission today, sir, after twelve hours yesterday?" I asked incredulously.

"Look, Smith, go out and take a look around. Check on their progress, let them know how far they are from the border. It's not a Scout mission," Brisa told me, knowing full well it was.

"Captain, they've had contact around the Rome plows almost every day they've been there," I protested to Brisa's back as he walked away.

Later, on the flight line, as I was loading belts of ammo into my minigun, Cisco walked up. "What're you doin', Atom?" he asked. "I thought Crab and Duck were flyin' Scouts today."

I told him about the mission Brisa gave me, and asked what he was doing that day. "Nothin', it's my day off. But if you want, I'll ride around with you," Cisco offered.

"Thanks, Cisco, that would be great. We'll try and take it easy today," I said, thinking to myself that Brisa could send me out without cover, but at least I had the best door gunner.

By sunrise we were strapped in and lifting off for the Rome plows. Orange haze covered the rice paddies and the sky above us turned deep shades of red and purple as we low-leveled out of Tay Ninh. The monsoons were on their way back to Vietnam and the days were getting a little cooler; it was a beautiful day for flying.

Finding the plows was no problem—they cleared a swath through the jungle two hundred yards wide wherever they went. The gigantic bulldozers got the name Rome plows from the town where their unusual steel blades were made—Rome, Georgia. On the left-hand side of the Rome blades was a thick spine of steel, which came to a point four feet in front of the blade. As the bulldozers lumbered through the jungle they would drive the steel spine into the side of the towering jungle trees, ripping off great chunks until the tree came crashing down.

At the head of the column of bulldozers we found the commanding officer. "Thanks for coming out, men. Can't hear a damn thing with these plows all around us," the captain yelled. "We're making good progress, figure we'll reach the border by eighteen hundred hours."

"Have you had any contact in the last twenty-four, sir?" I asked.

"Just a few mortar rounds early last night," he replied. "Radar picked them up on the zero-six-five-radial, three-hundred-plus meters." He explained over the roar of the plows that a patrol had gone out early that morning but had not found anything.

"We'll check it out," I assured him as we headed for our aircraft. The little LOH looked particularly vulnerable as the big bulldozers rumbled by on both sides.

About four hundred meters out on the 65-degree radial, only a hundred yards north of the swath that the Rome plows had been clearing, we found a three-acre clearing. We followed standard operating procedure and circled the field above the tree line. On the northwest side of the clearing we found a trail with what appeared to be enemy traffic; it was pretty old. The clearing itself consisted of some low bamboo clusters and shoulder-high brush, which was not very good cover, making it easy to find the mortar site. The mortars had been set up in the southwest corner, maybe four or five of them total, some twenty yards from the tree line. Once again the tracks we found indicated the enemy had left the area quite a bit earlier.

After reporting our findings to the CO of the plows, Cisco and I took care of the rest of the mission Brisa had assigned me. We checked the plows' progress in relation to the Cambodian border and looked for signs of the enemy ahead, behind, and on their flanks. The whole scene was as peaceful as a swarm of bulldozers tearing down the jungle.

By eleven o'clock Cisco and I had been flying for more than four hours, lunch time was approaching, and I was so tired that I was getting punchy. We decided that nothing much was happening around the bulldozers, and we might as well go back to Tay Ninh.

"Plows, White two-four, we're headin' back to Tay Ninh. What about this afternoon?" I asked. "You want us to come back out?" I was hoping he would say "no," allowing me to sneak off and sleep until Brisa found me.

"Negative, two-four. We'll be OK," the captain came back.

Our flight path to Tay Ninh took us within a mile of the mortar site, so I suggested to Cisco: "Let's take a last look at that field. Maybe they're setting up their mortars for another round tonight."

"Let's do it, Atom," Cisco agreed, always ready to go for it.

Maybe it was the two weeks of R&R or it could have been the fatigue, but it was definitely stupid. I flew right out into the middle of the clearing. For some reason, I didn't really think the NVA would have returned. As I flew over the tree line and out to the mortar sites, the only thing on my mind was: "Those trenches are here somewhere, I know it." Sure enough, there they were, off the right nose of the helicopter. I pulled back, slowing to fifty knots, and started a right turn. Over the intercom I suggested to Cisco, "Let's drop a few grenades in those trenches, let 'em know we've been here."

"I'm gettin' some ready already," he laughed.

By this time we were going only thirty knots, and I was slowing down even more, starting to line up on the target, waiting for Cisco to say he was ready. As I rolled out level, heading back toward the tree line, we began to parallel a trail running straight to the mortar sites—it took only one glance to notice signs of recent use. We were going about twenty knots, only fifteen feet above the ground; the sandal and bike imprints in the dirt were unmistakable.

Still wanting more proof, unable to believe what the fresh tracks meant, I tried to focus on one set of prints gliding by under our belly. There, jumping into the trail right behind our tail rotor, was an NVA soldier. Looking back, I noticed his black clothes and pith helmet first, and then the blazing AK-47. He was only twenty feet away, ten feet below us—then there were four, ten, twenty of them, right where we had flown—all shooting straight at us.

Cisco swung out of his open door, M60 bucking in his hands, shooting past our tail. I whipped around; it was clear in front of us, and for a second I started thinking again. The tree line's right there, we can make it, I told myself, safety is just over those trees. "Taking fire, taking fire!" I yelled reflexively over the radio to my nonexistent wingman.

In those first moments, inexplicably, I had not heard any of the many slugs that were hitting our helicopter. Perhaps the proximity of the hammering AK-47s was covering the sound, but as I yanked the collective into my armpit, I did hear the familiar and sickening sound of a fatally wounded engine tearing itself to pieces. It didn't matter! We had to get away, had to make it to the treetops a hundred feet ahead of us; I kept the collective up. Then I heard an unfamiliar sound, a horrible grinding like a giant pepper mill.

One of the NVA soldiers' first shots must have hit the main transmission. Only the large gears that drive the main rotor blades could make such a horrific noise, but I couldn't put the collective down,

somehow we were still climbing. We might not make
the trees, but it was obvious we couldn't stay there.

Slowly we climbed, clearing the tops by inches, the
engine losing power all the time. We made it over
the tree line, but didn't get much farther, maybe two
hundred feet. The rotor blades thrashed violently as
we settled between the tops of two great treetops. As
we disappeared into the jungle, the din of the helicopter tearing into the treetops was replaced by the
rush of branches over the fuselage and the occasional
tree limb snapping as we plummeted almost silently
to the ground some hundred or more feet below us.
The last part of the flight I can recall was throwing
the disabled controls around the cockpit in an attempt to swerve the helicopter away from an enormous limb that was coming up through the chin
bubble at my feet.

When I awoke, I had the distinct impression that
someone rather large had squashed me in my seat.
My crotch was only inches from my nose—then the
pain hit and I lost consciousness. The next time I
came around it was the smell of smoke and hot oil
and fuel that caught my attention. Fire! I thought,
terrified. Got to get out. . . . But when I tried to
move, the pain in my back knocked me out again.

I have no recollection of how it happened, but one
of the times I regained consciousness I found I was
lying outside the helicopter flat on my back. I didn't
know where I was, couldn't even see the helicopter,
and something was moving on my face. The hand I
brought up to investigate was covered with blood,
dark and thick. Wallowing through the blood were
large ants. Blood and ants were everywhere, on my
face and hands, the front of my fatigue shirt, even
my mouth was full of blood. I choked and tried to

spit out some of the thick mess, but nothing happened—on impact my jaw had been shattered by my steel chest protector.

By rolling over on my side I got the blood to run out of my mouth, and I could see the helicopter, almost fifty feet away. It didn't look like my LOH, smashed to half its height in a heap at the foot of an enormous tree—but Cisco was still in the back. He looked dead, his head hanging down, slumped against the forward bulkhead in the mangled aircraft, but I couldn't be sure.

Just about any movement knocked me out cold or paralyzed me with pain, but I found I could drag myself on my left side. When I got to Cisco I reached up and undid his seat belt, then pulled myself up to get him out of the smoking wreck, but all I managed to do was rock him back and forth. There was so little strength left in my body and each exertion disabled me with shocking pain radiating from my spine—so I quit.

Besides, Cisco looked worse than dead. Blood was running out of his mouth and into his lap—the aluminum floor below him was covered with the stuff. When I rocked him I could see the far side of his face was smashed and his left eye was hanging out of its socket. So I left him, pulled myself into the cockpit, and found the emergency radio. "I'm hurt. My back is broken and Cisco's dead," was my only transmission.

I have no idea how many times I slipped in and out of consciousness, but one of the last times I came around, Cisco was lying beside me outside the helicopter, and he was breathing. Another time my eyes opened for a moment, just long enough to focus on what looked like the barrel and front sight of an AK-47 inches from my face.

Of all people, it was Sharp who played the pivotal role in our surviving that crash. Sharp, the guy I had shown nothing but disrespect to, just happened to be landing at the Rome plows' command post at the same time we were getting shot down. He heard me say, "Taking fire, taking fire," and recognized my voice. I know how Sharp found us (the smoke from our engine made it through the trees), but how Sharp figured out we had been shot down, and what motivated him to go looking for us in the right area, I will never know, but will always be grateful—he saved our lives.

If Sharp had not heard my transmission and arrived at the scene of the crash as soon as he did, two things likely would have happened. First, the NVA, not hearing any other helicopters in the area, would have checked out the crash for radios, weapons, and prisoners. Finding us as disabled as we were, they would most likely have shot us. Even if the NVA had not come to get us, we would certainly have bled to death before anyone could have found us through normal flight following. The fact that Sharp even heard my call on the radio was extremely coincidental.

Only an aircraft within a mile radius tuned to the Rome plow frequency could have heard my transmission. Sharp was the only aircraft for miles. He had tuned in to the Rome plows just minutes before we were shot down and minutes later would have been on the ground, unable to hear my transmission. FM transmissions are line-of-sight, and Cisco and I were below the tree line, as was the Rome plow receiver, when we were shot down. Sharp was the only person who could have possibly heard that last call.

What Sharp did next was true to form, and the type of action that had earned the contempt of most of the pilots in the company. He climbed up to five thousand feet and circled until help arrived. The first to arrive, also true to form, was Crab. The CO at the bulldozer command post had called our company as soon as Sharp confirmed Cisco and I were down, and Crab immediately came to our rescue. His heroic efforts almost got him court-martialed, evidenced as follows:

STATEMENT

On 30 April 1970, at approximately 11:30, I was advised by WO-1 Arnold that WO-1 Smith was thought to have been shot down. I quickly checked with the people in operations, Capt. Brisa and CW-2 Garrett, and they informed me that WO-1 Smith had been shot down near LZ Kramer, but that nobody had an exact fix or knew of his condition. I advised them that I was going up for a UHF radio check in 984 and nothing further was said. When I got in the air, I made contact with WO-1 Sharp on UHF and he advised me that WO-1 Smith was down with a broken back and his gunner was in poor shape. They had seen smoke, but were not sure at that time if it was from the aircraft. I asked him if they needed any assistance, and he indicated the affirmative. I then called back to operations, advised them of the situation, and was requested to return home. From the information I received about the situation from WO-1 Sharp, I elected to continue to the crash site.

Crab had to write this statement in defense of his actions against Brisa's charge that he had disobeyed a direct order by going to our rescue. In my two years in the Army, I never witnessed or heard of such malicious and willful abuse of command.

When Crab arrived on the scene Sharp called on the radio and informed him, "Be advised, two-one, fuel's getting low, having trouble receiving on UHF. I'm heading back to Tay Ninh."

Crab took over the responsibility of directing the rescue operations. The Rome plows were on the way to the crash site, and their CO had called in a Blues team, a helicopter unit that specialized in rescue. The Blues landed in the clearing where we had come under fire and set up a defensive perimeter on the north side of the crash site. At the same time bulldozers cleared a road in from the south side for the tanks, armored personnel carriers, and infantry to get to us—they sent a small army after us.

Within an hour of being rescued Cisco and I were in the 45th Surgical Hospital in Tay Ninh. The drugs they gave me helped the pain in my back and made it easier to remain conscious, but I was far from comfortable. Because of my spinal injuries the doctors had immobilized me flat on my back on a special rig, and then left. Once again I found myself choking on my own blood, only this time I couldn't turn my head.

It took a while, but I finally devised a way to clear the blood that was oozing from my shattered jaw into my mouth. Periodically I would tilt my head back, sliding the coagulated blood into my throat, and then eject it with a forceful cough. It seemed as if they left me there for hours with nothing to do but blow blood wads into the air, which invariably fell back onto my face. When a doctor or nurse did come by it appeared that all they were interested in was asking me inane questions.

"What's your mom's name?" a doctor asked.

"*Whaa ha huck hu hair?*" I demanded. What the hell was this guy doing asking me about my dead mother when he should have been putting my face back together?

Apparently they were checking to see if I was going into shock while I waited to be medevacked to the main hospital in Long Binh. As long as they could get rational answers from me they knew I was safe. After what seemed like hours, they shot me up with something powerful and loaded my stretcher on a helicopter for the flight south. Before I slid under from the drugs, I remember thinking how happy I was to be back in a nice safe Huey again.

In Long Binh, while I was asleep, they shaved my mustache off, stuck in some intravenous feeding tubes, attached a urinary catheter, cut a seven-inch hole through my stomach muscles, performed an exploratory laparotomy (looking for damaged internal organs), stitched me back up, removed a few shattered teeth, put my lower jaw back together with wire and a reinforcing bar, stitched up my face, immobilized me on a special and very uncomfortable bed for my back, stuck a tube down my left nostril all the way into my left lung, and hooked me up to an artificial respirator.

15

Homeward Bound

Early May 1970

After drifting in and out of consciousness for two days in Long Binh's 24th Evacuation Hospital, I awoke for a moment on 2 May, my birthday. When I opened my eyes the first thing that caught my attention was a large black tube sticking out of my nose. The tube, about the same size as a garden hose, was hooked to a small clear-plastic machine that had three colored pistons going up and down—it looked like a toy.

With my comprehension slowed down by the pain-killers the medical staff was administering, it took me quite a while to realize that the pistons were moving up and down at the same rate as my breath was going in and out. The machine was helping me breathe through the tube in my nose. It was fascinating watching the little pistons move up and down and feeling the air move in and out of my lung. Then I coughed, and everything went to hell.

The air going out bumped into the air coming in. When I tried to pull the air back in, it felt as if the machine wanted the air to come out. I panicked, fighting the mechanical rhythm, and for a few anxious seconds did my best to suffocate myself. The machine actually had been designed to accommodate irregular breathing, but nothing like the snorts and blasts I was giving it. Fortunately the momentary panic wore me down to where the drugs could take over and put me back to sleep. The next time I awoke I was happy to see someone had taken me off the respirator.

From then on I awoke several times a day, usually just in time to see a nurse walk up to put me back under with a needle in my thigh. During one of my lucid periods I spotted an unconscious Cisco across the aisle and four beds up from me, wrapped in bandages.

Not long after that (it was hard to keep track of time) a doctor came to my bed and said, "Oh, you're up! I'll be right back." A few minutes later he was standing beside my bed with an enormous manila envelope. "I've got some X rays of your back here," the doctor said, pulling out big dark sheets with white smudges on them. "It doesn't look all bad, but you can never tell," he continued. "As you can see, you've got some crushed vertebrae that have actually splintered here, could be trouble, but there doesn't appear to be any nerve damage."

Then he went down to my feet and messed around with my toes. "Can you feel this?" he asked me. When I did not respond he looked up and noticed my wired jaw and said, "Oh, never mind," and began writing on a clipboard.

The next thing he did came as a real surprise. He pulled my bed sheet down to my knees, stuck his hand in my crotch, and said, "You won't be needing this thing anymore." With that simple phrase still bouncing around in my drug-fogged brain I felt my penis being torn off.

Up to that point I had been reluctant to communicate verbally because of my shattered jaw. However, when I thought that this maniac doctor had just emasculated me, I started screaming "HOP, *Whhh hu uunn?*"

My brain reeled in turmoil, eyes pleading for mercy, while the doctor stared at me with a puzzled expression. Finally he said, "Well, it looks like you felt that catheter come out," and walked away.

A little while later the nurse came back with a small pair of stainless steel scissors. "If you start to throw up," she said, "cut the little wires holding your teeth together and let it flow out." I did a quick estimate of the time it would take to cut the countless wires wedged in among my teeth and decided I had better not throw up. Following immediately behind her was another nurse with my shot. It was a relief to get back to the world of dreams.

At first staying awake was important to me, but once familiar with the routine and activities around me, I slept as much as possible. Directly across from me lay a Vietnamese woman who had a gaping black hole in the side of her face from her ear to her lower jaw. Several times a day a nurse would come by and wash out the hole while the woman moaned in pain. Once in the middle of the night, the soldier to the left of the Vietnamese lady woke us all up when he started screaming, "I'm bleeding, aaaaaaah, help, I'm bleeding." The lights came on and the orderly who came to his aid found an artery had ruptured in a wound on the soldier's forearm. The orderly took off running and came back with a pair of forceps. He jammed them into the wound and started fishing for the severed blood vessel. The moaning, bleeding, and screaming went on day and night in the little Quonset hut that served as our hospital ward.

Early one morning I awoke suffocating. The medical staff had disconnected me from the artificial breathing apparatus, but I was still breathing through the black pipe in my nose. Somehow the pipe had become plugged. I rang my bell (guys who could not yell for a nurse got a bell), and the nurse showed up. "It's too early for your shot," she scolded me.

"*Hhimm Hoooknng. Hhannn heth,*" I tried to explain with the little air I had, but she wasn't getting it. So I pointed to the hose, then down to my lung, and finally put my hands around my neck and started choking myself. A big smile lit up her face, and she chuckled, saying, "That's the best I've seen yet," and walked away.

A few stressful moments later the same nurse came back with a little electric pump that was connected to a glass jar by some clear plastic tubes. She put the contraption on the table beside my bed, picked up one of the longer tubes, and said, "Now you just slip this little tube down the one in your nose like this," and started sliding the tube into my nose.

"*Wwwhhh hhu hhuunng?*" I demanded.

"That's it," she cooed to me, not missing a beat. "Now you take it—that's it. Now slide it down until you feel it poke."

She couldn't be talking about the bottom of my lung, I thought, the tube will poke a hole in it. But a suffocating man is a desperate man and I slid the little tube in until it stopped (I could barely feel it in my lung). When I nodded that the tube had hit the bottom, she turned on the little electric pump. A few seconds later little gobs of mucus started dropping into the glass jar and my breathing returned to normal—a phlegm jam. Mucus built up in my lung and having to suction it out became a daily ritual.

Besides smiling, waving, and flashing the peace sign to Cisco, there wasn't a lot to do in the 24th Evacuation Hospital. My attitude, however, had improved since the first few days. It didn't take long to realize my wounds were not terminal. I had also come to grips with the possibility that I might have serious problems with my back. The strong narcotics the nurses were giving me barely took the edge off the pain, and I had trouble feeling and moving my legs and feet. However, on the plus side, I thought, if I was paralyzed the Army would give me a pension and I could get a Porsche with hand controls. The nicest part of it all, I figured, would be getting a comely nurse to help me in and out of the car. I also knew that I would never have to go back to combat—what a wonderful feeling.

The thing that most concerned me was why there wasn't any sympathy mail coming from home. I was terribly lonely, felt used, and desperately wanted to know that someone cared. As usual the problem was another Army screwup. They had sent Uncle Pat the following telegram:

The Secretary of the Army has asked me to inform you that your friend, Warrant Officer Thomas L. Smith, was slightly wounded in action in Vietnam on 30 April 1970 while pilot of a military aircraft on a combat operation when the aircraft was hit by hostile ground fire, crashed, but did not burn. He received a fractured mandible.

One of the first letters that did reach me was from Wolfman, who did not know that I had been shot down. In fact, he thought I had stayed out of Scouts since the first time I quit, back in December.

Atom Ant,

I sure was glad to hear from you after my first attempt to get a response out of one of your six writing legs—"It sure is great to hear from you!"

You must be feeling pretty short, other than your size, Ant, I sure hope you aren't getting upset about going home—Wolf joke.

Your letter left me with the impression of true trust between you and I. I really hold this close to my personal feelings. It's given me something of a feeling of achievement during the time I flew. I'm glad that I had the chance to fly with a person that really knew himself. The reason I stated that, was because you were truthful when quitting. You knew how important it is to fly with all consideration, therefore no one got hurt because of you. I think that's when you really know yourself, and you've already proved yourself as a Scout pilot and that in itself is good.

I hope Atom you can understand what I said because I'm sure glad you saw it out and knew when to quit. . . .

Atom, what I'm saying is I flew with the greatest people I've ever met and I'm so thankful for fate to be so kind to me in having the opportunity to live— that's what's happening!

Dig,
    Wolfman

Wolfman's feelings about me, Crab, and flying with us made me feel good. His emphasis on the fact that I knew when to quit Scouts made me feel a little foolish, but his words *no one got hurt because of you* made me cringe. The doctor informed me that Cisco had lost his left eye.

Cisco, who had volunteered to fly with me on his day off, always making jokes, acting like nothing mattered, but knowing full well that the mission I had been assigned would be dangerous. Cisco, the

nicest guy I had flown with, got hurt because of me—
because of my stupidity.

When letters did start arriving from family and
friends, they were packed full of sympathy and concern. Such as:

> "I'm really glad you didn't kill yourself, you stupid
> shit."

> "Today someone said that a young man has a
> greater chance of getting killed driving a car than he
> does in Vietnam. Or was that driving a car in Viet-
> nam?"

> "Tommy, the Stones are singing 'Let It Bleed,' I
> just picked some lilacs and they're smelling up the
> room. The sky is big and full of billowy clouds and
> I'm kind of drunk."

> "After a few months in the hospital you will prob-
> ably have such a hard-on you won't be able to blink
> your eyes."

> "When is the Army going to stop your plane sup-
> ply? Isn't this the third helo that has ditched you?"

> "You ought to write down a few of the stories you
> must have by now. They could be best sellers."

Uncle Pat and Aunt Kitty wrote me almost every
day, letters loaded with kind words and welcome
news from home. However, the most meaningful
feelings of sympathy and appreciation for what I had
done and what had happened to me came from the
simple words of a group of second graders. Judy was
teaching school and asked the eight-year-old kids in
her class if they would like to write me. They did.

"Dear Tom, I was sorry to hear what happened to you. How are you? I'm fine. I hope you can come home soon. What you did was very brave. Get well soon."

"Dear Tom, I am very sorry what happened in Vietnam. And I am glad you do all the things for us because you do it so well and I hope you get well soon. And when I was coming home the other day I saw a sqrirrle chasing another sqrirrle. And every where one went the other went to. And one chased one up a tree. And they never got home. And I do so well I got all As and an B you no why I got that mark because I try so hard."

"Dear Tom, I am sorry to hare abot your accident. How are you doing, Tom? I hope you come home from the hospital soon so you can do what you want to do. When you come home you can say hello to your friends at there homes to. Well I am saying hellow to you now to have fun. When you come home from the hospital I now you will have a smile when you come home from the hospital. Tom, I now how it is to be on fire becous my brother was on fire and he had a teribel accident on the stove because he wasent looking at the sleeve he had on. My brother is all better all ready he can do all things. I hope you will be ever to do that to."

"Dear Tom, I am sorry to hear about your accident. Get well soon. Be more careful."

There were over forty of those wonderful letters and each one was accompanied by a crayon drawing. My favorites were those depicting my escape from a crashed helicopter and the ones showing me in my hospital bed.

Things just got better and better every day. Crab

came down to visit and told me he was going to see to it that Brisa was held accountable for the way he handled his responsibilities. He had a statement with him which he had submitted to the brigade commander.

> On the evening of 30 April 1970, at about 20:00, I had a conference with Capt. Brisa on ways to correct the situation that had resulted in one of our LOHs being shot down that same day, with the crew being critically injured. Up to that point, he had been flying a single LOH with no cover or wing bird on scouting type missions with the Rome plows, over areas of known enemy activity. My recommendations at this time were to put a Scout team up to accomplish the mission, while at the same time affording safety to the crew under this situation. He rejected my proposal and I found myself scheduled to fly the mission the next day under the exact conditions of the prior day when I had seen my good friend, WO-1 Smith, and his gunner critically injured. I requested at this time to be taken off the mission on the grounds that it could not properly be accomplished in the manner he prescribed. It would be a waste of blade time and an unnecessary risk to personnel involved. He approved my request.
>
> The next morning, 1 May 1970, at about 09:00, Capt. Brisa called me to his office and informed me that I was grounded until further notice. No reason was given for this action and I was not advised of my rights or his intentions.

Crab disobeyed an order in coming to our rescue, one whose sole purpose was to deny us aid, and now he was trying to make sure Brisa would not treat other pilots the way he treated us. It was hard to top that for a worthwhile friend.

Cisco was also doing better, walking around with

a great big bandage on his face, joking and trying to score with the nurses. One of the first things he said to me was "I got a couple of the little bastards," trying to make us both feel better about our injuries.

The doctors could not fix his eye, but they were doing what they could to fix up his face. He explained the process to me. "They've stuffed the whole inside of my face with cotton."

"*Wwwh ffrr?*" I asked.

"What for? 'Cause I almost ate the intercom box when we hit the ground. Take a look at this," he said, pulling up the bandage. The side of his face looked like hamburger. "They went in through my nose," he went on, pointing to a piece of string hanging out of his left nostril. "Inside the face bone and packed a bunch of cotton back there to hold the bone in place while it heals." He paused for a while, then said, "I sure hope they know what the hell they're doin'."

When the big day came to take the cotton out, the doctor grabbed on the string in Cisco's nose and started pulling out a strand of cotton almost an inch thick. He extracted a foot of the packing, then another foot, and another. I thought I was hallucinating, or perhaps the doctor was an amateur magician. Cisco could not believe it either, the more cotton the doctor pulled out, the bigger Cisco's eye got. They must have pulled eight feet of that stuff out his nose.

Later Cisco came over to my bed. He had a dejected look that I knew was being faked. He was obviously setting me up for one of his jokes. "As if Scouts wasn't enough proof, Atom, now I got this," he complained miserably.

"*Whaa hu heen?*" I asked, setting him up.

"What do I mean? How could they have fit all that

cotton in there if I had any brains?" He laughed. I thought I was taking the whole thing pretty well, but Cisco was amazing for a guy who had just lost one of his eyes.

Shortly after Cisco became ambulatory Craig came down from Cu Chi to visit. He came walking over to my bed with Cisco; both of them were grinning from ear to ear.

"Good to see you, old buddy," he said sympathetically. It was great to see Craig. "Came to see you a few days ago. Before you woke up. That machine was breathing for you and you were making a lot of weird sounds, like a death rattle or something." He looked down at his hands and then back up at me. "Thought each breath was going to be your last." The look in Craig's eyes as he mumbled the last sentence told me how relieved he was.

"*Hank hu, haag,*" I said as sincerely as circumstances would allow.

"What?" Craig asked.

"I think he said, 'Thank you, Craig,' " Cisco interpreted for Craig, then turned to me and continued, "You're going to be thanking him even more when we get you out of here."

"*Hut hor?*" I asked.

Cisco looked under my bed and cheerfully pronounced, "Yeah, his bed's got wheels too." With that Cisco and Craig pulled my bed out from the wall and, IV bottles clinking together, wheeled me out of the Quonset hut. The nurse on duty hardly even noticed us.

Craig and Cisco wheeled me around on the boardwalks that connected the Quonset huts until they found an empty trash enclosure, big enough to hide my bed. Then Craig opened his flight jacket and pulled out a great big joint. "Thought you might need an attitude adjustment," he explained.

"*Aaaaa hite*," I tried. They both looked at me and cracked up. Minutes later we were all laughing hysterically as Craig and Cisco played runaway train on the boardwalk with my bed, with me in it.

A few hours later, after Craig and Cisco had parked me back in my Quonset hut, I started to feel sick. Quite a drama unfolded in my pot-soaked brain. I envisioned myself strangling on vomit, while trying to rip my teeth out. The images were overwhelming. Fortunately my paranoia helped me forget I was sick.

On 8 May they moved me by litter to the 249th General Hospital in Japan. Just before my plane left I got a note from an M. Stoughton at the Red Cross.

To: W.O. Thomas Smith
  The Red Cross has a free phone call for you to whomever you choose. Please go to the phone center—Red Cross Building.

It was very nice of them to make the offer, and my bed did have wheels; but, even if I could have gotten over to the Red Cross building, who could have understood me at the other end of the phone?

Shortly after Cisco and I arrived in Japan, Cisco was determined to be fit enough for travel to the mainland and he was shipped out. A few days later the dental surgeons determined my jaw was not healing correctly and rebroke it—with the net result of a couple more teeth lost. The surgeon who performed the operation wore glasses, and I was able to observe his gruesome bone-breaking technique in the reflection of his lenses. However, not all the news was bad. The orthopedic surgeon who checked me out announced in august fashion, "What's your problem? You're in perfect shape; get up and walk around."

It sounded like a great idea, so I slid my legs off the bed, pushed myself up, and, after a brief struggle, fell on my butt. My left leg buckled first, but my right was just about as worthless. On my second attempt I took it a little slower and before long I was wobbling along on my own.

On 25 May, after two weeks in Japan, I boarded a flight home. I didn't actually get to board it; they carried me aboard on a stretcher. Somehow the transportation people had not gotten the word that I could walk and booked me a litter instead of a seat. I thought at least I would get to sleep inside the windowless fuselage of the enormous transport plane on the way across the Pacific, but the moans and groans of the hundred or more wounded men alongside me made it impossible.

My next stop was Walter Reed Army Hospital outside Washington, DC. In the mess hall that night, as a special treat for making it home alive, I ate a piece of spaghetti, my first solid food in almost a month.

With my jaw so badly broken, the first few weeks I obtained all my nourishment through intravenous feeding tubes. Later, however, I started drinking my food. At meal times I went through the chow line, loading food on my plate just like everyone else. But instead of sitting down, I dumped the contents of my tray in a blender with my glass of milk, whipped it to a mush, and sucked it down with a straw through a hole the dentists had left between my teeth.

I had been dreaming about solid food for weeks, so I slid the pasta through a hole in my teeth, tongued it into a pulp, and swallowed it down—it tasted great.

Before long, the doctors took the braces and wire

out of my mouth and began letting me leave the
hospital for part of the day. This new freedom called
for even more of a celebration than a piece of spaghetti. I went shopping for civilian clothes and then
took a bus to Manhattan Porsche. The car that I
bought was so new it still had shipping paper over
the air intakes and convertible roof. I paid a little
more than eight thousand dollars for it, almost
exactly what I had saved from a year's work in
Vietnam.

Several days later they discharged me from Walter
Reed on thirty days' leave. Free at last, I thought, as
I slid behind the leather steering wheel of my silver
Porsche 911-T Targa.

Well, not completely free, I found out. Before I
went on leave I had to report to my new duty station,
Davidson Army Airfield at Fort Belvoir, Virginia. My
assignment was to the helicopter unit responsible for
the president's transportation around the capital area—
a worthy assignment, I thought. However, when I
reported to the officer on duty at Davidson Airfield
he informed me that, due to my extensive injuries,
instead of flying helicopters for the president, I
would be a laundry officer.

When I got home to Keene Valley, a letter from
Crab was waiting.

27 July 70

Atom Ant,
    You wouldn't believe the way things have been
working out around this place. But then I suppose
things are working out pretty well in Keene Valley
too. Did they assign you to a stateside unit yet or
will you remain casual?
    Well the bad news is that our dearly beloved Brisa

got relieved of his command. It's such a shame as he was career oriented.

The 1st Brigade has moved down to Bien Hoa and plan to stay, so did I. We're right next to the R&R center—Pegasus Pad—and it's OK.

Garret and J. Edgar leave in a month, so Loftin is the only real asshole left. Fred Bauser is in fine health and from what Ski says, Lady was in heat and Bauser got to work out. So maybe he'll be a father before too long. Mia and Goop made the move to Bien Hoa, but I guess Tuu was too close to her family in Tay Ninh. I've got to fly up and see her one of these months.

So let me know what you're up to and if you want anything from over here and what the Army is doing to screw you.

Crab

On the fourth of September, four months after being shot down, I was given an Honorable Discharge from the Army. It did not bother me that they had unceremoniously dumped me without concern for the problems my injuries were causing me; I was glad to be going home for good. Late that night, cruising up the Northway Turnpike just minutes from Keene Valley, flashing red lights lit up the night behind me. I took a quick look at my speedometer before slowing down—a little over 100 miles per hour.

The state trooper gave me a questioning look as he led me back to his patrol car. Finally he asked, "How come you stopped?"

"I thought I was supposed to," I said, thinking that was a strange question to ask.

"Most people going that speed aren't anxious to stop, that's all," he said, answering my unasked question.

We got into his car and as he wrote me a ticket we started talking. Before long he looked at me and asked, "So, how come you're in such a hurry?"

After patiently listening to a brief account of the last few months, he stared directly at me and asked, "Can you prove it?"

I showed him my hospital discharge papers, a profile of my injuries, my DD-214 (which listed my citations), and a few other pertinent papers I had in my car.

The officer nodded his head slowly as he finished examining the documents, then closed his ticket book. "Take it easy," he said, and shook my hand.

Glossary

AC: aircraft commander

AH-1-G: a Bell Cobra single-turbine assault helicopter designed as a weapons platform and crewed by two pilots in a tandem-seat configuration

AK-47: a semiautomatic and automatic rifle of Soviet design (from "avtomat Kalashnikova 1947") using 7.62mm ammunition issued to NVA and VC troops

AO: area of operations

APO: army post office

arch-light: code name for a B-52 bombing mission in which several of the aircraft simultaneously dropped a hundred or more bombs on a relatively small area

ARVN: Army of the Republic of [South] Vietnam

B-40: a short-range shoulder-launched rocket

B-52: a Boeing Stratofortress eight-jet long-range heavy bomber

BDA: bomb damage assessment

C-130: a Lockheed Hercules four-turbine cargo aircraft

C&C: see *command and control*

CH-47: a Boeing Chinook twin-turbine tandem-rotor medium-lift troop transport helicopter

CH-54: a Sikorsky Sky Crane twin-turbine heavy-lift helicopter

Charlie: a South Vietnamese soldier; see *VC*

Charlie Charlie: see *command and control*

Chinook: medium-lift helicopter; see *CH-47*

claymore: an antipersonnel land mine (charged with plastic explosive and shrapnel)

CO: commanding officer

Cobra: an assault helicopter; see *AH-1-G*

Command and Control: missions flown, usually in UH-1s, to assess U.S. and enemy troop activities

CP: command post

CS: a harassing (nonlethal) antipersonnel chemical warfare agent

CWO2: chief warrant officer, 2d grade; see *WO*

DC-3: a Douglas twin-reciprocating-engine cargo/passenger aircraft of the World War II era

DD-214: the form that provides a one-page summary of a person's military career

DEROS: date of expected return from overseas

dink: pejorative term for enemy soldier; see *gook*

EM: enlisted man

F-100: a North American single-jet fighter-bomber aircraft, typically armed with 500-pound bombs

F-105: a Republic Thunderchief single-jet fighter-bomber aircraft, typically armed with a 20mm cannon and 250-pound bombs

FAC: forward air controller

FM: frequency-modulated radio with line-of-sight transmission used primarily by ground troops and aircraft

frag: a fragmentation grenade

GI: U.S. Army infantry soldier (from "government issue")

gook: pejorative term for enemy soldier; see *dink*

grunt: U.S. Army or Marine Corps infantry soldier

HE: high explosive [munitions]

HHC: Headquarters and Headquarters Company of a U.S. Army brigade

Huey: a troop-carrying helicopter; see *UH-1*

KIA: killed in action

klick: kilometer (0.62 mile)

knot: 1.2 miles per hour (1 nautical mile per hour)

Loach: slang for LOH; see *OH-6*

LOH: light observation helicopter; see *Loach* and *OH-6*

LZ: landing zone (anything from a fifty-foot opening in the jungle canopy to a fire-support base)

M14: a semiautomatic rifle using 7.62mm ammunition

M16: a semiautomatic and automatic rifle using 5.56mm ammunition issued to U.S. troops

M60: a machine gun using 7.62mm ammunition

M79: a single-shot rifle that launches a 40mm exploding projectile

MACV: [U.S.] Military Assistance Command Vietnam

minigun: an aircraft machine gun using 7.62mm ammunition (a small rapid-fire gatling-type machine gun)

MP: military police

NVA: North Vietnamese Army

OH-6: a Hughes single-turbine four-seat light observation helicopter; also OH-6A

OH-58: a Bell single-turbine five-seat light observation helicopter that replaced the OH-6

OV-10: a North American–Rockwell Bronco twin-turbine reconnaissance aircraft

P-38: a Lockheed Lightning twin-jet fighter-bomber aircraft of the World War II era

peter-pilot: copilot

POL: a refueling area (from "petroleum, oil, and lubricants")

PX: post exchange

R&R: rest and relaxation (leave away from the combat zone)

recon: reconnaissance

ROTC: Reserve Officers' Training Corps (found on many university campuses)

RVN: Republic of [South] Vietnam

SKS: a bolt-action rifle using 7.62mm ammunition issued to NVA and VC troops

Sky Crane: a heavy-lift helicopter; see *CH-54*

Slick: a troop-carrying helicopter; see *UH-1*

TAC: flight school cadre (from "Tactical Air Command")

TH-55: a Hughes single-reciprocating-engine two-seat training helicopter; also TH-55A

TOC: tactical operations center

TOT: turbine outlet temperature

TR-4A: a British Triumph two-passenger sports car

UH-1: a Bell single-turbine fourteen-seat utility helicopter, referred to as a "Huey" or "Slick"; also "UH-1-C," "UH-1-D," and "UH-1-H"

VC: Vietcong (the South Vietnamese insurgency force; literally, "Red Vietnamese"), sometimes referred to as "Charlie"

Vietcong: see *VC*

Willy Pete: white phosphorus (the charge for incendiary and smoke munitions)

WO1: warrant officer, 1st grade; see *CWO2*

WOC: warrant officer candidate